The Headman and I

The Texas Pan American Series

The Headman and I

Ambiguity and Ambivalence
in the Fieldworking Experience

By Jean-Paul Dumont

University of Texas Press
Austin and London

The Texas Pan American Series is published with the assistance of a revolving publication fund established by the Pan American Sulphur Company.

Library of Congress Cataloging in Publication Data

Dumont, Jean-Paul, 1940–
    The headman and I.
    (Texas Pan American series)
    Bibliography: p.
    1. Ethnology—Field work. 2. Panare Indians. 3. Dumont, Jean-Paul,
1940–   4. Anthropologists—French—Biography. I. Title.
GN346.D85   301.2′07′2   78-8091
ISBN 0-292-73007-1

Design by Joanna Hill

For Elli,
Who Showed Me
Part of the Light

Contents

Illustrations

Figures

Maps

Plates

The problem of the value of truth presented
itself before us—or was it we who presented
ourselves before the problem? Which of us
is the Oedipus here? Which the Sphinx? It
would seem to be a rendezvous of questions
and notes of interrogation.

—Friedrich Nietzsche,
  Beyond Good and Evil

Acknowledgments

The fieldwork on which this study is based took place among the Panare Indians of Venezuelan Guiana between the summer of 1967 and the summer of 1969, while I was a doctoral candidate at the University of Pittsburgh. The field research was funded by grants from the Wenner-Gren Foundation for Anthropological Research (New York), the U.C.L.A. Latin American Center (Los Angeles), the Fundación Creole (Caracas), and an Andrew W. Mellon predoctoral fellowship (Pittsburgh), whose support I gratefully acknowledge. Additional fieldwork was undertaken during the winter of 1970 when I served as a film consultant for Granada Television (Manchester).

The fieldwork itself was greatly facilitated in Venezuela by the cooperation of the Instituto Caribe de Antropología y Sociología, the Instituto Venezolano de Investigaciones Científicas, the Servicio de Malariología, and the Universidad Central de Venezuela.

In 1976–77, while writing the manuscript, I received a professional leave of absence with partial salary from the University of Washington and a research training fellowship from the Social Science Research Council; I am indebted to the generosity of both institutions. I am no less thankful to the Language-Behavior Research Laboratory of the University of California at Berkeley for the office, aid, and facilities provided at that time, and especially to Brent Berlin and Paul Kay for the warmth of their hospitality.

From the inception of my project until its completion more than ten years have elapsed, and my intellectual debts have accumulated to such an extent that it would be impossible to list all those who have generously contributed their time, hospitality, and help. At the risk of being unfair, I shall make a few exceptions. The first is for the Panare people, from whom I select Marquito, the headman of Turiba Viejo, for reasons which I hope will become obvious when the reader enters further into this book. The second is for those who read, commented, criticized, and helped improve part or all of one or another manuscript version of this book: Alan Dundes, Kay Gee, Nelson Graburn, Hiroko Horikoshi-Roe, Judith Hudson, Charles Keyes, Dean MacCannell,

Margaret Nowak, Sherry Ortner, Peter Roe, Renato Rosaldo, Michelle Rosaldo, and Steve Tobias. In addition, I have a special debt of gratitude toward Robert A. Paul and Paul Rabinow, who were intimately involved with the gestation of this book, for their unflagging encouragement and stimulating friendship. Finally, this project would never have been completed without the constant moral assistance of my wife, Elli, who bravely suffered through every single page of every manuscript version of this book and managed to keep her cool when faced with the neurotic behavior of the author.

Editorial Note

The reader may find the following notes helpful. Unless otherwise specified, material originally in French or in Spanish has been translated into English by the author. Creole Spanish terms and Panare linguistic forms are always given in italics. Because no phonological description of the Panare language has yet been published, the following phonetic notation is only an approximation:

a as in m*a*t
e as in m*e*t
i as in d*i*m
o as in d*o*me
u as in d*o*om
ö as in d*u*mb
y as in *y*et
w as in *w*et
p
t
k
m
n as in *n*et in initial or intervocalic positions, as in ri*n*g otherwise
r this rolled *r* ranges from an almost *d* to an almost *l* and is a flap
s as in hu*ts* in initial or intervocalic positions, as in u*s* otherwise
c as in *c*hip in initial or intervocalic positions, as in *s*hip otherwise
x as in Spanish *j*ota or German a*ch*

Finally, in bibliographic references, the first date between brackets corresponds to the original date of publication of the source material, when it differs from the edition that has actually been consulted.

The Headman and I

1. *Introduction*

This book is about the Panare Indians of Venezuelan Guiana and me, the investigating anthropologist. I have already written a book about the Panare (Dumont 1976). True, it was more about Panare objects than about Panare subjects, more about "their thing" than about them. Now, as I am about to take a second look at the Panare, I wish to shift the focus of my analysis, reorienting it toward the goal of an anthropology of the subject. Not only will I continue to direct my gaze at them; in addition, I want to consider how they gaze at me. My effort will be directed toward perceiving, apprehending, and interpreting the "and" of the relationship which my fieldwork built between an "I" and a "they."

I emphatically do not intend to dwell myopically on either of two extremes: neither the self-indulgent emotions of a fieldworker vainly attempting, by confessional narratives, to create an introspective travelogue, nor the simpleminded obsession for the hard, computerizable, and computerized data which, with their positivistic aura, pass for the ultimate in scientific sophistication in some anthropological circles. Between these two different forms of the same monologue there must be room for something else.

This something else may be difficult to pinpoint, yet it is nothing other than the result of one's complete immersion in a foreign culture. What is at issue here is the recognition of a dialogue established, despite all odds, between an "I" and a "they"; in fact, it is the whole process of anthropologizing which takes place there, throughout the entire time "I" and "they" are associated. Although every single fieldworker must eventually face such a process, it comes as a surprise to me that few of my colleagues have paid more than lip service to it. Yet an ethnographer observes what he/she is prepared to observe, no more and no less; in other words, my preparation, my goal as a knowledge-absorber acts upon my material as a filter, that is, as a contrivance for freeing data acquisition from the suspended impurities of experience. In addition, my own cultural and psychic makeup is such that I do not observe passively: I act and react, toward and to something. This something happens to be a someone who is also acting toward and reacting to me. This particular kind of interaction, implied and brought about by immersion and insertion in a concrete fieldwork situation, determines both the locus of my discourse and its focal point. In this venture, I hope to gain some insight about "me" and "them"; otherwise I do not see the point of having gone "there." Thus, it might even be said that anthropology as such interests me minimally and that my attention at this point is turned rather toward anthropologizing. This is not to say that I do not recognize a great heuristic value in anthropological models; in fact, the reverse is true, since I freely use one or another depending upon my specific conceptual needs. The issue here, however, involves dialogue and interaction rather than one-sided displays of data and conclusions. In this attempt at interpreting my fieldwork experience, I am actually trying to answer only one question, namely: "Who (or what) was I for the Panare?"

Even though I am not a strict hermeneutician, I have not used the verb "interpret" haphazardly, and I can see a congruence between my use of this term and its definition by Palmer: "Interpretation . . . can refer to three rather different matters: an oral recitation, a reasonable explanation, and a translation from another language. . . . In all three cases, something foreign, strange, separated in time, space or experience is made familiar, present, comprehensible: something requiring representation, explanation or translation is somehow 'brought to understanding'—is interpreted" (1969: 14).

The interpretation of the relationship that existed between the Panare Indians and myself requires what I would like to call a return to the text, if I may use the word "text" in a metaphorical sense, referring to the development in time, the interweaving in the process of certain types of interactions. My interaction with the Panare is bounded in space and time. It began on a Saturday afternoon, September 2, 1967, when I first met Juanchito, the Panare headman of Pavichima on my first arrival at Caicara, and it ended on a cloudy morning in late February 1970, when I left the settlement of Turiba Viejo for good. It began and it ended. It is made up of a multiplicity of actions and manipulations, of performances which acquire their full meaning only a posteriori in reference to the context in which the interactive text developed.

The text is not only supposed to be meaningful—in fact loaded with meaning—but also amenable to description, even a "thick description" to use the expression which Geertz (1973: 7) borrowed from Ryle (1949). Yet such a thick description of the text, if it is to be an interpretation, also requires the interpretation of the context with which it interacts in a dialectical relationship. It should be clear that the context always, and by definition, precedes the text. Thus it follows that, in order to comprehend the relationship which I established with the Panare, it is necessary, although certainly not sufficient, first to acquire some familiarity with the way the Panare interact among themselves and with others, whoever these others may be.

Thus "context" in this case refers to the system of communication existing among the Panare, one that is both structural and eventual, possessing both form and content. "Text" here refers to something more fluid, more concrete, more difficult to apprehend, and can be said to require the use of "an actor-oriented method" which "attempts to understand the actor's view of his own social world. It involves analysis of the symbols which give meaning and through which understanding is possible, as well as the social and economic conditions within which these symbols operate; in other words, how experience is organized" (Rabinow 1975: 3).

In both the context and the text, one can recognize an ideal, normative aspect as well as an actual, behavioral one. It is the point of articulation of these two aspects which interests me. And it can be seen now that my original question, "Who was I for the Panare?" was but a pretext, in the ordinary sense of the term as well as in its etymological sense. For such a question—rather than the spontaneous and immediate answer given to it—continually informed my anthropologizing throughout the duration of my fieldwork. In many different ways, and imperceptibly for me at the time it was happening, the answer to this question was provided daily in the field. But in addition, the answer which now can be provided in a meditated, reflective, and interpretative way calls forth a whole set of other questions prompted by the first question.

A relationship between "I" and "they" is necessarily dialectical and eventuates in three logical, yet overlapping and, as it were, progressivo-regressive stages: a confrontation, a search for meaning, and, optimally, a recognition. These three stages correspond roughly to the three dialectical steps: thesis, antithesis, and synthesis. The confrontation corresponds to the initial situation in which I am I and they are they, each on his own terms. The search for meaning corresponds to the dialectic process in which an exchange takes place, one in which they figure me out and I figure them out, so to speak. Finally and optimally (which means that it does not necessarily happen), recognition takes place, at which point the other is recognized in his/her otherness.

Therefore, by taking the pretext of my initial question beyond an

investigation of text and context, I seek to detail the texture of my
social insertion among the Panare, the texture of anthropologizing. Is
this a texture of compatibility or of domination? Ultimately, does anthropology fall below its aim, thus remaining pure confrontation, even
an endorsement of ethnocide? Does it reach its aim, acceding to the
other's meaning? Is it capable of going beyond its aim, toward the
recognition of someone else's otherness? Such is the series of questions
which will mark the path of the present work, so that, starting from a
precise and definite anthropological praxis, I may in this way add my
modest contribution to the elaboration of a critique of anthropological
reason.

It goes without saying that this type of reflection does not occur
in a historical vacuum. Quite to the contrary, I am only pursuing an
effort which, one way or the other, has already been undertaken. No
matter how critical and even polemical, the following pages still constitute a tribute of sorts to my predecessors, since it is in reading them
that I acquired a taste for anthropological reflection.

Jim Watson reports that one day the late Ralph Linton asked a
graduate student, already back from the field for some time, how the
writing of his dissertation was coming. " 'Oh, it should move along
quite well,' replies the student, "once I get through beating the life out
of my material' " (Watson 1972: 299). Authenticated or apocryphal,
this anecdote rings true to most anthropologists, I am sure. And yet,
I sometimes wonder whether most of anthropology has not embarked
on the same ill-fated course as this mercifully anonymous student.
Even practically speaking, there are good reasons for maintaining the
liveliness of the experience. Put facetiously, a little life in our work
will not kill us. But more seriously, there are imperative theoretical
reasons for doing so.

Few sociocultural anthropologists have confined themselves to the
participant-observation method in their fieldwork. But practically all
anthropologists have used this method, through which they maintain
the required "balance between empathic involvement and disciplined
detachment" (Mead 1973: 248) with the human group they study. In
her perceptive narration of her four fieldworking experiences, Powdermaker expresses herself in almost identical terms: "The self concept of many anthropologists seems to have one characteristic in common: the image of stepping in and out of society, of being involved
and detached" (1966: 289–290). Yet, the publications of anthropologists have long consisted of "objective" monographs in which their
presence in the field has been bracketed out, as if the "empathic in-

volvement" had been repressed for the sake of a hoped-for "detachment."

In this sense, the founders of modern anthropology such as Boas, Kroeber, Radcliffe-Brown, and Evans-Pritchard, to mention only a few, are all detached, and this is purposely so. Indeed it was the status of anthropology as a science which was at stake with them. To eliminate the perceiving subject, i.e., themselves as participant-observers, from their reports was an attempt at both a more factual objectivity than that of their predecessors and a stronger grasp of social and cultural realities. In fact, they were reacting strongly against two kinds of people.

Freilich identifies this reaction in reporting

> *the following statements of Lowie and Evans-Pritchard: "Able travellers mingled fancy with observation, indulged in the superficial psychologizing that duped Klemm and otherwise twisted the facts from initial bias" (Lowie 1937: 70). The missionaries and administrators, although frequently "men of greater culture than the gentlemen of fortune of earlier times" (Evans-Pritchard 1964: 67) were themselves often far from objective in describing primitive society and culture. Their data was therefore also a "twisting of the facts." By the time the synthesizers (of the 19th century) had added their own interpretations and had completed their attempts to fit the data into preconceived theories of evolution and progress, descriptions of primitive society were far removed from the reality being depicted (Freilich 1970: 7, footnote).*

This effort toward more objectivity had paradoxical consequences. More thorough fieldwork was undertaken, and more "empathic involvement" was achieved in the field experience from which their predecessors had been detached, either because they were superficial and prejudiced observers or because they were armchair anthropologists who synthesized from afar. At the same time, the more that "involved sympathy" emerged during the fieldwork experience, the more "disciplined detachment" was found in the published reports under the pretext of objectivity. As late as 1960, Casagrande could write the following: "Field research is a challenging scientific undertaking, an adventure of both the mind and the spirit. It is also a memorable *human* experience, yet most anthropological writings tend to obscure the fact" (1960: xii, his emphasis). But twelve years later, Kimball and Watson could still write: "It is no small irony that in a field where personal involvement is both deep and inevitable the literature is largely committed to the third person. This must be no small part of the reason that the experiential field has remained indeterminate" (1972: 7).

Anthropologists' reluctance to speak of their field experience is reported by Freilich in the following terms: "The sparsity of writings on anthropological field methods and field experiences is explained by, first, a fieldwork culture that underemphasizes methodology and supports private rather than public communications of field experiences, and, second, the 'rewards' field workers receive for keeping their errors and their personalities hidden and for maintaining a romantic attachment to the fieldwork mystique" (1970: 36).

Because anthropology is "the most scientific of humanities, the most humanistic of sciences" as Wolf (1964: 88) succinctly puts it, it would be inconceivable that an "involved" fieldworker could successfully repress his/her own perceiving self without "leaks." One of the earliest of these came from Malinowski himself, who did so much in the way of elevating anthropology to its present status, in writing about the Trobrianders in the introduction to his magistral *Argonauts of the Western Pacific*: "I began to feel that I was indeed in touch with the natives, and this is certainly the preliminary condition of being able to carry on successful field work" ([1922] 1961: 8). Despite his minute descriptions of how he worked in the field, infinitely more light is shed on his field experience by his now famous *Diary*, which was certainly not meant to be published and which, significantly, was not released before 1967.

Since Malinowski's lengthy introduction, the literature on fieldwork has exploded. But as late as the fifties, such a distinguished anthropologist as Laura Bohannan used a double protection to relate her fieldwork experience in West Africa: she fictionalized it and also used a pseudonym (Bowen 1954). The fact that the next most successful fieldwork account was also written by a woman (Powdermaker 1966) cannot be taken lightly. Since Margaret Mead had already become also the most formidable public relations agent for American anthropology, it suggests that women, all of whom had already established their reputations on the straight course of traditional anthropology, were left with the task of conjuring the impurities of experience. They had to cope with the blood, sweat, and tears aspect of fieldwork—feelings and sentiments included—while the men were exclusively doing "the real thing."

With an outpouring of sex, grass, rock, and dollars came the vibrant sixties, and a deluge of fieldwork literature. It had become not only permissible but hip, then cool, for people who were neither to speak of the fieldwork experience in anthropology. It is in this climate of opinion that Malinowski's *Diary* was released to an avid public and whole books were devoted to fieldwork, from *Behind Many Masks* (Berreman 1962) to *Marginal Natives* (Freilich 1970), not to mention the immensely successful introductory chapters to monographs such as *Yanomamö: The Fierce People* (Chagnon 1968) and the honest efforts of our female colleagues in *Women in the Field* (Golde 1970).

With few exceptions—among which *The High Valley* (Read 1965) and *Never in Anger* (Briggs 1970) definitely stand out—most of this literature is confessional, undoubtedly informative about its authors and the sixties. At the same time, and not unexpectedly, it is very repetitive. The human group that the anthropologist studied became the pretext for his/her lyricism, and by the same token almost disappeared. The "balance between empathic involvement and disciplined detachment" does not exist here any more than before. Moreover, the subject of the anthropological experience was condemned to an introspective monologue and remained unable to introduce an authentic dialogue with the people under scrutiny. A mere juxtaposition of self-consciousness and objective data does not reflect the role of the anthropologist in the field at all but rather obscures it.

Accurately, Rabinow notes that those works which have dealt with the question of participant observation "have varied a great deal in keenness of perception and grace of style, but they all cling to the key assumption that the field experience itself is basically separable from the mainstream of theory in anthropology—that the enterprise of inquiring is essentially discontinuous from its results" (1977: 5). And yet, I would like to take a stance less severe than Rabinow's as a judge of this literature. Indeed, I perceive its self-indulgence. But I also prefer to see in it the begun, yet unfinished, movement of a programmatic dialectic, the antithesis foretelling the synthesis to come.

As Freilich puts it, "the critical tool in anthropological research is the researcher himself" (1970: 33). This tool is self-conscious, as pointed out by Powdermaker: "A peculiar character of field work in anthropology and in other social sciences is that the scientist has to communicate with the objects studied and they with him, and that he is part of the situation studied" (1966: 286–287). Turning away from the American tradition which leaves me hopeful but unsatisfied, I perceive a greater, albeit still flawed, awareness in the French tradition.

This is mainly due to Lévi-Strauss' momentous *Tristes Tropiques*

([1955] 1974), which renewed a philosophical and literary genre
initiated in the sixteenth century by Montaigne ([1774] 1955) and
continued by innumerable *Philosophical Voyages* and other *Sentimental Journeys*. Of course, British writers such as Young ([1792]
1969) and Sterne ([1768] 1967) come to mind, but Lévi-Strauss'
style is decidedly more reminiscent of Chateaubriand's *Voyage en
Amérique* ([1827] 1964). Someday, if this has not already been
done, someone will profitably compare the former's description of
Santos with the latter's of Philadelphia.

I read *Tristes Tropiques* avidly as a teenager, as did a whole generation of French anthropologists who had suddenly discovered their
vocation. I read it with blind passion, over and over again, and I now
feel awkward in noticing some imperfections in it, as if some ungrace-
ful wart had just appeared on the otherwise perfect smile of this intellectual Giaconda. Lévi-Strauss had done some fieldwork, but nothing comparable to that of his Anglo-Saxon colleagues. Anthropologists
have remained reticent with this book, which is "treated . . . either as
a fine piece of French literature or, snidely and true to form, as an
overcompensation for the author's shortcomings in the bush" (Rabinow 1977: 4). Of course, the crux of the problem was radically different, for the criticism in turn reveals the reluctance, if not the sheer
inability, of anthropologists to cope with Lévi-Strauss' lucid effort at
integrating anthropological theory and anthropological praxis. The
difficulty lies elsewhere, in the timid and unsystematic aspect of the
attempt.

Masterful as it remains, *Tristes Tropiques* carries the mark of the
analytical thought which begot it. Despite Lévi-Strauss' perceptiveness,
the tragedy of the events he had to struggle with, and the psychological stress to which he was submitted, in his book, at least, he remains
outside. The events are described, discussed, digested, integrated, and
ultimately structured by a subject whose awareness remains exterior to
them. Consciousness does not seem to result from the experience of
otherness. It rather seems the intellectual apprehension of an alienated
elsewhere by an abstracted and withdrawn subject. In other words,
even in the deep of the bush, rain or shine, his mastermind is at work
or at play. There is no back and forth movement between experience
and consciousness. Things and beings, including Lévi-Strauss himself, are objectified for the benefit of an omnipotent consciousness.
Even in the field, he is still superbly, if uncomfortably, ensconced in
the Louis XV armchair of Jean-Jacques Rousseau. This problem is
pointed out by Lévi-Strauss himself, who recalls the year 1928, when
he dropped out of law school to become a full-time philosophy stu-

dent. He contrasts the attitudes of law and medicine students with their arts and sciences counterparts and speaks of the latter in a revealing way, for it qualifies him too:

> *As for the future scholar or researcher, his aim is commensurable only with the time-span of the universe. Nothing could be more mistaken, then, than to lead him to believe that their choice is a form of commitment; even when they think it is, the commitment does not consist in their accepting a particular datum and identifying themselves with one or other of its functions and in accepting the personal opportunities and risks it involves, but in judging it from the outside, as if they themselves were not part of it; their commitment is just their own special way of remaining uncommitted. In this respect, teaching and research are not to be confused with training for a profession. Their greatness and their misfortune is that they are a refuge or a mission (*[1955] 1974: 54–55*).*

What ultimately leaves me dissatisfied with *Tristes Tropiques* is not the absence of dialectics, but that dialectics are not pushed far enough. When I turn to the last page, I have witnessed the dialogue between abstract objects—the Caduveo, Bororo, Nambikwara, and Tupi-Kawahib among others—and an abstract subject—not Lévi-Strauss himself but as *res cogitans*. At the most, I find there an inter-objectivity where I had hoped for an intersubjectivity. My experience, as well as my consciousness, of anthropology is different. In the tradition of his book, I recognize that the theory and the praxis of anthropology are inseparably united. But I wish to go one step further in the examination of their relationship. As pointed out by Rabinow, "all cultural activity is experiential, . . . fieldwork is a distinctive type of cultural activity, and . . . it is this activity which defines the discipline. But what should be the very strength of anthropology—its experiential, reflective, and critical activity—has been eliminated as a valid area of inquiry by an attachment to a positivistic view of science, which I find radically inappropriate in a field which claims to study humanity" (1977: 5).

My main concern here will be the reintroduction of the concrete subject as the necessary condition of any anthropological understanding. Clearly, my feelings as a fieldworker are per se of no interest whatsoever to the profession. Similarly, the people I studied are per se an illusion, for there is no essence of a tribal group. What exists, however, is a concrete situation in which "I," the anthropologist, and

Though it is rather an unequal relationship, I imagine.

"they," the studied people, came together in a series of interactions which deeply affected our mutual perception. By definition, the situation is dialectic, so that "I" and "they" transformed each other.

Furthermore, and taking this dialectic seriously, it becomes possible to perceive that the anthropologizing subject is the occasion, the pretext, and the locus of a drama that he/she is to reflect upon. As a consequence, in fieldworking I indeed become a tool, but a reflective one, that is, a heuristic device. I become less instrumental than operational. Hence the necessity of using myself as a discovery procedure, for the chain reaction that our meeting induced will allow me to perceive the studied culture and society in action. The studied people are not there, passively waiting for me to take their picture. Nothing seems more fictitious to me now than the classic monograph in which a human group is drawn and quartered along the traditional categories of social, economic, religious, and other so-called organizations and everything holds together. Moreover, the more modern attempts at studying culture change hardly fare any better, for although they are not trapped out of time, their time is mechanistic, at any rate unreal, and cut off from any historical dialectic.

In my opinion, the point is to reintroduce the process of anthropologizing into the results of anthropology. Consciousness is not a given, floating out of a concrete situation, but a process of acquisition. In this process, the incidental and the anecdotal become of paramount importance. For this is how the anthropologist is encultured and acculturated[1] by the people he/she lives with. The changes one is subjected to, as well as the changes one introduces, are not impure epiphenomena. Quite to the contrary, as every fieldworker has experienced, they are discovery procedures through which the very articulations of the studied culture and society manifest themselves. Instead of focusing either on objects of study or on the perceiving subjects, and in so doing blurring both, it seems to me that we should focus on the happening of anthropology itself, that is, on these impurities through which an authentic understanding can be constituted "between the West and the rest" (Sahlins 1976: 54).

---

[1]Enculturation refers to the process through which an individual, in general a child, is taught the proper ways of behaving, thinking, and expressing feelings in his/her own culture. Acculturation, on the other hand, refers to the process of culture change which occurs within one culture under the external pressure of another. In other words, enculturation is the process of socialization of an individual within his/her own culture, while acculturation is the more or less forced social change which results from interethnic contact.

In this respect, my work emphasizes not an objective viewpoint but a multiplicity of viewpoints, all of which passed through the warping prism of my consciousness. I have not attempted to test anything, only to understand the relationship that fieldwork created. I thus find myself in complete agreement with Mead when she writes: "There is no such thing as an unbiased report upon any social situation. An unbiased report is, from the standpoint of its relevance to the ethos, no report at all; it is comparable to a colorblind man reporting on a sunset" (1949: 299).

The present work is ultimately a modest effort in the direction of self-reflectivity, even a timid one, as I realize. More programmatic than actualized, less achieved than to be achieved, the statement of Redfield which resounds in my memory is still in order: "In me, man and anthropologist do not separate themselves sharply; I used to think I could bring about that separation in scientific work about humanity. Now I have come to confess that I have not effected it, and indeed think it is not possible to do so" (1953: 165). And yet, as I understand it, this is the path toward listening to what "the rest" are telling us with voices that are no longer faint, despite their progressive depletion.

It is both appropriate and urgent for "the West" to answer the legitimate anger of an Oglala Sioux (Deloria 1969, 1970), and through him to answer the Old Indians as well as the New Indians: Custer died for our sins indeed, but from now on, you talk, we listen.

Part I:

Entering the Field

2. A Confrontation on the Outskirts

Enveloped in the comfort of a refreshing late afternoon breeze, I found it difficult to overcome the fascination of hues and reflections on the swollen waters of the river. Dozens of fishermen in dugout canoes were repeatedly circling upstream and then downstream, casting identical nets with grace and precision. A couple of American travelers who interrupted my reverie were discouraged from engaging in further conversation. I was strolling on the Paseo Orinoco, killing time. The sun began to set, and for a few moments the whole sky was shot through with pinks and purples. I thought of *Tristes Tropiques* and smiled to myself, to the sun, to Ciudad Bolivar, to memories, to nothing in particular and to everything at once. The waters were quite high, fairly close to the parapet of the promenade. I was still in C.B., as Americans called it, recalling their own initialed city, L.A. I wanted to verify what everyone had told me: it really would be impossible to enter Panare territory at that time of year.

From the DC-3 on which I flew the following morning to Caicara I could overlook the whole situation: a very, very inundated one. On my right, that is, north of the Orinoco, all the flat, desert-like *llanos* of Anzoategui State were gently soaking in water. On my left, south of the Orinoco, I could see the northern edge of the Guiano-Amazonian forest. Midway, we passed over the confluence with the Río Caura and then quickly reached that with the Río Cuchivero. Somewhere between these two points, at Maripa, the blacktop road which had been following the right bank since Ciudad Bolivar ended, and the landscape began to change. The Guiana became more mountainous, with eroded, flat-topped *mesas* isolated in the savanna-covered plain. As we approached the *cerro* of Caicara, I saw the Orinoco flowing around the Guianese shield. Across the river was the little town of Cabruta. From there a ferry was struggling across the rushing waters to reach Caicara with its eclectic cargo.

For an outsider, access to Caicara depends on the time of year. During the rainy season, the regular flights from Caracas or Ciudad

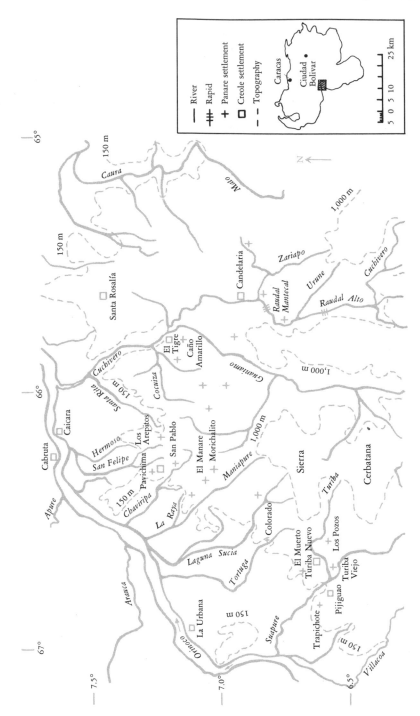

Map 1. *Panare territory*

Bolivar are the only means of approach. During the dry season, however, Caicara is less dependent upon air traffic; at the time of my journey it was a twelve-hour jeep ride from Ciudad Bolivar or Caracas,
since both roads were then in the process of being tarred and were not
completed until 1970.

Caicara was a pioneer town of about five thousand inhabitants
whose population was inflated at the time of my arrival by a number
of Creoles—the Venezuelan peasants—who were waiting patiently
with relatives and friends for the receding of the waters on their savannas. In Caicara, the Panare world ends or begins, depending upon
one's viewpoint. But as my cabdriver's jeep slogged through the muddy gullies in the streets of the town, I realized that my entrance to the
territory was not to be immediate.

Catching his breath between two bottles of frozen rather than
merely cold beer, a *ganadero* (cowboy) explained to me that access to
Panare settlements offered no major difficulty in the dry season, but
ahora no, señor. While most of his fellow townspeople were dozing,
thus escaping the crush of the early afternoon heat, he continued his
end of the conversation, going beyond what I had solicited. "They are
not savages [*bravos*]; they are tame [*mansitos*]. They come here to
town quite often during the dry season [*verano*]."

I could not get a word in edgewise. "They come to our farm
[*hato*] too; we give them food. There is even one who bears my name;
he is my *compadre*." My Spanish was still quite rusty and I had some
difficulty following his rapid monologue. He laughed and made a
successful effort to burp. "Ah, you want to speak about the Panare. I
know a lot. Since I was a kid . . . When they came here, they used to
stay with my *compadre* Carlos Ochoa. You bet [*claro*]. You don't
know him; he is dead. He crashed two years ago in the upper Cuchivero. He has two sisters who live here, but they are afraid of getting
malaria. They are old; they don't like to have Panare hanging around
anymore."

I asked him where the Panare stayed when they came to town,
which gave him time to open another bottle. "Anywhere." "What do
you mean, anywhere?" "In abandoned houses, anywhere. In fact, now
they drop in at Don Carlos'." I looked confused. *"El evangélico, sabe?*
They sling their hammocks in his backyard. Nobody else gives them
food here. Sometimes they also come to the priests. Much less though."
Either his speech was becoming less and less coherent with the cumulative effect of so much beer or else my efforts to follow his Spanish
were beginning to regress, probably both.

Don Carlos and his wife are an American couple, Protestant mis-

sionaries who have spent some twenty years in Caicara. With them I
found generous yet guarded hospitality. While he was showing me his
notebooks of Panare vocabulary, his wife began lecturing and preach-
ing to me, which irked me. Would I bring hard liquor to the Panare?
It was prohibited by law. The word of the Lord must be brought to
the Indians. Clearly, she had mixed feelings about anthropologists, but
her husband was more informative. No, the Panare did not usually
show up in Caicara during the rainy season, but there were some here
now. Don Carlos asked me whether I wanted to see them. Because of
stage fright, apprehension, or self-consciousness, I hesitated before
agreeing.

My first encounter could not have been called a smashing success.
Juancho, the headman of the local group of Pavichima, was a small
man in his late fifties who had shown up in Creole attire to help himself to the food prepared by the missionaries. He had come to Caicara
with his daughter and two of her sons. The youngest child was sick
and had to be hospitalized, so the party would stay in town until the
boy's release from the hospital. In his confrontation with me, Juancho
was reserved and shy, uttering a few phrases from time to time, but I
could not understand a word he was saying and could not even determine whether he was speaking Spanish or Panare. I do not know what
I had expected, but I felt annoyed, powerless, and frustrated, and I
withdrew. Much later Juancho explained to me that he had thought I
was an *Americano*, that is, in Panare parlance, a Protestant missionary.

In the following days I made a nuisance of myself, desperately
trying to engage people in conversation, if only to familiarize myself
with the sounds of the language. But it became clear that I was not
going to get very far in this way. Juancho's daughter bent her head
toward the ground whenever I addressed her, remaining absolutely
still and saying absolutely nothing. Juancho and his grandson were not
much better, for after half an hour of my interference they decided to
go *paseando* (to take a walk). More interesting to them was a group
of about thirty Indians who had just arrived in town. Where were
they from? Why did they come here? Where were they going? I never
found out. They were not Panare; the Panare told me that they were
Guaribo, but the visitors themselves claimed in Spanish to be Piapoco.
The Creoles disagreed as to who they were. What was certain was that
Juancho and his family enjoyed seeing them, examining their baskets
with curiosity, and leaving me to my linguistic worries.

On September 5, Vicente and his son arrived, having hitched a
boat ride from their local group on the middle Cuchivero. Insofar as I
could judge at that time, their accent was different, but their reaction

to me was the same as Juancho's. Vicente was in his early thirties, a tall man ready to laugh. He was the headman of his group and was not very eager to spend much time with me. He had come to Caicara to choose some blowguns from Don Carlos' stock, an incident which may seem curious and to which I will return later. He, too, as I later found out, thought I was a missionary.

By this time several things were already quite clear: I would not learn anything in this place; the season was bad for undertaking a survey of Panare groups; Don Carlos, who was providing hospitality, food, and shelter, had a supply of blowguns; and I, from the Panare point of view, was a nobody. Juan Pablo, the Spanish rendering of my first name, did not fool them at all, and they had no use for me whatsoever. *¿Qué regalando?* they asked me in trade-Spanish, "What do you have to give?" Then and there I had nothing, but I told them I would later bring knives, machetes, etc. They added a more specific request: "If you come, don't forget to bring beads."

The Panare love small white beads and pale blue-green ones. Men wear a string of them tightly fastened above each bicep, while women wear strings of them as necklaces. These beads are imported from Czechoslovakia, Japan, Taiwan, and Hong Kong, but since their importation is taxed by the Venezuelan government at the rate of 100 Bs[2] per kilo, the Panare cannot easily obtain them. The request of Vicente and Juancho was therefore perfectly clear: bring the impossible and prove that you are worth something to us. I had nothing to offer; I did not exist, and was perceived in a strictly economic context, as a potential gift-giver reduced to my exchange value.

By November 22 the waters had completely receded, and the sun had already begun to scorch the rejuvenated vegetation of the savanna. At this time I undertook my survey of the Panare settlements. With the logistic support of the local Service of Malariology, which chauffeured and guided me, I finally did reach Panare territory. It soon became apparent, however, that my frontal attack on the Panare problem was to be further delayed.

The Service of Malariology was a very efficient institution in Venezuela which had practically eradicated malaria from its territory. Its employees were local men, that is Creoles, who would ride a mule or walk to reach settlements which were inaccessible to jeeps or canoes. I was completely dependent on them for my survey of Panare settlements, since they knew the locations well from their regular visits. But being local Creoles, they had kinfolk, friends, acquaintances, that

---

2 "Bs" stand for "Bolivars," the Venezuelan currency. At the time of my fieldwork, the rate of exchange was approximately 5 Bs to the U.S. dollar.

is, a whole social network in the area. It was precisely this social depth which remained between me and the Panare, a middle zone which was to be both the condition of my access to the Panare and an obstacle to it.

Since the Creoles were to be mediators, both screening and facilitating a cultural brokerage between myself and the Panare, some light must now be shed upon my relationship with them. Right from the start, it was evident that they were prepared to react to me as a member of a specific social class rather than as an interacting individual. While I addressed them as I was expected to—on a first-name basis—this, to my naïve amazement, was not reciprocated. Instead, I was introduced as *el doctor de los Indios* and spoken to with *si, doctor; no, doctor*. This unearned title conferred on a then graduate student in fact made things less ambiguous for them: it clarified my status and implied the specific role I was expected to play. Such a "doctorate," it turned out, was conferred on anyone coming from a city who in one way or another could be considered an expert of sorts. Further observation showed that a simple knowledge of the three Rs was enough to qualify in terms of expertise, but the category of city-dweller, even for a foreigner, could only be attained by appearing to have wealth. In sum, the primary qualification for "doctorhood" was recognizable membership in the bourgeois class. Relative education, wealth, whiteness, and familiarity with urban centers were all opposed to the Creoles' perception of themselves. As one man expressed it, "We are ignorant, we are poor, yet as far as this home is concerned, we are completely at your orders."

Of course the servi(ab)le aspect was mostly cognitive, little more than a stereotypic formula of greeting. Nonetheless, the self-deprecation was repeatedly emphasized, since I was perceived as a representative of the dominant class in the hierarchy of complex Venezuelan society. Had I not been sent to study the Indians by the government? I had the blessings of only one regional administration, yet that was clearance enough.

Invested with the aura of political power, I did have a few vague obligations, such as behaving "doctorwise" and giving academic explanations beyond my competence. Absolute knowledge was my bag, and I could certainly explain space satellites or cancer, that is, the infinitely big and the infinitely small. That I could not repair a radio was hardly believable. But on the other hand I also had two definite rights. I had almost unlimited access to the group's knowledge—and most individuals were more than eager to talk to me ad nauseam—and I

What does the anthropologist represent?

also had an unrestricted right to hospitality, a right I abused for a long time because I failed to understand that the chicken stew prepared in my honor was a special addition to the meal of boiled rice which would have been consumed in my absence.

At the same time I was exhibited by the Creoles, who were extending their hospitality purely at the whim of their personal network, since I was believed to have power, and therefore, to a limited yet real extent, was power. As such, I was manipulated like any other symbol, involved in a web of symbolic action. The rationale for this is easy to understand. Having arrived at a particular Creole home, I had, from my host's point of view, established a tacit contract with him: I had picked his house rather than his neighbor's. Insofar as the most subtle inequalities could immediately be perceived in this hierarchical society, he had been invested with some power himself, due to his ability to provide the *doctor* with a service which his neighbor had not done. He had obligated me. Besides, the same neighbor, ridden with curiosity, would not fail to drop by for a cup of coffee when I was around. In a way, the host was thus able to "produce" me, which was a symbolic way of remaining upwardly mobile. As long as I was indebted to my host, I provided an occasion to activate his network, to reinforce the solidarity of a group of people, and to boost that group's relative status. Quite unknowingly, I had become a Durkheimian catalyst. I quickly became aware of my political role as well when I discovered, after a few days of surveying, that no matter where our hammocks were slung for the night or where we were taking a coffee break, it was always at the house of a member of the same political faction.

Meanwhile, days were passing, and I had made brief visits to some fifteen Panare settlements. Clearly, my Creole guides were diligently orienting me, but they were not eager to spend too much time in any one settlement. At Guarataro, I hardly had time to sketch the plan of the settlement while one of my Creole guides was talking to the man "in charge." The fact that a Panare settlement could have no *capitán* was such an anomaly to the Creoles that it could only be met with disbelief.

A few Panare men, less shy and less busy than the others, voluntarily entered into a conversation in trade-Spanish which I did not have to join. My future role had already been defined for the Panare by the Creoles: "The *doctor* is coming to learn your language." This indeed was the simplest way to define my intentions. I could count about thirty people in this *churuata*, the Panare communal dwelling. I unsuccessfully attempted for the *n*th time to understand and to be understood by another person. Clearly, few if any Panare men spoke anything more than limited trade-Spanish. I was still looking for a bilingual, and all evidence agreed: there were only two possibilities.

Servando Vitriaga was a slim, twenty-year-old Creole who had spent part of his childhood in close contact with a Panare settlement on the middle Cuchivero through vicissitudes that I could never reconstruct with any accuracy. Despite my natural scepticism at his "I know everything," his command of the Panare language was adequate, as he had acquired it at a tender age. The hospital at Caicara employed him part-time as an interpreter for the Panare, but the archbishop of Ciudad Bolivar, who was planning to open a mission among the Panare, had made him a job offer which I could not match. Accompanying me *en la selva* (to the bush), when he could live more comfortably in Ciudad Bolivar, offered no appeal to his political, social, or economic aspirations. For my part, I was not enthusiastic about him either, since I suspected that his ethnocentrism would have a negative effect on my acceptance by the Panare. Fortunately—as I thought at the time—there was an alternative, and I turned toward Pedro Castro, a real Panare.

Pedro was a small, sturdy, fortyish man who spoke Spanish fluently enough for my purposes. He had been baptized in his infancy by a now deceased Creole who had made a gift of his name to the young boy in the course of proselytism. The son of his godfather introduced me to him with great pride: "He is used to working for us Creoles." Not much more information was provided at the time—in particular, the circumstances of his "working for us." Actually, for many years he had been a wage laborer for the Creoles, but for that very reason had virtually been expelled from his own local group. At any rate, he certainly was a unique person to work with. Despite the loss of his upper incisors and his incessant tobacco chewing, he was a native speaker. The Creoles had emphasized to him that since he liked to work with *civilizados*, it certainly would be a great opportunity for him to work for *el doctor* for 10 Bs a day, a proposition which also enabled me to avoid haggling over his salary, since the amount had been suggested without any intervention on my part.

His enthusiasm was of short duration, however, when I mentioned that I was going to stay a year or so in a single Panare settlement. He was willing to teach me the Panare language, but since he was living like a Creole, there was no way to convince him to go back to living among his own people. I had no choice but to offer to work with him in Caicara, which was as glamorous to him as Ciudad Bolivar had been to the first bilingual. As a matter of fact, he was even reluctant to interpret at all in the Panare settlements in which we stopped on our way to the town, remaining absolutely silent there. This was not the ideal situation, yet I was happy to get the chance to jot down some Panare words in my notebook. On the other hand, I was learning very little from Pedro directly; I could see that he was trapped between two cultures, that of the Panare, who had rejected him, and that of the Creoles, who would not accept him except as a wage laborer.

Being brought to a Panare settlement was torture for him. Dressed in Creole attire, he would vainly attempt to pass for a Creole; yet in Caicara, when I tried to tape his utterances, he would protest that he could not speak into a microphone because I would then steal his voice—a typical Panare reaction. I was not giving him the opportunity he desired, and this increased the ambiguity of his cultural identity more than either of us wanted. In addition, he turned out to be fairly counter-productive in the Panare settlements. Either he would not interpret anything or the Panare would maintain an ostracizing silence in his presence, cutting me off completely from any access to them. This gave me a very poor introduction to their world, exactly the kind of first impression I had hoped to avoid by surveying Panare settlements with a native speaker.

As it turned out, the situation had infinitely more symbolic depth than I could grasp at the time. Too many actors were involved in this minidrama, the development of which was certainly beyond my control. The Panare at that time were a goal for me, the unknown element I was trying to get at. But between us I had substituted an interpreter whom they considered at best a weirdo and at worst a renegade, a neither-nor with whom they did not know how to cope.

My association with Pedro had a minimally functional yield. This was unfortunate, but the convergence of our paths was doomed from the start. As I understand it now, this association was never as fortuitous as I had first hoped it would be, in part because the Creoles had been instrumental in my hiring him. In fact, although they had mentioned Servando Vitriaga as an alternative, they had never pushed for him as they had for Pedro Castro. I had been easily convinced of the suitability of the latter, not only because I could neither afford the Creole interpreter nor convince him to work for me, but also because in my view a Creole interpreter was a worse alternative than a native Panare. In many respects the Creoles had won a logical game of political strategy in their mediation between me—the bourgeois—and Pedro—the Indian. In their eyes, Pedro represented what the Panare should be: the successful Indian who had finally arrived at "civilization." He was an *indígena*, it was true, but a properly dressed one; a wage laborer, but a hard worker; an *irracional*, but one who had finally come to grips with the world of rational economic behavior. Pedro was a deserving man who was entirely at their mercy, and the Creoles felt good about freely giving him a little extra help in the right direction.

Conversely, in their eyes I was a bourgeois who stooped to conquer, who stooped to their world. How could they oblige me more than by producing for me the Creole equivalent of a "noble savage"? Of course, they were also producing me in the same way throughout their social networks. In their mediation between Pedro Castro and me, they had manipulated both of us to their political advantage. Pedro and I had become the dupes of the game, for I did not help his social integration among the Creoles any more than he helped my cultural introduction to the Panare. We had one and only one point of convergence, since we were going in opposite directions—he toward the Western world, I toward the Panare. We could not go anywhere together, since we had little power to bestow on each other, and soon we were waving at each other from diverging paths. Henceforth I would have to act alone. Thus it was that I settled with the local group of Turiba Viejo on December 14, 1967.

3. *Without and Within*

Turiba Nuevo, despite the novelty implied by its name, is quite literally a dead end, the end of the truck path. Located on the lower part of the river from which it derives its name, this Creole village is a bumpy twelve-hour jeep ride away from Caicara in the dry season when the rivers can be forded. During the rainy season, only an occasional light plane lands on the poorly maintained strip of grassland. At that time of year, any freight has to come up the river, thus replicating the journey made around 1910 by the earliest Creole pioneers, who had paddled upstream on the Orinoco, passed La Urbana (a small river port some 60 km WNW of Turiba), traveled up the Río Suapure as far as its confluence with the Río Turiba, and finally settled in the savanna, on the edge of the Guianese shield.

The first Creole settlers had found this flat savanna hospitable, and for that reason Turiba Nuevo had been built there. Being located at the edge of a fertile forest cover, the village had the advantages of being at the juncture between two types of environments: the lowlands of the Orinoco basin and the highlands of the Guianese shield. Thus the settlers could rely on the grasslands for their animal husbandry and the edge of the forest for some slash-and-burn cultivation. Most important of all, they could fix their eyes upon the mirage of wealth, a dream of revenge upon their poverty.

But the reality was somehow different. Most of the 600 Creoles who were living in Turiba Nuevo were not too well off. Poorly dressed, poorly fed, living in scattered mud *ranchos*, they had little if anything with which to attract and retain the schoolteachers or nurses who, during their training, had already tasted the sweet savor of urban life. Thus the arrival of a plane, truck, or canoe constituted a noteworthy interruption in the monotony of their daily routine. Such occurrences quickly became the occasion for a social gathering, where they could look for a traveler, a package, perhaps a message . . . but most of all some gossip about the vast "outside world"—which rarely referred to anything more cosmopolitan than La Urbana, Caicara, or

Ciudad Bolivar. But these events were extraordinary happenings. On
a day-to-day basis, the focal point of the village was the government-
held Station, where basic supplies could be bought at controlled prices
and where one could be almost certain of finding the occasion for
some social interaction.

Turiba was an easy point from which to *meterse en el monte*, that
is, to enter the northeastern edge of the extended Guiano-Amazonian
tropical forest and look for rubber and chicle as well as tonka beans.
Such marketable resources were plentiful in the area, and transporting
them by canoe to La Urbana or Caicara offered no major difficulty.
When I arrived, however, even the mirage of imminent wealth had
dried up, since the market for these goods had collapsed a few years
previously as a result of the synthetic manufacturing of their by-
products, and the diamond rush which occurred in and after December
1969 had not even been dreamed about yet. The village was striving,
though not exactly thriving.

Irregularly but frequently, Panare Indians from the local groups
of El Muerto, Los Pozos, Turiba Viejo, and, to a lesser extent, Colorado would come to the Creole outpost, strolling, *paseando*, as they
would say in trade-Spanish, paying a visit there or just passing by on
their way to another settlement. Their own settlement, Turiba Viejo,
"Old" Turiba, was so called because it was there that the Creole pioneers had first settled in 1910. Shortly thereafter, they had decided to
move a few kilometers upstream to their present location, Turiba
Nuevo. At that time, it appears that there were no Panare in the area.
Now, however, all this was but a blurred memory, as the self-made
"Colonel" Domingo Flores, leader of the first group of Creole settlers,
had been resting in peace under six feet of earth for almost a year.

The Panare memory was hardly any better. *Kulye kanokampe,
kuliptu kanokampe*, I was told by Marquito, who, if not the most
talkative of my Panare informants, was one of the most knowledgeable
regarding his own traditions: "many years ago, very many years ago."
He was not saying that the Panare had been created at that time, but
that it was then that they had been given their present aspect by the
demiurge Manataci, the androgynous anaconda who was sometimes
visible as the rainbow, at other times audible as the thunder. Except
for this mythical faith, Panare history, as we understand it, had no
more depth or extension than the too shallow memory of my best informants, whose preoccupations were decidedly in the present. Marquito, like any other Panare, was making history in the existential
present of his concrete behavior and could not care less about historical
consciousness. The origin of his people was not a historical issue but

an etiological reference, something which could be re-presented and was therefore relevant in that way only. Clearly, there were events which had taken place in that period of time between Panare origins and the present, but these were transparent and did not require explanation.

Yet myth and history do coincide at one point: the Panare's emergence at the source of the Río Cuchivero. Documents published prior to the Second World War concur in assigning this same territory to the Panare: 7° N latitude, 66° W longitude (Koch-Gruenberg 1922: 235). In 1944, however, two authors, Antolínez and López Ramírez, independently described a much more extensive territory for the Panare, one which accurately matched the region they occupied at the time of my fieldwork. What actually did happen, of course, nobody knows for sure, but some prudent reconstruction may be ventured.

The Panare, who belong to the Carib linguistic family, were located in the upper Cuchivero basin during the eighteenth century. The Indian groups who had once been located on the right bank of the Orinoco between the courses of the Suapure and the Cuchivero had become extinct by 1850 as a side effect of earlier contacts with the expanding Western world. A vast territory was left almost empty, since the Creoles, who were just beginning to settle in the area, at first remained quite close to the bank of the Orinoco. Liberated from the demographic pressure which would have contained them had they stayed in the upper Cuchivero, the Panare began to expand to the northwest, progressively occupying the territory they now share marginally with the Creoles, as reflected by the situation at Turiba.

Regarding the recent past of the Panare in the Turiba area, the Creoles, somehow more historically minded, have a better memory than the Panare themselves, and ultimately the two testimonies do agree. A composite yet coherent image of that fissioning past can be approximated. I have previously described it as follows:

> *Around 1930, two Panare brothers-in-law, both born in Ochi (now disappeared) in approximately 1895, left their birthplace to settle on their own at La Raya on the southern edge of the Sierra Cerbatana, about 80 km northeast of Turiba. About ten years later, a split of La Raya led to the establishment of three new settlements. The founders of La Raya left it and followed the edge of the Cerbatana on its western side; Manuel Hernández settled at El Paujil, while José Medina settled farther north at Morichalito. A third group departed. Heading southeast, Manuel Blanco settled first at Los Gallitos, which has since be-*

come the Creole village of Turiba Nuevo. The first contact be-
tween Panare and Creoles took place there. Finding it a conven-
ient place propitious for cattle breeding, the Creoles began
building their mud houses around Los Gallitos. In 1945, in order
to avoid both the Creoles and their cattle, the Indians had to
move, and their village split again: one party, headed by Casa-
nova Viejo, established itself at El Muerto, about 10 km north of
Turiba; the other one, headed by Manuel Blanco, crossed the
Turiba River and founded Guamure, only 5 km northeast of
Turiba. Guamure split again in 1964: a group settled at Los
Pozos, about 10 km south of Guamure, while Manuel Blanco
went to Turiba Viejo, the original settlement of the Creole col-
onists. When, in December 1967, a few weeks after the death of
this headman, I myself arrived at Turiba Viejo, there was no
Panare settlement south of the Suapure River (Dumont 1976:
23–24).

Turiba Viejo was thus the southwesternmost settlement in the Panare territory, located at 6° 35′ 58″ N latitude, 66° 42′ 12″ W longitude. This roughly triangular area, delimited by the right bank of the
Orinoco and two of its tributaries—the Suapure and the Cuchivero—
constitutes the northwestern tip of the Guianese shield, around which
the Orinoco flows in rather leisurely fashion. In this territory, all
rivers flow from the rocky formations of the Guianese shield toward
the Orinoco, and most of them are too short to be navigable. Falls and
rapids on their upper courses further impede navigation, although the
meandering lower courses can easily be forded during the dry season.

The highly eroded Guianese shield is a system of mountains which
becomes more and more loosely connected as it approaches the Orinoco, at which point the flat-topped, steep-flanked *cerros* are separated
from one another by small plains. The dominant landscape here is the
Guiano-Amazonian tropical rain forest, here and there interspersed
with small savannas, particularly on the flat mountain tops. Along the
right bank of the Orinoco, a 10- to 80-km-wide floodplain presents a
rather desolate landscape in which scraggly grasslands compete for
living space with desert-like stretches of sand. Sparse and stunted
trees occasionally grow in the savanna, the monotony of which is elsewhere broken by clusters of palm trees which manage to thrive in
shallow little depressions and by gallery forests which meander here
and there against the distant horizon of the blue mountains.

With the first rains of April/May, the cracked crust of the soil
changes into the oozing mud of a gigantic swamp, where the vegeta-

tion, scorched since October/November, rejuvenates rapidly. Yet, inundated or withered, the savanna offers many more contrasts than the
forest, which wages a losing war with the savanna on the plain. In the
forest, the constantly humid air never reaches a very high temperature,
due mainly to the thick foliage overhead which provides an efficient
sunshade, while in the openness of the sun-scorched savanna, the at-
mosphere virtually quivers.

This polarization of space between closed forest and open savanna
is not something I alone felt. Both the Panare and the Creoles perceive
this with acuity, although they do so in opposite ways. The Creoles are
people of the savanna, the place to which they have adapted and to
which they belong. However boring and less than providential, this
dull environment, where hunger and ennui slowly consume their lives,
is nonetheless home. But for them the forest is entirely different, the
very locus of desire, invested with colorful phantasms which are carefully inflated by those who have stayed for some time in its bosom. *La
selva* is not only a maternal figure, offering an unlimited share of attractive and elusive goods, but also a female figure who abandons herself lasciviously only to the most daring *machos*. Back in the savanna,
they relate inexhaustible accounts of their adventures: the mythified
trials to which they have been subjected, the jaguars and snakes they
had to kill, the demands of a remote and scary El Dorado peopled with
nymphomaniac Amazons. What they bring back from this commerce
with the forest are memories to build on, a mind trip. In most cases,
they come back in the same way they penetrate the forest: with only
their machetes, a word which refers properly to the bush knife and
figuratively to the erected member—both tools about whose use they
are always ready to brag.

For the Panare, the situation is reversed. They are at home in the
thickness of the forest. Although they have to share it with spirits less
to be revered than to be feared, this is where they hunt and gather;
this is where they establish their gardens. For the Panare, adventure
begins with the profane world of the savanna. Even though their main
settlements are not established in the depths of the forest, and even
though Creole and Panare territories overlap, the savanna is clearly the
home of the Creoles. This environment is also exploited to some extent by the Panare, but it is mainly the avenue to a wholly different
style of adaptation, with its tempting attractions and fearful wonders,
its horses and cows, its trucks and airplanes, its electricity and radio
sets, its clothes and metal tools, its shotguns and plastic goods; in
short, a world difficult to manipulate.

Half-daring, half-restrained, the Panare settle midway between the sacred and the profane, *a la pata del cerro*, that is, in the foothills where the plain ends and the forest and savanna confront each other in vain. There, close to a source of water, the Panare clear a roughly circular space on a slightly slanting terrain, using the natural slope of the ground to prevent the water from stagnating. In the center of this space, with its back to the mountain and its sides flanked by several workshop-huts, they erect their communal dwelling, the *churuata*. This word is used in Venezuela for any communal Indian dwelling. The Panare, however, call theirs *pereka*, although this latter term has a wider connotation than the former, since it can refer to the whole settlement in general, as well as to any particular *churuata*, in which as few as fifteen and as many as fifty individuals may live.

The whole Panare population is dispersed in about fifty local groups which maintain a minimum distance of 15 km (approximately a two-hour walking distance) between themselves. From a territorial viewpoint, each local group thus constitutes a discrete unit. Political conflicts between groups are thus virtually eliminated, since they do not compete for the same resources. Indeed, the gardens are cleared in a forest location very close to the *churuata*, while predatory activities are carried out within a maximum radius of 15 km from that building, conceived as a center. Truly speaking, there is not one Panare territory, but, from an emic standpoint, there are Panare territories, not unified at all by any shared institutions or tribal consciousness. In addition, the boundaries of each "experienced" territory continue to fluctuate, to be subject to the group's mobility, and no individual, even if he/she marries within the local group of origin, will ever spend his/her entire life within the same *churuata*. In fact, after eight to ten years, in terms of time and energy expended, it is less costly to build a new *churuata* and to clear new gardens nearby than to repair an old, leaking building and cultivate gardens which become more and more remote year after year.

The construction of new dwelling places is also a result of fissioning which is occasioned by political conflicts within the local group. Often linked to population growth and triggered by adultery, these cleavages between members of a formerly unified group compel the departing party to build a new *churuata* in the new place of residence. Finally, the death of the headman or of a shaman involves, ideally if not always actually, the burning down of the *churuata*. In all these cases, the communal dwelling place is seen as overwhelmingly temporary, an immediate response rather than an enduring institution. In addition, the lack of land tenure associated with slash-and-burn horticulture, and little if any ecological pressure in this respect, gives the

Panare great leeway in terms of mobility. Thus even the territory itself of a single local group lacks being, as it were, and its actuality is only existential. It is a space which is temporarily located, dependent on historical contingency, in short, "lived."

The space which surrounds the settlement is not amorphous, though, for the opposition between savanna and forest is clearly perceived by the Panare. Although they exploit both types of environment, they are more systematic in their use of the resources of the forest than of those of the savanna. Only the soil of the forest is fertile, and, of course, this is where gardens are cultivated. In addition, the forest is the place where big game such as tapirs and peccaries are tracked during collective hunts, and it is by means of these endeavors that men acquire the prestige necessary to gain access to women. The forest is also peopled with spirits one had better avoid, particularly at night, when they can become most dangerous. Ultimately, this environment is a world somehow sacred, one to be manipulated with care, while the savanna is mainly the profane world of the Creoles. True, the savanna offers a plentiful supply of fish (principally during the dry season), but success at fish poisoning does not provide prestige comparable to that of hunting. Although the savanna has small game to be hunted individually, it is generally not even conceived of as a predatory space at all.

The savanna, however, is the locus of commercial exchanges with the Creoles. Since buying/selling is the modality of that exchange, anything and everything of worth has a value which is convertible into a general equivalent: Venezuelan currency. Consequently, the savanna is neither the space where one helps oneself nor the space where one gives and receives; it is the place for trading. The forest, however, is the exact opposite, for here one helps oneself *ad libitum*. In its bosom dwell the wild plant and animal masters, who are generous. Without having to counter-give, the Panare receive the "children of the forest" (*icpankin*) from these masters, just so long as they hunt, fish, and gather with moderation. Thus trade in the savanna is clearly opposed to predatory activities in the forest. In addition, both "free" hunting, fishing, and gathering and "paid-for" trading are opposed to the gift/ counter-gift exchanges that regulate relations among the Panare. And both activities are similarly opposed to horticulture, where that which is planted must first be "given" to the cultivated gardens so as to force the gardens to "counter-give," that is, to bring forth a harvest. Thus, the Panare may be seen to place themselves between two opposed worlds which they mediate within their inhabited space. Located between the profane and still natural space of the savanna and the already supernatural space of the forest, the Panare settlement represents cultural space *par excellence*.

Turiba Viejo was no exception. A few days after my arrival, I climbed the hill behind the settlement. Turiba Viejo was at my feet, just at the juncture of the savanna and the forest. Its various paths radiated from the cleanly swept central clearing, the *churuata* looked like the inverted keel of a boat, and eleven workshop-huts were neatly laid out along the sides of the *churuata*. Down below, carefree children were playing. I could see the garden clearings forming a distinct break in the dark green of the forest, and I could approximate more than actually see the course of the Río Turiba through the screen of trees.

Mirón, who had accompanied me, extended his arm in the general direction of Turiba Nuevo, hidden behind a stretch of sylvan mountains; then he pointed to different Panare settlements which could not be seen. Finally, indicating the savanna, he began an unsolicited enumeration of all that it represented to him, an endless paradigm. Cows were the most attractive item, although like most Panare he had always been quite afraid of them. This one animal represented a lot of meat but came without the excitement or chancy outcome of hunting. And saltwater was the most extravagant thing that he had

Pl. 1. *The settlement of Turiba Viejo*

ever heard of; it existed far away, beyond Caracas. The fact that my *churuata* lay beyond the saltwater like that of the *Americano* was neither easy for me to explain nor easy for him to grasp. Truly, my homeland was off limits for him. His world was here, transparent to him, although still quite mysterious to me.

Saltwater was a mind-blowing experience for the few men of Turiba Viejo who had seen it, heard it, smelled it, and tasted it, according to the four senses that the Panare recognize. So was the air- and noise-pollution of Caracas. Phantasms and memories were intertwined in the account untiringly given by Domingo Barrios: "Too many people, too much traffic. They even drink that saltwater which runs in their homes." "Do you drink it too?" Andrés asked me. My denial did not carry much conviction for anybody around. "You lie," stated Marquito's son, with a big smile on his face. "Yes, you are a big liar," commented a child who had until then remained silent in the conversation.

In the dry season of 1965, Raúl Leoni, then president of Venezuela, had hopped by Turiba to pay a brief visit to his remote constituents. On his way back to the capital, he offered to take Marquito and Felipe for a week's visit to Caracas, a proposal which—their curiosity overcoming apprehension—they immediately accepted. As can be imagined, such an event was an extraordinary occurrence, unprecedented and not to be replicated.

Apart from myself, very few totally foreign visitors ever came to "visit" Turiba Viejo. It happened only once during my stay, in February 1968, when the archbishop of Ciudad Bolivar, modern messiah, dropped from the sky in full archiepiscopal regalia and spent a whole hour inspecting the situation. The entire group of Panare men had been busy felling trees in preparation for new gardens. *Kanowa*! someone yelled suddenly. The word could refer to any means of water, land, or sea transportation. I could not hear anything yet, but everyone had stopped working and was carefully listening now. "It is coming here!" Everyone dashed back to the *churuata*. Arriving last of all—panting—I saw Monseñor there, next to the helicopter, flanked by his pilot and Servando Vitriaga, his interpreter, all facing the compact group of curious men. Women were also peeping at the show, but they did so furtively and from afar. Domingo Barrios and Felipe Casanova took care of the conversation with the strangers, since Marquito, the headman, was never very talkative, often remaining silent unless directly addressed. An adolescent pointed to His Excellency's robe and declared that he was dressed like a Creole woman, a comment which provoked general giggling.

Shortly after the helicopter had taken off, Domingo Barrios asked me, "What was he looking for?" I did not know exactly and said so, to which he replied, "He is a real big headman of the Creoles. You, you know nothing. You are not even a small headman." One of his sons added, "The other man can speak," referring to the interpreter. "He is not like you; you are dumb and you lie." His brother joined the conversation: "You walk; he flies. We would rather have him around than you. He would give us machetes and beads. You ask many questions but you do not give. Not enough."

That was a real blow to my prestige. They were reminding me of what I had promised them when I first arrived. That was not enough either. I should bring more goods, since I was rich. And if I was not rich, why did I stay around instead of going back to look for more goods to bring them? The truth of the matter was that I was having a very hard time competing with a helicopter. Domingo Barrios and his sons knew that well and were using this opportunity to put some pressure on me to stimulate and increase my generosity. They also knew, however, that they had received no gift whatsoever from the archbishop's party, who had only made some vague promises about an unreal future. Given this situation, the most promising individual to manipulate was clearly me. The principle of interaction was made quite explicit: "You want to know, you have to pay." The helicopter thus served to remind me of two facts of my social position: my economic function in the group and my political nothingness. Since I did not give that much, I could not be that powerful in their eyes. Nevertheless, by evening they had at least momentarily forgotten my stinginess and were describing over and over again "the big metal bird yet small transportation-means which had brought the robed man." The incident had provided a nice diversion in their daily routine.

In that respect, my first visit to Turiba Viejo was quite similar. It happened while I was conducting my preliminary survey. The Service of Malariology people from Caicara were unable to arrange a trip for me to the southwestern Panare groups, since, administratively, the latter fell under the jurisdiction of their counterparts in La Urbana. The quickest and easiest way out of this dilemma was for me to get a jeep ride from the Guardia Nacional. As I should have suspected from the beginning, had I not been so naïvely confident in my gendarme driver, the undertaking turned out to be far from ideal, a reconnaissance more in the military sense than the academic.

After having lost an unbelievable amount of time en route, and subsequently having had to cancel our visits to two out of three projected groups, we finally arrived at Tyriba Nuevo. My arrival at the village with such an escort duly impressed the Creoles, but, as they said, Guardia Nacional or not, the Panare were still two hours away by foot, and there was no jeep path to Turiba Viejo. Mellowed—or rather softened—by the delights of Caicara, the gendarme was not at all eager to rough it and spend an extra night in the wilderness. Besides, he did not deem it proper for a fully accredited anthropologist to walk when he could order several young villagers to open up a path for his jeep. So he did.

To reach Turiba Viejo in this way took us roughly as much time as if we had walked. We had to pass through a stretch of forest, ford a stream (which we barely managed), and finally cross a long expanse of bumpy savanna, where we followed the well-trodden Panare path leading almost to Turiba Viejo itself. By jeep we reached the gallery forest which follows the meandering Turiba River. The settlement was across the river, but it could not be seen. For the next few hundred meters we had to walk through the forest to get to the riverbank. We still could not see the *churuata* and, with the breeze agitating the foliage, we could not even hear any noise coming from there, although our arrival, of course, had not gone unnoticed. Panare dogs barked at us while Andrés paddled across the river in an unstable dugout canoe which I was to see capsize several times thereafter.

My party was greeted on the other side by virtually the entire male population of the local group, while the women remained safely at a distance, intrigued and amused. The roaring of our jeep had been heard from far away; never had such a vehicle come here before. Our arrival was an occasion for interrupting the monotony of daily chores, and everybody took advantage of the opportunity to get a peek at us. The children were wearing a string around the waist—their only clothing—while a number of women had pulled a Creole dress over their loincloths or had draped themselves in blankets. All the men were wearing a loincloth except one.

He was Domingo Barrios and he had had all the time he needed to dress up in a manner befitting the occasion: pants, jacket, hat, and sunglasses. It was most fortunate that he was ready, for the rank-minded gendarme attacked immediately: "Who is the chief here?" He used the term *capitán*, by which the Creoles refer to the Panare headman. To this, Domingo Barrios gave a less than accurate response, pretending that he, in fact, was the *capitán* and acting accordingly. In this way he dealt with intruders. In reality he was not the group's headman, but was allowed to play that role because he was a rather glib speaker. Actually, the headman had been Manuel Blanco, but he had had the misfortune to pass away three weeks earlier. Marquito, a shy introvert who was then the headman-elect, was not inclined to deal with such nonsense.

The Creoles assume that there must be one and only one headman per Panare local group. Projecting their conception of coercive power onto the Panare, they always wish to deal with the *capitán*. In fact, although the Panare do make a distinction between shaman (*tukuraxtey*) and headman (*iyan*), the political authority of a headman is legitimized by a religious sanction: his shamanistic initiation. As a result, there are local groups in which there is no headman, that is, groups where nobody has gone through the shamanistic initiation. Conversely, there are groups in which more than one man is potentially qualified to be headman without actually being so. For the Creoles —who refer to themselves as *racionales*—this is the ultimate proof, crystal-clear evidence that the Panare are *irracionales*. On the other hand, the Panare are aware that vis-à-vis the Creoles they have to have a chief. So quite often, after having stated the unacceptable truth that there is no headman in the local group, they will proceed to get out of the problem by coming up with an ad hoc headman—in the present case, Domingo Barrios.

The situation was slightly more complicated at Turiba Viejo, where the recent death of Manuel Blanco had left a vacuum of au-

Pl. 2. *Marquito (*unyey-TV1*), headman of Turiba Viejo*

Pl. 3. *Domingo Barrios* (töna-*TV 4*), *during the fish poisoning of a pond*

thority in the group which would last until his replacement by Marquito. But Marquito would only become the headman, properly speaking, when Manuel Blanco had entirely disappeared, a relatively lengthy process which required more than his mere physical death and burial.

Meanwhile, Domingo Barrios—who was neither the group's headman nor about to become so—was welcoming our party because he was a shaman and in that capacity could act with some authority. In addition, one of his roles was as a mediator with the Creoles, as exemplified by his behavior during the visit of the archbishop. He knew enough about the Creole way to shake hands and give the embrace (*abrazo*) and could speak profusely in trade-Spanish, raising the volume of his voice to match that of his Creole interlocutor. In short, he was able to behave in a way the Creoles could understand, and they generally liked him. Actually, he was well aware of the limits of his Creole competence and performed accordingly, that is, with a sort of quantitative exaggeration which enabled him to improve its quality, as if overperforming was a way of making up for its shortcomings. Somehow, he was even able to make a show of it, something I discovered with time. Never at a loss in dealing with the Creoles, he was neither a fool nor a deviant. While Pedro Castro was entirely trapped in his role, Domingo Barrios was not. The latter, entirely at ease within his own culture, was only putting on a show in which he overacted with delight— to the great amusement of his companions. In fact, he knew enough to remain within the limits of both the Creole and the Panare code of behavior. Above all, he was a master at double entendre, making fools of the Creoles in ways they could not understand, while the Panare could not help but notice his facetious caricatures. For instance, he would deliberately raise his voice when speaking with a Creole, something he would never do otherwise except when he was mimicking the Creole for a Panare public—and in that context he would overdo it even more, speaking at the top of his lungs.

We had hardly disembarked from the canoe and were still unable to see the *churuata*, which, obscured by vegetation, was some 50 meters away from the riverbank, when Domingo Barrios asked us *¿Qué buscando?* ("What are you looking for?"). Before I had time to formulate an answer, the gendarme took the lead so that I could not get in a word: "He is a doctor, a big *capitán* sent by Caracas. You better treat him well. Otherwise I will come back and put you in jail. He is good. He will bring gifts."

To be sure, that was an introduction, but it was even worse than I had feared, and I thought I would die of embarrassment. Obviously, both Domingo Barrios and the gendarme were playing a power game in which I was the pawn, and each was eager to demonstrate his authority to the other.

We walked swiftly toward the *churuata*. The clearing where the *churuata* and the surrounding workshop-huts are located constitutes the core of the settlement. Its maximum extension, however, includes not only the clearing but also the water source and the gardens. Women rarely venture out of this perimeter, which encloses the sphere of their daily activities. If a woman does leave this area, she is almost always preceded by her husband, or her father or brother if she is unmarried. During collective travels undertaken by the whole local group, the Panare—who ignore navigation except for the rare purpose of crossing unfordable rivers—walk single file on narrow paths, with the group of men always preceding the group of women. An individual's place in the file is thus sexually determined, except for breastfed children, who are carried by their mothers. Weaned children walk in front of their parent of the same sex. It is thus as if the men were constantly maintaining, almost containing, the women behind them or inside the perimeter that men freely and commonly transgress.

The Panare are not completely sedentary, for at the peak of the dry season, they abandon their settlement for an open-air campsite in a forest clearing where they sling their hammocks, generally within a kilometer of the main settlement. The spatial organization of the camp is similar to that of the *churuata*, and the residential unit remains compact, as the whole group moves together. Conversely, at the peak of the rainy season, the nuclear or polygynous families within the group scatter in different directions, each to occupy a *rancho*. These small buildings are often located more than a half-hour's walking distance from the main settlement but still within the territory where predatory activities are carried out. Although in general one or two families will still remain in the main settlement, the group is dispersed, and as such it does not exist anymore. Except for these two movements, which each last about a month, members of the local group spend the rest of the year within the main settlement, performing most of their daytime activities in the workshop-huts.

But it was the *churuata* I was led to see first. To get into the building, we first had to bend and pass through an entrance tunnel. The interior was pitch black. The thatching of the roof, extending to the ground, provided good protection against the sun. The building was almost deserted, with its empty hammocks neatly strung up higher than our heads to allow free passage underneath. It was impossible not to perceive a certain coziness in this protected space. A glance was enough to see that the *churuata* was built according to the same pattern as the workshop-hut, although the former was much larger. No workshop-hut exceeded 8 m in length, while the *churuata* was about 20 m long, 12 m wide, and 8 m high. It had been entirely rethatched the previous year, so it was in excellent shape.

The Panare build their houses at the very beginning of the rainy season. The small workshop-huts and *ranchos* are a private concern and are constructed by one man alone or with the help of a kinsman. But the *churuata* is of concern to the whole group, and it is the responsibility of all the men to undertake its construction as well as its maintenance. In fact, anything which requires collective participation—such as the common meals, the rituals, and so on—takes place within the *churuata* or in its immediate vicinity, while that which concerns a married man and his family of procreation takes place in the workshop-hut. At dawn or at dusk, for instance, the whole group of initiated males assembles in front of the *churuata* and there shares a common meal, while the whole group of females, who always eat separately on the side or in the back of the *churuata*, shares their meal with uninitiated boys.

Each morning at daybreak, after the communal night's sleep in the *churuata*, the local group disperses to the familial workshop-huts. At night each family comes out of these private buildings to resettle in the *churuata*. As is often the case in other ethnographic contexts, the house itself is a microcosm made in the image of the macrocosm.

Domingo Barrios offered us a refreshing calabashful of manioc beer. It had been kept cool in a kettle at the foot of the central pillar which, as I learned later, was the center of the world around which the Panare weltanschauung was organized. If I had not been so subservient to the distorting empiricism of ethnographic observation, I might, indeed, have perceived at that time that this pillar extended well beyond its visible aspect, to the point where it intersected Manataci's rainbow during the daytime and the Milky Way at night. Only the eyes of a Westerner could not see that. I might have noticed as well that the log erected in the clearing in front of the *churuata* was likewise an *axis mundi* and that each separate center represented *the axis mundi*, by means of which access to the supernatural was possible: access to the demiurge who had shaped the present world and access to the domain of the souls of the dead, the Milky Way. But at the time I did not, because I did not yet speak Panare and because my accompanying gendarme was growing more and more impatient to leave. Had I not by now seen everything I could possibly want to see? As he pressingly pointed out, "You've seen one, you've seen them all."

4. *Of Nuts and Fools*

"What do you want?" Asked either in trade-Spanish (*¿Qué bus-cando?*) or in Panare (*nexpa ipimpwö aman?*), the question was in-escapable, as was the need to formulate an answer. To formulate, per-chance to fabricate. Yet, as I scribble now with mixed emotions, some ten years after it really happened, as I am doing my best to recapture the quality of this anthropological experience, I cannot help but per-ceive the blind power game I was playing. The irony of it all is the paradoxical blend of absolute good faith and absolute bad faith in which the game was played and displayed. I had a ready-made answer, "I want to learn your language," the actual meaning of which I did not question; my only worry was that my linguistic and gestural ability would not express it clearly enough to be understood by the Panare at large. Today this answer deserves a bit of explanation, even though at that time it did satisfy me completely, particularly when I saw—or thought I saw—that I had made myself understood.

The rationale for my answer ran something like this. My French, Cartesian, rationalistic self was about to study Panare culture; in other words, the Panare were the objects of my study. They knew something I wanted to know. Since knowledge is power, I had to acquire some sort of power in their eyes in order to accede in turn to their knowl-edge, which ultimately would be further transformed into my power. I dare say the problem was to induce the exchange, the transformation. And there was not the least doubt in my mind that the difficulty was to be divided into as many parts as possible; I was going to be analyti-cal to the tips of my toes. For a while, the Panare of Turiba Viejo re-mained a group of largely undifferentiated people, a colony of Durk-heimian ants, as it were; they were indeed my Ph.D. material. The data to be rehashed and regurgitated in my dissertation would remain inaccessible, however, without the hymenopterous friends who would become my collaborators, in the usual as well as—I am afraid—the derogatory meaning of the term. Even before making friends, I had to be tolerated, if not accepted, and justify my intrusion. This was not going to happen, I thought, if I was uninterpretable, so I offered a self-interpretation, a stereotyped may-I-introduce-myself which was fittingly the most neutral one I could think of: learning their language. Being a half-truth, it was a half-lie (language was only a tool), but I could live with it. Of course, given my threatening introduction by the gendarme, and the shield that the vast Western world imposed between them and me, the Panare had little, if any, political choice in accepting me. Language was but a pretense, since they now had to cope with me. Today, I wonder whether my eagerness to rationalize, validate, and justify my presence was not more for my own sake than for theirs, whether it was not a defense mechanism against my fear of being rejected. Now I see it more as a self-assuring projection of what appeared to be the total opacity, the uninterpretability of Panare reality, an expression of the culture shock I was undergoing. I thought that being analytical about it was foolproof, whereas I should have thought a little less and felt a little more. My anxiety about the whole situation was not to be expressed, but repressed, and I would appear as self-assured as I possibly could, while I knew damn well the stakes of the game: one goof and I was out of anthropology and the remote glimmering of an academic career.

The reason I am dwelling rather heavily on this embarrassing self-exposure is emphatically *not* a belief that it reflects any kind of uniqueness or originality. Quite to the contrary, I firmly believe these feelings to be fairly common in any fieldwork experience, even commonplace to the point of triviality; but, more importantly, they are part of the experience and a constitutive part at that. In other words, their exposure, revealing as it is, represents an effort of consciousness concerning the dialectics of the anthropological process, for it is in tackling the problem of the subjectivity of the experience, not by hiding it, that some understanding of it can be achieved. What is explored here is the evolution of the discrepancies which were creeping in between what I believed I was doing and what I was indeed doing, between a rationale and a mere rationalization. I strongly suspect there was less rationale and more rationalization than I hoped for, and this, in turn, was interpreted and misinterpreted *ad libitum* by the different individuals I came into contact with. More specifically, I am attempting to demystify the persistent and tenacious myth of anthropological objectivity.

Clearly, there is indeed an objective reality outside of what I have perceived, but it is not the one I have perceived, nor is it the one—I am sorry to report—my "objectivist" colleagues perceive. The argument will certainly be raised that social scientists have not waited for me to discover the implications of Heisenberg's (1958) principle in their respective domains. Little more than lip service has been paid to it, as in the case of Lévi-Strauss, who writes: "Man is no longer satisfied with knowing; as he knows more, he sees himself knowing, and the true object of his research becomes more and more, every day, this indivisible coupling of humanity transforming the world and transforming itself in the process" ([1973] 1976: 303).

And yet this does not prevent him from striving, throughout all of his formidable works, from aiming for "positive knowledge," as if, despite his claims to the contrary, the relation of incertitude was something simply unavoidable. Neither does this prevent him from dismissing in one broad sweep both phenomenology and existentialism:

> *Phenomenology I found objectionable in that it postulated a kind of continuity between experience and reality. I agreed that the latter encompasses and explains the former, but I had learned from my three sources of inspiration that the transition between one order and the other is discontinuous; that to reach reality one has first to reject experience, and then subsequently to reintegrate it into an objective synthesis devoid of any sentimentality. As for the intellectual movement which was to reach its peak in existentialism, it seemed to me to be anything but a legitimate form of reflection, because of its overindulgent attitude towards the illusions of subjectivity ([1955] 1974: 58).*

The problem seems even worse across the Atlantic, where Lévi-Strauss' most vociferous opponent, Harris, entirely ignores the relation of incertitude, shielding himself behind "etic statements [which] depend upon phenomenal distinctions judged appropriate by the community of scientific observers" (1968: 575). Regretfully, only Harris himself cannot perceive the idealism built into this position—rather than the materialism to which it falsely pretends—for he reintroduces into his field, as surreptitiously as unconsciously, the worst of metaphysics in refusing to consider his acting part in the anthropological process. More precisely, Harris takes shelter behind the consensus of the scientific community, which can be strongly suspected of sharing a priori a similar if not identical ideology, that of the Western world, so that two "independent" scientists will agree to see in the Pleiades a star cluster in the same way that two "independent" Panare will agree to see in the same Pleiades a mythical being.

The fact that ultimately neither Lévi-Strauss nor Harris reaches the positive objectivity they wish to enjoy seems to be proven by their strongly reciprocal inability to understand each other, since there are, after all, a French anthropology and an American anthropology, while there is no such comparable difference between, for instance, French and American physics or chemistry.

In order to avoid the logical positivism of the first and the vulgar materialism of the second—leading in both cases to an ill-disguised solipsism—the central position occupied by the observer in the anthropological process must not only be taken into serious consideration but must also be questioned constantly. It does not seem sufficient to me merely to restate the banal but often disregarded fact that the investigator's attitude influences, affects, and therefore changes the behavior of the investigated. After all, physicists have turned what looked at first like a handicap into a discovery procedure. But, in translating physics directly into anthropology, a little something has been left out, namely, that it is admittedly difficult to fear, to hate, to mourn, to fall in love with . . . in other words, to *feel for* a light particle. Even in those cases where some attempt has been made to notice the impact of the investigator on the behavior of the investigated, nothing has yet really been said about what happened to the investigator—more precisely, nothing about the dialectics of the process, nothing about the way in which it influences, affects, and changes the data collection.

That a good deal of distance must be taken along with the tantalizing temptations of objectivization is illustrated in a brilliant way by Leiris, who describes or, rather, evokes a nineteenth-century copy of a Pompeian painting which hangs in his office at the Musée de l'Homme:

> *The copyist, aiming probably to faithfully document the original work, produced instead a different image. The copy, executed in an inflated and hackneyed manner, is doubly anachronistic. The style, at once naïve and painterly, as far removed from the spirit of our age as from the spirit of the original, endows the nineteenth-century reproduction with a singular charm (1976: 269).*[3]

A page later, with his usual lucidity, Leiris remarks:

> *This nineteenth-century copy represents pictorial derision, even nose-thumbing, at the science of cultures. A copyist, acting in*

[3]No translation can do justice to the elegance of Leiris' style. He actually wrote: ". . . copie assurément fidèle dans l'esprit de son auteur (qui ne visait probablement qu'à établir un document) mais traitée en un style rondouillard

> good faith, succeeded in transforming a vestige of ancient Rome
> into something which could be a mock-up of a second-rate set
> for a production of The Magic Flute. Perhaps we, as observers
> of societies far removed from our own, commit equal errors in
> interpretation. When we think we have sketched a true portrait
> of another culture, perhaps in fact we have only interpreted it
> according to our own biases, and present-day reflections of other
> cultures, so faithfully executed by our standards, may well ap-
> pear laughable when cultural perspectives have shifted (1976:
> 270).[4]

If there is some pretension on my part, it is to assume interpretation with a minimum of lucidity, to perform a kind of second-degree
anthropology, an anthropology of anthropology, by reinserting my "I"
into the process, as part of the process. This is because time, in my
opinion, has the same distancing effect as space. If going to exotic cultures is a way of better perceiving what is going on in one's own, it
seems to me legitimate to say that a temporal delay also somehow provides a wise viewpoint: both being "away" and reflecting "after" place
things in perspective, something that did not escape the attention of
Lévi-Strauss when he wrote at the beginning of *Tristes Tropiques*:
"Time, in an unexpected way, has extended its isthmus between life
and myself; twenty years of forgetfulness were required before I could
establish communion with my earlier experience, which I had sought
the world over without understanding its significance or appreciating
its essence" ([1955] 1974: 44).

When I try to recapture, in its lived thickness, that elsewhere and
that past, I am constantly compelled to sidetrack and backtrack. Once
more I am about to describe my entering into Panare culture; another
entrance, another viewpoint. I can give several reasons for this. First,
anthropological time is a duration and not a succession of instants,
and it would be utterly trifling to follow, step by step, the actual se-

---

et pompier aussi désuet par rapport à nous qu'aberrant par rapport à l'original, ce qui dote cette oeuvre doublement anachronique, et naïve en même
temps que savante, d'un charme singulier" (1976: 269).

    [4]The original French reads: "Dérision picturale et, ce qui va plus loin,
pied de nez à la science des cultures puisque, si un copiste de bonne foi a pu
transformer un beau vestige romain en maquette pour mauvaise mise en scène
de *La Flûte enchantée*, cela induit à penser qu'il peut en être de même de tous
nos travaux d'observateurs de sociétés éloignées des nôtres et que, quand il
nous semble avoir tracé de l'une d'elles un portrait ressemblant, nous n'avons
peut-être fait qu'interpréter selon nos modes et fournir une image qui paraîtra
risible lorsque ces modes auront changé" (1976: 270).

quence of events. Second, entering the field is probably the most dramatic and traumatic event, the most shocking one in that duration; its multiple facets are not immediately revealed, and its meanings appear only in retrospect. In addition, one never leaves the field, so to speak; one only enters and re-enters it. By this I mean that the fact of leaving, despite its emotional valences, is of little yield, whereas the repetition of the entrances provides the most significant tensions of symbolic interactions. There is no *veni, vidi, vici* in anthropological comprehension, no sudden revelation, only a lengthy process in which some aspects of a culture will progressively become less obscure, but this is articulated around certain privileged events which acquire a certain saliency: the entrances. Finally, there is a strictly psychological reason. Entrance is a time of maximum sensitivity on the part of both the anthropologist and the people he/she studies. Such sensitivity cannot be sustained and becomes progressively eroded and blurred by the routine of daily interaction.

In that light, I would like to return to the question with which this chapter began, to the answer I so eagerly provided, and to the power play it involved. Such an answer was part of a strategy resulting from an essentially naïve but reassuring conception of what a traditional culture was all about. When I wanted to make a quip about the nature of the anthropological enterprise, the most appropriate metaphor I could think of at the time was the cracking of a nutshell. To myself I represented culture as the walnut, a hard shell enclosing a delicately flavored and intricately designed kernel. There were only three ways of getting to the kernel. The nutcracker technique crushes the kernel as it breaks the shell, as characterized by the expansion of the Western world; I was determined to have no part in that. Ideally, I would have liked to be a small, not really voracious worm which sneaks in, surreptitiously, just to peek, peep, or peer at what is inside. But realistically, there was a third solution—to insert a knife blade at the base of the walnut and use it as a lever to open up the shell with minimal damage, so that I could stare and gaze at the unbroken kernel. In and of itself, the political and psychoanalytical—illusory and deceptive—biases of such a lust for *Macht* seem to me, in retrospect, too self-obvious to deserve much further elaboration. How one adequately links this nut theory to the praxis of a fool remains to be illustrated by the history of my arrival, of this new entrance into Turiba Viejo.

I knew all too well that my formal declaration of intention concerning the language would require a more practical substantiation, namely some down-to-earth type of leverage, if I was to succeed in investigating Panare culture. I planned to use several means to achieve it, which were soon entirely successful in at least one respect, in that I managed to make a total fool of myself.

I had brought with me a sizable quantity of fishing lines, hooks, bush knives, and the like; I had also brought an ample supply of medicines, thanks to the Service of Malariology. My upbringing in a medical family, my chance induction into the French Army Medical Corps, and last-minute crash instruction by my father had taught me how to place a tourniquet, set a fracture, give injections, and other basic *dos* and *don'ts*. I was thus quite ready for the "illegal" practice of medicine, but my confidence was greatly enhanced when a rural doctor, who had been based in La Urbana and was known by the people of Turiba Viejo, decided, out of sheer friendship, to help install me in the settlement.

When all my gear had been carried safely across the river, Domingo Barrios was suddenly confronted with the absolute reality of my arrival. Once more trousered, shirted, and sunglassed, he welcomed us rather coldly. Our presence was troublesome, because we had arrived right in the middle of the preparation for a *waxpoto*, the festival of the dead, which was to begin that night. We knew this already, as we had shared the small pickup truck which had brought us and my gear from Turiba Nuevo with the group from Los Pozos headed by Anacleto, an extra load of a dozen Panare. Painted in red from head to toe with achiote, they were in fairly high spirits, probably less in anticipation of the feast to come than because they were already full of manioc beer. Domingo Barrios cheered up when Anacleto described to him the goods I was bringing, and the quasi-infinite supply I had left behind me in the Creole settlement as a reserve. Anacleto's hyperbolic gestures, inspired by a certain degree of intoxication, told the whole story; I did not need to understand their dialogue to realize what was being said. Domingo Barrios seemed further relieved to see that the Creoles, having unloaded the truck, had already left.

But nothing could have seemed more portentous to me, or could better have fitted my plans, than when he told us that Marquito was sick in his hammock. I asked to see him; he was suffering from an acute manioc-beer hangover that two antacid tablets soon took care of. I was thrilled; the headman's quick relief had its immediate reward, for the doctor and I were shown to a workshop-hut in which to store my impedimenta and sling our hammocks. It had been built by Marquito, but he was using it only for storage, having built a newer one next to it where he and his immediate family performed their daily

Pl. 4. *Anacleto* (tose-LP67), *headman of Los Pozos*

activities. Because it was his, because it was an extra one, because he
was the headman, and because we were the "good guys" with medicines and various other goods, I would be able to stay there. The hut
was open in front, which meant I would have no privacy, but it gave
me a great opportunity to control what was going on in the settlement
—or so I thought. This was an illusion. True, I was visible and therefore public, so that anybody at any time felt free to come and visit,
but at the same time I was under constant surveillance. In addition,
almost anything could be hidden from me, as I was to discover to my
growing despair.

At any rate, it may easily be imagined with what naïve relief I
sat in my hammock, playing with gusto the sterile trinkets-and-beads
game with my would-be friends in the hope of encouraging their further collaboration. I gave two bush knives to Marquito as headman
and one to each adult male in the group. In giving away medicines
and manufactured goods, I was truly bartering; I was extending short-
term credit for doctorizable data. But the truth of the matter was that
I was much too successful at playing my own game, and the harbingers
of trouble were not long in appearing. I had wanted to assume a role
meaningful to the Panare. I succeeded much beyond my hopes, to the

point of smothering entanglement. Rather than remaining uninterpretable, I was, if anything, overinterpreted, and the levers with which I had intended to open the walnut sprang back at me. And it hurt.

Within a few days I was on my own, medically and otherwise, and before long the novelty of my medical help and my gifts of lines and hooks, as well as the initial excitement they had provoked, had worn off. My gift giving took on the status of a routine activity. In fact, I was treated as I deserved, as an inexhaustible provider. People approached me constantly; one had a headache, one had lost his fishing hook, one wanted this, one wanted that, endlessly. I hardly had time to do any work of my own. Then one day two incidents occurred, almost simultaneously, which forced me to react, thereby adjusting my approach.

Domingo Flores, a young man at that time still a bachelor, came to see me with a scratch on his thigh. It was so tiny and superficial that no blood had even been drawn to the surface of the skin. I told him so and turned down his request for mercurochrome. Less than a minute later, he came back bleeding profusely. I could not believe it. Where the scratch had been, there was now an honest-to-God cut he had inflicted himself with his knife so that I would believe. I wanted blood in order to cure, so here it was. In utter anger, and not without guilt about what I was discovering to be my power, I sent him to hell; his mother and several men came to plead his case, to no avail. Soon after, a boy, the youngest son of Marquito, came to ask me for two hooks; I had given him some that very morning, but he said he had lost them. Still upset by the first event, I angrily denied him his second request. Practically everybody who was in the settlement came to the front of my hut in protest. Not only was I "ignorant," but a "miser." How come I did not want to give or to cure? Why could I not go to Caracas to bring more supplies? Why was I such a bad guy? Why was I so ugly too? How come my wives were not here with me? Why did I not go back home? I held firm, although I was panicked at what I perceived as the explosiveness of the situation. I explained that only in the early morning would I treat the genuinely sick individuals, and that I would give goods only as payment for services; I made it plain and clear. How come I was such a liar? Everybody appeared very angry at me, and nobody spoke to me for the rest of the day. When I hit my hammock that night, I was very depressed. The morning after, things resumed—to my surprise—their normally smooth course of interaction, and henceforth a more moderate and regulated flow of demands was presented to me. I was relieved.

Both incidents were quite revealing of the symbolic overtones which prevail in the establishment of relations in the field. The more I wanted to play a role, the more the Panare would attempt, and to a large extent successfully, to take advantage of it. They would test their power against mine. My goods and services were up for grabs. Since I was seen as powerful, I had to be endlessly generous, because the basis of my power in the group had been precisely my generosity, which I in turn had seen as the key to my acceptance in the group. In addition, this unlimited access to goods they imputed to me showed that they perceived me as a metonymy of the Western world, where everything they do not possess is found in plenty. So far, I had been considered a *tosempe iyan*, a "big headman," now, more humanly, I would be no more than a small one. Clearly, my economic and medical roles had been failures in establishing a rapport with them from my viewpoint, because so far I had presented only an opportunity for them to acquire goods and to manipulate me in so doing.

In fact, by that time, the Panare already had a pretty good idea who I might be, but I had not advanced much in my knowledge of them, even though in retrospect I had made some progress in understanding. Although I had failed to notice, so far they had been better anthropologists toward me than I had been toward them, for they had spontaneously done what I had hoped for, namely, given me an identity.

Despite the real and not negligible interest that my services represented, they were, in fact, minimal: hardly anybody was really sick, and my gifts of metal tools were not enormous. Yet, since they did not throw me out, what was it which prevented them from rejecting me? Clearly, I will never be sure of the degree of coercion involved in my presence. Ruling out the possibility that they ever took seriously my pretense of studying linguistics, did they feel really threatened by the gendarme's introductory speech, or did they realize that some gifts from me were better than none? Although both had an impact, these reasons were not sufficiently convincing. The essence of the answer seems to me to be elsewhere, although I fully realize that it was I who forced them into a relationship with me, and not the reverse. Without completely solving my medical and gift-giving problems, we both had adjusted enough to the new deal, and I was beginning to make sense to them in a way I had not at all anticipated.

The incipient communication and the subsequent identity I was about to acquire resulted—partly at least—from a policy of applied structuralism on my part, although its barely formulated and half-conscious character should prevent me from calling it policy. It was more a practical and spontaneous thought, that which Lévi-Strauss

Pl. 5. *How Juan-Pablo Martinez' son* kanapwey-*TV 14 viewed me*

([1962] 1966) would call "savage." From the start I had two fear-
some shadows from which I wanted to separate myself: the Creoles
and the missionaries. I was not an *ötnyepa*, not an Indian—that was
immediately obvious. Therefore, I was a *tatto*, a Creole (or, rather, a
non-Indian); but if I had to be *that*, there was no reason for me not to
manipulate commutations in the series of correlations and oppositions
that would unveil my "true" position. To that purpose, I used procedures of two types: synthetic ones to differentiate myself globally
and analytic ones to operationalize relevant features.

The Protestant missionaries—for their Catholic counterparts had
not yet made any impact in the area and were hardly known by the
Panare of Turiba Viejo—were defined as *Americano*. When Marquito

asked me whether I was one of them, I denied it on geographical
grounds which I tried in vain to establish. It made more sense to him
that I could not be an *Americano* because of my chain-smoking. Such
empirical evidence was clearly more powerful a statement than my
geographical rhetoric. But to give away cigarettes to Marquito and the
other men who had gathered with us was an argument which, to my
surprise, fell short of being totally convincing, because the Panare
cultivate a fair amount of tobacco in their own gardens. In daily usage,
tobacco mixed into a paste with water and ashes is held between the
lower lip and the teeth. It is only during the shamanistic cure that the
officiant blows tobacco on the suffering part of his patient's body.
Therefore, tobacco is not a free form which I could have manipulated
at will; although individuals enjoyed the fact that I offered them cigarettes from time to time, they were not constantly bumming them from
me, contrary to the experience of most anthropologists. In fact, tobacco was already a bounded symbol in their culture, so that smoking,
being significant in a different context, could not serve in this one as
well. In addition, smoking and cigarette offering, prohibited as they
may have been by the Protestant missionaries, were placing me on a
par with the Creoles at large.

Yet, another incident that took place during the *waxpoto*, shortly
after my installation, helped differentiate me definitely from the
missionaries. It must have been late afternoon. Except for infants, the
whole male population of the settlement was gathered close to the
sugarcane press where manioc-beer preparation had taken place earlier
that day. They were feverishly busy preparing the ornaments they
would hang on their backs for the performance of the ritual at dusk.
These ornaments are made out of palm leaves (from the tree *osa-yo*,
Sp. *cucurito*) that the adult males of the group had cut in the forest
earlier on the way to the gardens. For each individual, the palm leaves
are cut lengthwise so as to form a small yellow and green "cape" to be
strapped around the forehead with a piece of bark. Topping the cape,
and standing up at the back of the head, another bit of yellow palm
leaf is attached. This latter item is not spread out like the cape but set
up straight and ornamented in diverse ways by carving, cutting out, or
more elaborate plaiting and caning. Since these ornaments were discarded every morning and made afresh each day that the ceremonial
lasted, I had ample occasion to watch their manufacture, although I
did not discover much about the significance of these free variations.
In fact, this ritual was too good to be true; it began as I arrived, and I
had not the faintest idea what was really going on. Yet, one day, while
Domingo Barrios was making his ceremonial ornament with the other

Pl. 6. *The* waxpoto *ritual*

men of the settlement, I saw him shaping its head part into what I
could not help but interpret as a Christian cross. It was striking because there was—and had been in the previous days—no motif of that
sort, involving two perpendicular bits of palm leaf instead of the single
vertical one. When I inquired, he answered that it was a *kru* (an obvious borrowing from the Spanish *cruz*). It puzzled me highly and I
pressed him further. He explained matter-of-factly that he was doing
like the *tatto* and, as I feigned not to understand, he added: like the
Americano. The smiles and laughter of the other men showed that
they at least were amused by the answer. I was pondering whether he
was joking or serious, when he led me to what I felt was shaky ground
by asking: *tinca ryo aman?* which meant "do you know (about)
God?" and might be interpreted as "do you believe in God?" Had I
been more fluent in Panare at that time, I would have liked to answer,
"I have heard of Him, but do not believe in Him." Short of that, I
decided to answer negatively, to his disbelief and to the disbelief of
his companions, who had all read perfectly my hesitation in answering.
    I was thinking about this puzzling motif, about the Panare rein-
terpretation of this sacred form, now deprived of any content other
than its sacredness, about its sudden recycling in a death ritual, and

about the historical contingency as well as the historical necessity of my disturbing presence and its side effects. While all this was running through my head, Domingo Barrios slipped away and soon came back with half a flask of rum of unknown origin and dubious taste. The testing nature of the gulp I was demandingly invited to swallow— amazing on another plane because I never saw anybody among the Panare drink rum during my stay, and the flask, contents and container, were still part of Domingo Barrios' "treasure" when I left Turiba Viejo—did not escape me any more than it did my delighted companions. As if to hammer home his point, Domingo Barrios belched and muttered, more to himself than to inform anybody in particular, "He is not *Americano*."

I would now like to show how I established such a discontinuity in a different way, although I would not like to give the impression of succession to these events which were, on the contrary, all happening more or less simultaneously. Experience itself is a synthetic continuum, a duration in the Bergsonian sense ([1889] 1960), into which I am introducing the artificial cuts that the linearity of my discourse requires. In fact, given the prejudice of the Creoles toward the Indians, to which I had been exposed from the start, I thought that I had to dissociate myself maximally from the Creoles. There was evidently no point in claiming that I was not a *tatto*, the common term for Creole, because in reality the terms refers to everybody who is not Indian. No point, either, in "going native." As Wagner so vividly puts it, "The would-be native could only enter a world of his own creation, like a schizophrenic or that apocryphal Chinese painter who, pursued by creditors, painted a goose on the wall, mounted it, and flew away" (1975: 9).

It was more a question of attitude, a gestalt that my relationship to the Panare should take, something holistic. Moreover, it was a question of cultural loyalty, vis-à-vis myself as much as vis-à-vis the Panare. For, to be frank, I was dizzy, and slightly headachy I might add, under the impact of too much and too many cultural shocks. Within hardly more than a year, I had left France, come to and left the U.S., arrived in Venezuela, had a taste of the Caracas bourgeois way of life—and had now left the Creoles in order to enter Panare culture. The point is this: to whom was I to be loyal in this culturally contradictory and conflicting situation? Clearly not to everybody, since I experienced them differently. Apart from myself, it is clear that my primary loyalty could not be to the Creoles, but only to the Panare. If each group had remained totally distinct from the other without any overlapping, I could have split—I should say "schized"—my attitude with more nuances toward the members of each society. I do not believe I could have done so, and, at any rate, I did not. And because I was "with" the Panare, I dissociated myself from the Creoles to the point of being unfair, a fact which, I am sure, is transparent from the previous chapter. Wrongly or rightly, I felt that I had to make a choice when I was involved in any kind of social interaction between Panare and Creoles. It was not then a theoretical problem, but an extremely concrete one with which I always felt uneasy.

Often, when on a trek with a couple of Panare men, we would stop by a Creole *rancho*, without my being forewarned that this would occur. Was I then to accept the cup of coffee offered by the Creole— the proper form of greeting in his culture—while my Panare companions would be offered none? Or was I to offend my Creole host by a refusal? This may seem to be making a mountain out of a molehill, for in most cases I accepted the cup of coffee and guiltily drank it without any nefarious consequence other than my own inner and nebulous feeling of contradiction. Yet, on at least one occasion, this was no projection of mine, but a real problem. Guzmán and Felipe Casanova had invited me to come looking for electric eels along the Turiba River. They had provided me with the harpoon I had requested but also, in order to add some piquancy to my company, an unsolicited loincloth they insisted I should wear. As I was promised that we would stay close to the settlement and that we would not stop by any Creole settlement, I accepted, to everybody's amusement, including my own. Thus equipped, I learned a couple of lessons.

The first was a memorable one, I may add, for I soon complained of what I believed were mosquito bites on my legs, as we were silently wandering and scrutinizing the riverbank for the deep and shadowy spots where eels are to be seen. Yet, as Felipe remarked, there was not one mosquito around, but he took a look at my legs anyway and sneered at me, having spotted hundreds of *inkiciri* on them. This unforgettable term refers to almost microscopic red ticks which were busily burrowing into my skin, leaving on its surface an infinity of hardly visible dots. Felipe and Guzmán first proceeded to pluck them out one by one with a small sharpened stick, but quickly got discouraged by the quantitative aspect of the problem. Then, they resolved to sacrifice half their tobacco provision to rub my legs to smother the ticks. On a smooth skin, relief comes quickly after only a minute quantity of tobacco has been used, but the hairy legs of the anthropologist would have required much more tobacco than their daily supply.

Meanwhile, the pain was becoming rather insufferable, and I somehow felt hopeful when they suggested kerosene rubbing as the only solution, to the efficacy of which I can gratefully attest. However, getting hold of some kerosene meant reaching the nearest Creole house, about a kilometer away. Because pain had softened my will as well as my concern over my garb, I resorted to going and begging for kerosene and thus made what a Creole could only consider an immodest appearance. What part of his stupor was staged for the purpose of dramatizing his disapproval, I will never know, but it took the Creole a while before accepting the reality of it being me, *el doctor de los Indios*. Interestingly, I have blocked the memory of his name, which tends to indicate that my apprehension, softened as it may have been, and his stupor were fairly complementary in expressing the unacceptability of the encounter.

As much as I was longing for deliverance, I was offered coffee before kerosene. Having been offered no coffee and having left me in Creole hands, Guzmán and Felipe Casanova resumed their quest for eels, agreeing that they would pick me up on their way back to the settlement. The kerosene application and the subsequent ablutions at the river brought me prompt relief—physical, not moral, for, in that respect, the worst was yet to come.

From the Creole viewpoint I was on the verge of indecent exposure, and I had to borrow from my host a pair of worn-out pants and a shirt that he himself was all too relieved to lend me. From then on, I was "clean," and interaction with the Creole resumed, superficially at least, as if nothing had happened. I was offered food. Unfortunately, the plate of soupy rice was served to me, piping hot, at the very moment the two Panare men arrived, dragging behind them half a dozen eels. Now I was trapped; I could not refuse to eat the food, I could not suggest buying some for the Panare, and I could not share mine with them either—all of these would have been totally unacceptable from the Creole viewpoint. Patiently, Guzmán and Felipe squatted silently, waiting for the Creole man and myself to finish a meal that I ate as expeditiously as humanly feasible.

We departed. The two Panare men made no comment whatsoever, although they maintained a rather hostile silence until I stumbled on a root and fell flat on the trail. Both of them finally manifested their anger at me. Instead of laughing at the incident to mock my clumsiness, their normal reaction, they raised the pitch of their voices as they talked to me, the normal Panare way of expressing anger. By the same token, they displayed some Socratic irony at my expense. "Are you hungry? Is your stomach empty?" they questioned rhetorically, and then addressed each other: "His clothing is beautiful; is he not a big Creole?" They concluded, "You want to know, but you know nothing and you are a big miser, a liar too." Guzmán added, "What did you give me lately? Nothing."

Later that day, back in the settlement, I had enough sense not to redeem my sense of guilt with any gifts, and the incident died by itself without further repercussion. But it was clear to me that it was because I was a sort of Creole that I had relapsed into my imputed "Creoleness," that the whole event had been an unfortunate hindrance in the process of my acquisition of a proper identity.

I have chosen to relate this particular incident at length, rather than other similar ones, because it encapsulates in its development most, if not all, of the complexities of the triangular interaction which was at stake between the Creoles, the Panare, and me. Here I see a prototype of my own ambiguity, which was ubiquitously pervading any single act I undertook. In having to interact with Creoles in the presence of the Panare, but without any participation of the latter other than their withdrawn presence, in their eyes I was replaced, relocated, if not rejected, on the other side—that is, I was interpreted anew as a Creole myself. And this is because, beyond the vanity of my efforts at not acting—hence not being—Creole, there was a more immediately perceived contrast, an imperative cleavage that the Panare drew between *ötnyepa* and *tatto*, between themselves and non-Indians, in the catchall category in which I was, to my distress, blurred with the Creoles.

However, such an inflicted classification was infinitely more complex than it may seem from the dry binary opposition I have presented thus far. In fact, if I am able to see now that in the context of my interaction with the Creoles the Panare pushed me back, so to speak, into the Creole category—if they did reclassify me in that way—it is because I also see that I had somehow been successful to a certain extent in being somebody different from the Creoles in the context of my interaction with the Panare alone, through other means which I am now about to relate.

I have alluded above to the admitted illusions of "going native," an exercise in bad taste. But, as distasteful as it appears, it may very well be, at the same time, the flawed and naïve version of a practical effort toward intersubjectivity in the anthropological process. Altogether, in the spontaneity it reflects and in the praxis it expresses, it seems to me less disturbing, although far more decried, than the dogmatic imperialism of "objective" anthropology, a form of "bourgeois rationalism" where "paradoxically, at the extremes of reductionism the distinction between materialism and idealism vanishes" (Paul and Rabinow 1976: 122, footnote). In both cases, the tautology of the soliloquy thus generated is evident.[5] However, if I use both as referential topics, it is indeed because they constitute a problem, as I have shown throughout this chapter. Their seductions and the oscillations they bring about are constant temptations, as defense mechanisms, for the fieldworker submitted to the stress of culture shock, insecure as he/she is before the novelty and unpredictability of the situation. In both cases, the concreteness of the situation, in other words, reality, is lost in favor of a parallel discourse where travelogue and cultural materialism meet in their resemblance to a psychotic discourse, upon which experience has no grasp whatsoever.

The problem is not to eliminate the distortions of subjectivity and objectivity, but mainly to reinstall experience in its place; in other words, to let it happen, to accept the radical character of the fieldworking experience. Once subjectivism and objectivism are rejected, what is left to turn to? The answer was given to me indirectly in the field and amounts to the experience of intersubjectivity. As little as I was prepared for it—no more and no less so than anybody else—it came about almost surreptitiously in the process of anthropological reciprocity. If I, the anthropologist, was knowing them, the natives, the reverse was also taking place too. Intersubjectivity depends exclusively upon the possibility of establishing a dialogue, that is, upon the rever-

[5]It may be useful at this point to recall Scholte's accurate remark: "A so-called value-free perspective in principle embodies and in fact perpetuates a normative ideology" (1969: 434). That objectivity represents an alienation from reality, and a good example of false consciousness is stated in almost similar terms by at least two different scholars. For Diamond, "The notion that data can somehow exist independently of a paradigm, even if unconscious, is obviously an illusion: such data could be no more than an infinite catalogue of random observations. Goethe put the matter succinctly: 'The highest wisdom would be to understand that every fact is already theory' " (1969: 425). There goes British empiricism, and here goes cultural materialism. According to Sahlins, "a praxis theory based on pragmatic interests and 'objective' conditions is the secondary form of a cultural illusion, and its elaborate empirical and statistical offspring, the 'etic' investigations of our social sciences, the intellectual titillation of an 'emic' mystification" (1976: 220). Consequently, objectivity has to be recognized for what it is: a myth, in fact, the myth of scientism perpetuated to the point of triumph in anthropological circles to this very day. Nash and Wintrob (1972) perceive this scientism as an inheritance from the previous century and in this respect would agree with Habermas' statement: "The philosophy of science that has emerged since the mid-nineteenth century as the heir of the theory of knowledge is methodology pursued with a scientistic self-understanding of the sciences. 'Scientism' means science's belief in itself: that is, the conviction that we can no longer understand science as *one* form of possible knowledge, but rather must identify knowledge with science" ([1968] 1971: 4, his emphasis).

sal of perspective whereby not only are the natives anthropologized—
they are also, in turn, anthropologizing. Now I should insist that it was
not planned on my part, at least not entirely, as I myself was not particularly immune to the defense mechanisms to which I have alluded
above. Rather, at first I saw my answering all sorts of questions about
myself and my culture as a hindrance to real work, but also as a necessary chore which turned out to be instrumental in helping me out of
my existential nothingness. In that respect, two factors, one behavioral,
the other aspectual, proved to be crucial. They represent no more than
an illustration of the process to which I was submitted.

The first one concerned my sexual behavior. To the Panare, of
course, it appeared bizarre, not to say suspicious, that I was settling
with them for an undetermined period of time without a female companion, even more so when, to their shocked amusement, they saw that
I myself was cooking, an exclusively female activity in their culture.
I was made acutely aware of the sexual threat I represented to them by
different incidents which were coherent once put together.

On the one hand, Creole men were claiming in rather frustrated
voices that there was no way to have an affair with a Panare woman.
Quite evidently, if they were stating this, it was because some had tried
without any success. On the other hand, Domingo Barrios had been
explicit on this matter from the start by warning me, "there is no
woman here," the meaning of which could not have been clearer. Obviously, if he and several other men of the group confirmed it, if he
felt obligated to state this right away, it was because some Creoles had
previously made sexual requests, if not demands. I later heard com-
plaints about lecherous Creoles leering at Panare women. Not from
sheer virtue on my part, but because I had to make virtue of necessity,
I replied to Domingo Barrios that, back home, I already had two wives
and was not the least bit interested in women. I carefully and dutifully
repeated this overstatement each time I visited a new Panare settlement and fairly often, before I had asked or stated anything, I was
told, "there is no woman here."

My attitude was therefore in strong contrast to that imputed to
the Creoles, as well as to their actual behavior, for many times a Panare
man encountering a Creole would be asked—jokingly to be sure, but
that does not make it less significant—whether he could not obtain a
Panare woman. Part of the Creole's rationale for formulating this desire was that the polygyny of the Panare was acting as an erotic stimu-
lant on the sexual fantasies of the titillated Creoles who, given their
nominal Christianity, disapproved of it. But coming back to my overstatement about women and the continent behavior it entailed, I hit

the jackpot in dissociating myself rather radically from the Creoles. On this account, I had basically the correct intuition that pretending to be married would favor my acceptance.

Even more striking to the Panare was my claim of having two wives, a sure indication of prestige in their culture. Not unexpectedly, my assertion was met with total disbelief until I could produce for Marquito what could pass for empirical proof, namely, snapshots of my two sisters-in-law. Having thus substantiated my claim, I passed for a "big headman" in my companion's eyes. More importantly, his next remark resounded like chimes in my ears: *tatto ickye aman*, "You are not a Creole." It appeared to me to be a success, but it had one other consequence; it left me in the middle of nowhere, "a no one man from a nowhere land." Clearly, Marquito's statement was not to be interpreted too literally; it was not a sudden revelation for him that, after all, I was somebody entirely different from the Creoles, but it was nevertheless a step in the direction of establishing a fine line of distinction. In order to take advantage of the possibility which had opened with Marquito's remark, I still had to acquire a new valence within the classification from which I had just been partially disengaged. This was still hardly perceptible, for so far I had been referred to and addressed exclusively as *tatto*. In other words, I had been labeled, but not named. I was already classed, yet anonymous, still within the Creole category; I had failed to establish a category of my own.

Clearly, as long as I was no one other than just another Creole, my investigation remained stunted, and I could not collect names of individuals, the most excruciating "must" I was confronted with in the field. Since I myself did not "exist," there was no reason why my informants should unveil their "existence." When I asked individuals for their names, they were genuinely puzzled and wanted to know why I was asking, for which I had no ready-made answer, at least none that I could elaborate with my minimal knowledge of the Panare language.

The attempt to stimulate a response by stating that my name was Juan-Pablo repeatedly met with failure. In fact, to the questions *sunka aice*, "What is your name?" or *nö aman*, "Who are you?" I invariably obtained a frustrating and puzzling answer of the type, "you already know," followed by the Spanish name—Felipe, Domingo, Andrés, etc.—by which a man was known among the Creoles. When I inquired about a woman, the most likely answer was *aic-pwi*, "She has no name." I was beginning to worry seriously about the likelihood of a taboo on personal names. I spent weeks asking for, begging, imploring names in vain before a son of Domingo Barrios invited me to his

garden and revealed several "true" names of male members of the settlement but strongly refused to reveal his own. I paid him generously
and came back to the settlement only to discover that the "truth" was
shocking: I had been given dirty names in the grand style. Only decency prevents me from showing more explicitly how I made a total
fool of myself, to the delight of my audience, when I tried to use these
names.

One day, however, in one single incident, my imputed bigamy
and the pilosity of my body, the extent of which struck and puzzled
the Panare, were lumped together to produce not only what then appeared to me the most unexpected chain reaction I could imagine, but
also what, in fact, was nothing else than an elaboration of Marquito's
earlier remark.

Since I had proved my bigamy, I was regularly asked to exhibit
the pictures of "my two wives," with the invariable giggling reaction
it induced, a sanction which I did not fully understand. But I dutifully
complied with the requests, satisfied to obtain bits and pieces of information with this stimulus. In this way, I learned who was married to
whom in the settlement. Marquito had two wives, so had Anacleto of
Los Pozos, and so had Felipe Casanova, but Domingo Barrios had
only one wife. I also learned the words *pwi* for wife and *tamu* for
husband, and their extension to refer to and address potential spouses.
But I could not take advantage of this fresh knowledge effectively to
further my kinship investigation because of my ignorance of Panare
personal names, even though I could recognize the different members
of the settlement.

I was concerned that this situation might be prolonged endlessly,
when Domingo Barrios asked me once more to let him see one of the
snapshots; at first, he stared at it upside down, then, turning it in all
directions, gave it a thorough examination. All this time he had been
silent, sitting on a biscuit box in my hut, but I knew he was going to
make some remark. *Asa pwi aman, korepe; ayape kamonton; ayapiptu,*
"You have two wives, good; they are pretty, very pretty." I was a bit
surprised, because nobody had made any comment of that sort before.
He paused, sighed, and, still looking at the picture, stated, *tame aman,*
"You are ugly." It was said in a soft, almost moaning voice. Nevertheless, it could be overheard distinctly in the surrounding huts, from
which contained laughter resounded.

Marquito came to my hut. He, generally so poised and restrained,
could not hold back his laughter when he reiterated my ugliness. With
a rapidity and precision which took me totally off guard, he plucked
out a clump of my chest hair, which he brandished under my nose,

repeating, "ugly, ugly chest hair." With the same vivacity, he pulled vigorously at my beard with the exclamation, "ugly, ugly face hair," which brought tears of pain to my eyes. He was about to do the same with my armpit, but I prevented him from doing so just in time.

He and Domingo Barrios proceeded to give me a lengthy explanation. Although I could not follow their exchange verbatim—it was full of puns, as I could judge by the reactions provoked in the surrounding huts—I could grasp its general outline. Altogether, the message was clear, and mention of my body hair was recurrent enough. A full description of my hairy body was given, with its *uyipo* (head hair), *tansipo* (facial hair), *kupuyipo* (chest hair), *pestoyipo* (thigh hair), *nasipo* (pubic hair), and some fifteen other anatomical categories. All this superfluous hair of mine was excellent terrain for ticks and other bugs—with that, I had to agree. How could body paint be applied to the skin with so much hair? I would have to shave everything, to depilate my entire body. But, above all, my beard was beyond belief. "Ugly as a howler monkey," Domingo Barrios insisted. Marquito asked, "Are they all hairy in your settlement?"

The question was a godsend, for it provided me not only with a way out of a situation which was beginning to bother me, but also with the occasion to perform a totally successful trick. I showed them three passport-size photographs of bearded relatives: a picture of one of my brothers and two different pictures of my father which could pass for two different individuals. Both Domingo Barrios and Marquito were flabbergasted and took the matter very seriously. *Atawonptu apo tansipoto pereka-iman*, asked Marquito, "Absolutely every male is bearded in your settlement?" Blessing this flawed, but encouraging, induction I obviously answered in the affirmative.

To support my assertion, I pulled out my copy of the Petit Larousse. It was obvious that, with their slanted eyes and straight hair, Chairman Mao and General Giap were *ötnyepa*. It was obvious, too, that JFK and Johnson were "shaven *tatto*." But, sweet triumph, Freud and Marx, Lincoln and Trotsky, Santa Claus and the Almighty were like my bearded father and brother, all relatives of mine; they were *français*, a word Marquito was amused to be unable to pronounce properly. They were ugly; they were bigamous; they were bearded; they were *tansipoto*. From now on, I would be referred to and addressed by that term, *tansipoto*, "the bearded one." Only when somebody was angry at me would I regress to the *statu quo ante*, to the status of a vulgar Creole, and thus be called *tatto*.

My beard had therefore been construed as a powerful symbol through which I lost my anonymity. I now belonged less to a subclass

of *tatto* who were all *tansipoto* than to a fuzzy set of ugly and bigamous *tansipoto* who lived far away, beyond the saltwater. Being thus
categorized, I would thereafter be finally and definitively identified
with no problem. The proof of this was administered to me by Domingo Barrios, who was still examining the pictures with Marquito—
both now surrounded by practically the whole male population of the
settlement—in their euphoria at having "discovered" me. More facetious than serious, Domingo called me *yim*, which I knew to mean
"father." That he was about my age, if not slightly older, was of no
concern. A few minutes later, Marquito's son Julio called me *puka*, a
man's name, as I was to discover almost immediately.

To collect the name of each inhabitant of the settlement had now
become all but a game. What had happened was that I had been neither rejected nor adopted, but merely accepted. However, that acceptance
could only come after an identification. The exhibition of family pictures had suddenly given me the social depth necessary and sufficient
to carry with it an identity. Now that I was reviewing all the pictures
with my companions and, at Marquito's request, giving the French
names of each character, every single one of these characters was now
renamed in Panare fashion by Marquito, who amused himself tremendously with this game.

As can easily be imagined, I took my identity very seriously, and
entered into my new and faked adoption with passion. Since Domingo
Barrios was my son, Marquito was my *yako*, my "brother." Suddenly,
the whole kinship terminology of the Panare was up for grabs for
the avid anthropologist. I had acquired a classificatory valence which
suppressed, momentarily at least, the logical scandal of my own presence in Turiba Viejo. The joke of my adoption had been played in
order to defuse, to de-dramatize such a presence.

Communication was then established, since they and I had re-
spectively identified ourselves in opposition to each other as well as to
the Creoles. As long as I remained an unexplained and intruding presence, I was dangerous, being a sort of Yahveh, the one who cannot be
named. I was there but I did not exist. In a way, I had a pure name
—my body was in itself a sign, but a sign without reference. In losing
my sanctity by showing actual or pretended family pictures, I had
allowed my categorization, and the complicity of naming had been
brought about as I stooped to my profane dimension. It will be noticed
that such a naming was strictly phatic—it was the unique guarantee
that communication had been established. Indeed, communication demands a preliminary classification of the involved locutors into categories compatible with that communication.

To sum up, the minidrama that I have just related indicates, perhaps demonstrates, how reality, ethnographic reality, is actively constructed, not to say invented. My existence had finally emerged. They and I were now in a new situation, being involved in a new relation of compatibility that neither the extremes of subjectivism nor of objectivism, with the relations of dominance that they imply, could have brought forth. I had finally entered Panare culture.

Part II:

Social Insertion

5. *Social Time and Social Space as Context*

In the previous chapters, I have dwelt much more heavily upon the text than upon the context of my interaction with the Panare of Turiba Viejo. The interaction between "I" and "they" needed to be made explicit in the light of a process—the flow of events that has just been exposed. Such a flow is like a behavioral discourse, linear and cumulative. By this I mean that each event entered into dialectic relation with all previous events and thus not only had a meaning of its own but modified in retrospect the meaning of the whole text.

Yet, in order for my interaction with the Panare to be fully understood, focusing on the text, although necessary, is not sufficient: no behavioral text is without its corresponding context. Undoubtedly, as shown by the text, meaning is achieved, yet meaning has already been ascribed, because the context provides in its structure the negative constraints which limit the array of potentialities for the text. The context, thus, constitutes the necessarily preexisting frame within which the text can be elaborated. As I have shown in the previous chapter, the Panare and I were able to create and manipulate my status and my role vis-à-vis themselves, but this was only possible with respect to and against the background of other relations. I was able to distinguish myself from the Creoles because there was a certain mode of relationship, a certain type of expectation in the Creole-Panare relationship. Similarly, if I was to be given a name and a kinship relation within the group, no matter what degree of playfulness it may have involved, this could only be done in the context of the social relations that the Panare maintain among themselves. At the same time, it should be clear that both the ascription and the achievement of meaning are dialectic; but we should be careful to recognize the three different types of dialectic movement that are involved here.

The first type is easy to grasp, if not necessarily to analyze. It refers to the time and to the rhythm of the behavioral discourse and involves the way in which an event acquires its significance from past events and also, by its mere occurrence, modifies the significance of these same past events. It is the constitutive aspect of the meaning of the text, its achieving quality, the cultural construct with which an American symbolist such as Geertz finds himself at ease.

The second type of dialectic is opposite and altogether antithetic to the first one, as it concerns the context, that is, that which preexists, conditions, and determines the achievement. It refers to the code according to which the message is emitted. It is easy to recognize here not only a vocabulary but also an analytical procedure familiar to a French structuralist such as Lévi-Strauss. Hence the meaning is already constituted. And it proceeds from a different dialectic, for it is constituted as the social memory of former discourses which codify and operationalize the present discourse.

But I am now confronted with, at best, a difficult paradox and, at worst, a blatant contradiction, the resolution of which is nothing other than the third type of dialectic alluded to above. For it seems to be either/or. Either meaning is process or it is result. Either it comes out of the unfolding of the text or it is already there in the context. From a methodological viewpoint, either phenomenological empathy *or* structuralist logic is valid. Either Geertz or Lévi-Strauss, and after all neither of them appears terribly impressed by the other. But in fact, is it really necessary to endorse the dichotomy between event and structure, and its so terribly occidental avatars such as subjectivity and objectivity, humanism and science, percept and concept, and the like? In doing so, are we not the victims of our heuristic procedures, surreptitiously reified?

Actually, except for heuristic purposes, event and structure are inseparable; they interpenetrate each other to such an extent that in the concreteness of an experience, they can hardly be discerned. There is no discourse without grammar, and similarly no grammar without discourse. But what seems to me much less trivial is that every discourse is not—partly or totally—grammatical, and that such ungrammaticalities may—and only may—under certain circumstances become grammatical. The mistake may become rule. Event and structure assault each other constantly in the dialectics of lived experience, and concrete behavioral interaction is nothing else than their practical synthesis. This is where, in my opinion, both Lévi-Strauss and Geertz fall short in their interpretative attempts, for—if I may venture this gory metaphor—the first gives us bones on which there is little flesh, while the second offers plenty of flesh that has been boned. In both cases, something is missing from the body of experience.

Therefore, the task which is now before me can be identified as the articulation between event and structure. Because of the intermeshing of the two, structural elements are to be found in the preceding discussion of events. I have shown previously how my view of the Panare and their view of me, prejudiced as each may have been, were not only confronted but met at one point: that of my "adoption." The paradoxically gradual and yet radical shift which occurred in our relationship was an event which in turn became structural. Once it had happened, its contingency turned into necessity.

Leaving the relations of the Panare with the outside world for later consideration, I will now consider the relations that they maintain among themselves. Thus the whole weight of Panare social relations must be brought to the foreground, for the following reasons. I was neither an Indian nor a Creole and, in the fieldworking situation, I had partial traits of both, the most spectacular of which was undoubtedly my "adoption." I could not interpret properly what it entailed and what it meant for me and for them at the time it happened, because that would have involved a prior knowledge of precisely what I was in the process of learning. It would have implied understanding of the context prior to the unfolding of the text. My interpretation is therefore an attempt to elicit what I experienced in the light of what I now know. Thus, I will begin here, reversing the succession of actual events, with an exposition of my understanding of Panare social relations which will later shed some light on my interaction with my kin at Turiba Viejo, that is, not only on the text, but also on the texture of our mutual discourse. I now have to return less to Turiba Viejo, the point of my insertion into the Panare world, than to the Panare world itself. Before returning to the concreteness of experience, I will be concerned here with social organization per se, the abstract frame of Panare social relations, which constituted—partially at least—a code for our concrete interaction.

A Panare residential unit is localized around its *churuata*, the communal dwelling that the Panare call *pereka*. The proper translation of this word is "house," but it often is metaphorically extended to refer to the whole local group, including its inhabitants. The residential unit itself, that is, the members of the local group, can be referred to by the term *tapatakyen*, so that two Panare individuals settled at Turiba Viejo belong by definition to the same *tapatakyen*. The demographic variation which exists among different local groups is rather wide—they range from about fifteen to sixty individuals. An interpretation, if not an explanation, of these two figures should be useful to show how the Panare conceptualize themselves in relation to space, something which seems to me of paramount importance and which I have emphasized repeatedly in previous writings (Dumont 1972, 1974*a*, 1974*b*, 1976).

The lower demographic limit of a *tapatakyen* is determined by the male mode of work, more precisely by the composition of collective hunting parties organized to spear peccaries, anteaters, and, above all, tapirs. As far as hunting, but also fishing and gathering, are concerned, the Panare have two different modes of work, individual and collective. To call the first of these an individual mode of work may appear misleading, for at no time will a man go out in the bush by himself; for the sake of security and also companionship, he will always be accompanied by another. The kinship relationship between them may vary greatly and thus does not seem very relevant, and, in fact, the product thus obtained is not immediately shared, although it will eventually be redistributed in the common meal. On the other hand, for a collective hunting expedition to take place, more than two individuals are required, the smallest number being three. The minimum size of a local group (*tapatakyen*) is determined by the presence of the three hunters necessary and sufficient to undertake a collective hunt.

In this respect, the two smallest local groups that I have encountered confirmed this interpretation. The first was a group in the Sierra Cerbatana headed by Guariqueño (*naxtö*-GQ501),[6] who had married two sisters, *into*-GQ505 and *acim*-GQ506. His group consisted of sixteen individuals: himself, his two wives, and his thirteen children, two sons and five daughters from his first wife, and one son and five daughters from his second wife. None of the children was married, but the two sons of *into* were adults and constituted, with their father, the only three hunters of the group.

While this first example represents a logical limit in group size that has endured over time, the second one shows a historical limit of a group at its genesis. The composition of the group of Ramón Gallardo (*unyey*-TR59) is given here as of the day of its fission from Turiba Viejo during the dry season of 1969. He had married two sis-

---

[6]As will be explained below, men have a Spanish name as well as a Panare name, while women have no Spanish name. To each Panare name I have added a classification tag consisting of two letters and/or one or more integers. Deceased individuals are identified only by number. The letters identify the group of residence, and the integers are a serial number. Hence, the wives of Guariqueño and of Ramón Gallardo may not be confused; although they bear the same names, they have different identification tags.

ters, *into*-TR60 and *acim*-159, the latter having died. His group was made up of seven individuals, all adults. In addition to Ramón Gallardo, it included three of his children (one son and two daughters by his late wife, *acim*), his wife (*into*), one of *into*'s daughters by a former marriage, and the latter's husband. Here again, we find three adult males who make the undertaking of a collective hunting expedition possible (see fig. 6).

Below this minimum, the group can no longer function culturally, and the only solution for it is to fuse with another. The Panare see this drastic solution as a terrible humiliation, for they do not perceive a fusion between two groups as a political alliance, but rather as the "submission" of a smaller group to a larger one, the greatest humiliation being for the "absorbed" headman. Yet, the implications that this could have for social stratification remain latent for a simple reason. The Panare are in full population expansion, and I know of no group which has been absorbed, only of groups which have recently been born. Therefore, the evocation of such fusion is nothing but a phantasm, but a phantasm which indicates clearly the loss of being that it would entail for the "submitted" group: its symbolic and social death. Its headman, in addition to being humiliated, is no longer an *iyan* and thus loses his status and the role attached to it. Although the former headman would not lose his role as a shaman, I did not need to share the Panare phantasm to understand, in sympathy with my informant, how little prestige a fallen headman would enjoy as a shaman. Felipe Casanova (*naxtö*-TV17), from whom I first learned about this, and who was neither headman nor shaman, summed up his interpretation of this envisioned disaster in these two Spanish words: *casi muerto*.

The reader may wonder why I am pursuing this imagined event, for which I have no empirical evidence whatsoever. There are two reasons. The first is that it allows me to introduce a distinction between the statuses of headman and shaman. Both are marked in relation to time, but conceptually, the shaman is located entirely on the side of permanence, of the supernatural which he manipulates. Quite to the contrary, the headman is located on the side of impermanence, of historical time. In a way, by his initiation, the shaman has received the seal of an incorruptible *essence*, while the status of headman implies a more risky and dramatic *existence*. *Casi muerto*, said Felipe Casanova of the unhappy headman, but he did not say anything of the sort about an unhappy shaman. A shaman is alive or dead. He is alive if he can control the terrible spirits in his chest, which make him powerful; he is dead when he has been overcome by these spirits. It is one or the other, all alive or all dead.

These contradictory perceptions of time bring me back to a very concrete space. I once asked what would happen if a headman died, actually, rather than metaphorically. The metonymic relationship of a headman to his group is such that his death brings about a spatial change. The deceased headman is buried, but the location of all burial places is very quickly forgotten (or "forgotten"). Below we will encounter another type of social amnesia when we cope with the names of the dead. In both cases, it is not a conscious prohibition, a taboo, for when I asked the grief-ridden Felipe Casanova where he had buried his day-old baby a few days after its burial, he showed me the spot, but nobody could tell me where Manuel Blanco had been buried. Furthermore, in theory at least, if not always in practice, the *churuata* of the deceased headman as well as all his belongings are supposed to be burned. Symbolically then, the death of the leader is thus the death of the group, whose space is temporally destroyed, almost erased. Properly speaking, and at least momentarily, the group loses its locus. Being destroyed, it has become atopic, and the contingency of temporal irreversibility has been spatialized. Of course, this norm, like any other norm, can be and is indeed manipulated, so that in fact a great variety of practices occur at the empirical level. At Turiba Viejo, after the death of Manuel Blanco (*töna*-157), the *churuata* had been built too recently to be sacrificed on an ideological altar; besides, the gardens were really close, the location of the settlement was convenient, so the *churuata* was spared. Instead, a play on words was used, as I was made aware much later by his son Juan-Pablo Martinez (*unyey*-TV11). The word *pereka* referred to any thatched building, so it was acceptable to burn Manuel Blanco's old workshop-hut (which was leaking anyway) rather than the *churuata*. Incidentally, his belongings had been piled up in the hut in the morning, but when Domingo Flores (*manyan*-TV26), another son of Manuel Blanco, struck the match to set the fire, all metal tools had disappeared, being withdrawn from use for a month or two before reappearing discreetly in the hands of the dead man's sons.

Nevertheless, whether it be *the pereka* or *a pereka* that is destroyed, the structural aspect of the problem remains the same: a temporal cause always has a spatial effect. In addition, this effect is negative, censorship rather than expostulation—the aim is always to erase even the trace, the memory of the dead headman.

But what is true at a symbolic level is also true at a social one. In fact, the composition of the local group is evidently based upon kinship links, and the headman is the keystone of this kinship construction, as can be seen from the respective groups of Guariqueño and

Ramón Gallardo. Actually, the conscious model of the *tapatakyen* is the extended bilateral family of the man who is at the highest genealogical level. As can be expected of any such model, the corresponding empirical reality varies considerably, and yet the social cohesion of the local group is structurally upset whenever the headman's death occurs. Sooner or later, the group will be subjected to some adjustment in its composition, to some rearrangement of its kinship space to achieve a neat balance. Practically, the residential unit is likely to enter a process of fission—at worst, to burst in all directions, or, less radically, to suffer the loss of one or two families which do not "fit" anymore because death has severed the actual ties which linked them to the rest of the *tapatakyen*. Characteristically, fission is more likely to happen when the local group has reached its upper demographic limit.

In contrast to the lower limit, which was determined by the mode of work, the upper limit is determined by the mode of production.[7] Beyond some sixty individuals, everything remaining equal, the yield of collective hunting begins to drop sharply. Yet success in hunting big game, and particularly tapirs, determines the acquisition of prestige, which in turn determines access to women. Whenever big game becomes more scarce, the blame is placed upon the headman, and it is mainly his prestige which is tarnished. Since he has no coercive power, only authority, this taint has two consequences. First, there is a slow trickle of individuals away from the group, which is made possible through bilocal residence. The conscious postmarital residence model for the Panare is uxorilocal, which is reinforced by the practice of bride-service that a man performs for his father-in-law. Often, upon

[7]In Sahlins' discussion of the "familial mode of production" (1968: 75–81) or "domestic mode of production" (1972: 41–148), the expression is used *lato sensu*, and it would be difficult to abstract a concise definition. However, Godelier defines it quite rigorously: "The mode of production *stricto sensu* [can be defined as] the combination, which can reproduce itself, of productive forces and of specific social relations of production which determine the structure and the form of the process of production and of exchange of material goods within an historically determined society" (1973: 18). A mode of production *lato sensu* can be defined as the ensemble of economic and social relations which correspond to a specific mode of production *stricto sensu*.

The mode of production which is unique for a given tribal group is not to be confused with the modes of work, which are multiple. In the context of a given tribal group, horticulture and hunting may involve two modes of work. Yet, they belong to a specific mode of production and do not constitute two different modes of production. The mode of work—that is, the combination of social relations, environment, and technology—as well as the social relations created by the appropriation and control of the means of production and of the products of work constitute the mode of production.

expiration of this service after a year or so, the married couple maintains this uxorilocal residence. But there are a great many counter-examples to this tendency in the empirical reality, as we shall see at Turiba Viejo. In fact, once the bride-service has been performed, there will be a tendency for the in-marrying man to withdraw to his group of origin, away from his wife's group, if it appears unsuccessful in terms of hunting. The second consequence is the creation of tension within the group that leads to its fission, with the pretext of a woman's sexual misbehavior.

In fact, the historical and cyclical aspect of such spatial and horizontal adjustments of the group's membership is relatively easy to understand. A prestigious headman tends to attract (married) individuals to his group, and he does so as long as his group is able to increase its big-game production without introducing any change in the process of production or, above all, any increase in the time of work. In these conditions, a local group may fairly rapidly reach a plateau beyond which the collective hunting yield decreases. Concomitantly, the size of the group will sooner or later decrease until the yield of collective hunting rises again. The system is self-regulated in such a way that, ultimately, variations in the production of big game determine fluctuations in group size. Yet the covariance is not simultaneous, but lagging. In effect, the demographic attraction or repulsion exerted by a group is always delayed in relation to its increase or decrease in big-game production, and this is mainly observable at the upper level, where group attraction is based upon an acquired and persistent reputation for success in hunting. A group may still be accommodating newcomers, although its game production has already begun to decrease. At the lower level, economic recovery is almost immediately perceptible for the *tapatakyen* members, thus stopping them from drifting away. As a matter of fact, I know of no group which has gone from above sixty individuals to below twenty.

Such population fluctuations in the local groups are predicated upon the politics of what I would like to call the space of kinship. In addition to being a member of a certain group, the residential unit, an individual also belongs to a certain category, that of the *pyaka*. An approximate but acceptable rendition of this term is "kindred," that is, the ensemble of individuals to whom an individual feels closely related, following the rule of bilateral descent. The extension of the *pyaka* varies considerably depending upon the circumstances, such that a second cousin with whom one has been closely associated in youth may ultimately be included, while an actual maternal uncle whom one has never seen may be excluded. Clearly, everybody has close relatives in the local group; thus one's *pyaka* and *tapatakyen* always overlap to a greater or lesser extent without, of course, ever coinciding perfectly.

The one individual for whom the overlapping is the greatest is generally the headman, whose bilateral extended family constitutes the core of the local group. To this core, in-marrying spouses and some of their kin are aggregated following a sort of building-block construction. For, in order to be a member of a given local group, an individual needs to have at least one primary relative in it.[8] Consequently, an individual may, in theory at least, choose where to settle from a rather vast array of local groups, even though practically the choice is much more restricted, since it is ultimately determined by the previous moves of close relatives and spouse.

This is only possible because of the bilateral principle of descent among the Panare, who have no lineages, clans, or any other descent groups which would persist through time. In fact, this is further evidenced by the fact that some individuals could not even remember the names of their own father or mother. For any practical purpose, descent is thus of little importance among the Panare, who are little concerned with genealogical depth. Indirect evidence for this can be given by a brief examination of the Panare naming system.

Babies have no real personal names. Until a child is weaned, he or she is referred to and addressed as *nyamca*. For instance, the son of Guzmán (*puka*-TV20) at Turiba Viejo was constantly called by that term by his parents. This, of course, brought about some confusion, for everybody in his age group was called the same thing. Most of the time, however, possible confusion is avoided, since such young children interact mostly with their parents, unless there is more than one *nyamca* in a given family. In referring to a male infant, however, there is always a way of avoiding ambiguity by using the converse of a teknonym,[9] in this case *pukankin*, "the child of *puka*." A female child would have been referred to as her mother's child rather than as her father's child; hence in this case it would have been *acimkin*, "the child of *acim*," which was the Panare name of Guzmán's wife (*acim-*

[8]According to Murdock, "the term *primary relatives* is applied to those who belong to the same nuclear family as a particular person—his father, mother, sisters, and brothers in his family of orientation, and his husband or wife, his sons, and his daughters in his family of procreation" ([1949] 1965: 94, his emphasis).

[9]According to Murdock, "in its most typical form [teknonymy] consists in calling a person who has a child 'father (or mother) of So-and-so,' combining the parental term with the child's name, instead of using a personal name or a kinship term" ([1949] 1965: 97). Conversely, the Panare call a child "son (or daughter) of So-and-so."

TV49). Even a fetus is referred to by the word *nyamca*, as I was to discover when Guzmán rubbed his wife's belly to convince me that she was pregnant. The word *nyamca* categorizes an individual from conception to weaning, and it conceptualizes all *nyamca* in relation to their elders. Fetus or infant, a *nyamca* is therefore no more than a would-be human being, as yet undifferentiated.

At the opposite end of the life cycle, I found that the dead were already undifferentiated, because they were quickly forgotten. Although there is no formal taboo on their names, a sort of social amnesia impedes the remembrance of such names. Some individuals, particularly older ones, who could not remember the name of a primary kin, would tell me as an excuse that their deaths had occurred a long time ago, too long ago for them to remember. Being a young man, Guzmán remembered well that his deceased father's name was Rodiana (*tose*-160), but he failed to remember that Rodiana's father was Rufo (*puka*-155). A fortiori, he had no idea that Rufo's father had been Basilio (*töna*-150). In most cases, to go back two generations in genealogies was nearly impossible. In fact, the very concept of genealogy is totally alien to the Panare way of thinking. In societies where names belong to clans, lineages, or similar groupings, there may be a need to reuse the names of deceased members, so that it makes sense to taboo the names of the dead. But in Panare social organization, which does not emphasize any descent principle, there is no pressure to remember the names of the dead, whose souls are all flowing in the anonymity of the Milky Way.

It is easy to see that infants and the dead are treated in a similar and opposite way by the Panare. While any infant is still a *nyamca*, any dead person is already a soul, in both cases outside the core of Panare culture. The infants, still close to nature in their "uncult" behavior, are yet to be encultured, while the dead are already segregated from culture and thrown out into the supernatural world, as permutable stars in the Milky Way. The only point of this classification seems to be highly ideological. The infants are not yet with us, the dead are no longer with us, and thus none of them can gain any individuality. This could hardly be more strongly emphasized than when Felipe Casanova (*naxtö*-TV17), whom I was asking about the siblings of his father, answered me, "Never mind, they are dead."

With the living, the matter was scarcely any easier to elicit. After their weaning, children are quite informally given a name by either or both parents. These names are chosen from two sets, one for males (*ciköxpwö, cipöron, etana, ikuren, köpwö, menyakari, simon, tukari,* etc.) and one for females (*arawa, asipa, ciruwa, esara, kainyam, karapwi, karime, kömusin, kucono, maara, makuin, mectetu, pemo, tikiri, tupören, wamo,* etc.). These names are only temporary, and when boys are initiated or girls have their first menses, these names are replaced by permanent ones bestowed by the settlement members of the same sex as the child. However, at first, to my amazement and soon to my dismay, there are only six permanent names for males (*manyan, naxtö, puka, töna, tose, unyey*) and four permanent names for females (*acim, aton, into, matö*). In all these cases, the name attribution is not submitted to any other determination, and for any individual any name can be freely selected within one of the categories: male child, female child, male adult, female adult. Since the Panare have no social units other than the residential group, the names are neither the property of a group nor transmitted by inheritance. It is easy to understand how these personal names favor rather than prevent confusion. In effect, although people tend to choose names for the initiated children from those which are not in use by the elder members of a family, this is only a tendency and certainly not a necessity. In addition, if a couple has five adult daughters, two of them must have the same name. Even worse, due to sororal polygyny, a man may have married two women bearing the same name. Under these conditions, genealogical investigation became an uncanny puzzle, although there were other ways to identify individuals when some doubt arose. The social context, nicknames, teknonym converses, kinship terms, and residential units did eradicate some possible confusion. But above all, men had Spanish names acquired from the Creoles, so that it was very unlikely that two men would have both the same Creole name and the same Panare name: in fact, although one man out of six was a *puka* and there was at least one other Guzmán in a different settlement, there was to the best of my knowledge only one man who was both Guzmán and *puka*, at any rate only one whose *tapatakyen* was Turiba Viejo.

The problem was slightly more tricky with women. Guzmán's wife, *acim*-TV49, also had a Spanish name, Luisa Flores. Guzmán did not know that, and not even she could remember it. I learned it from her father, Marquito (*unyey*-TV1), who apparently was the only one in the settlement to know and remember this name, the accuracy of which was later confirmed for me by the Creoles. In fact, whenever a woman acquires a Creole name, it falls very quickly into disuse and oblivion, with only her closest kin possibly remembering what it is. I will come back to this particular problem later, but for the moment will note that, for all practical and investigative purposes, it was as if women had no name other than one of the four Panare adult female names.[10] Both the small number of names available and the lack of concern for ancestors' names not only hampered my investigation, but also seriously flattened the kinship domain, as we shall see from the way in which names are used in daily life.

The second difficulty emerged directly from this flattening. Instead of looking at kinship in an ancestor-oriented way, that is to say "vertically," social relations were determined "horizontally." Bilateral descent, that is, the acquisition of one's status at birth from both parents, plays a very unimportant practical role among the Panare. But, on the contrary, marriage bonds are of extreme importance, which can easily be shown.

Direct sister-exchange is the archetypal model of and model for Panare marriage, and therefore there is no reason to be surprised by the high frequency of marriages between bilateral cross-cousins to be found in ethnographic reality. According to such a model, two men who are not siblings swap sisters in such a way that in the next generation any man will marry a woman who is both his MoBrDa[11] and his FaSiDa, thus reproducing, generation after generation, bilateral cross-cousin marriages[12] (see fig. 1). It is pure convention in this case to see men exchanging women, for obviously this is symmetric; we could just as well say that two women who are not siblings swap brothers in such a way that in the next generation any woman will marry a man who is both her MoBrSo and her FaSiSo. The only justification for this convention is that men largely retain political control over women's movements rather than the reverse.

In practice, however, the Panare do not systematically follow the logic of the model, for the problem here is not to maintain an affinal relationship between nonexistent unilineal descent groups, but to maintain ties between residential groups. In fact, the Panare actually express their marriage preferences in terms of space. To be sure, to marry a bilateral cross-cousin is somehow ideal, but this is not what a Panare

[10]To aid the reader, I hereafter give a Spanish pseudonym to the main female characters in this book. These pseudonyms are clearly ad hoc creations on my part.

[11]I have used conventional abbreviations for kinship relations: Fa for father, Mo for mother, Br for brother, Si for sister, So for son, Da for daughter, Hu for husband, Wi for wife. Hence, MoBrDa, for instance, reads "mother's brother's daughter."

[12]Two cousins are parallel-cousins if the linking parents are of the same sex; two cousins are cross-cousins if the linking parents are of opposite sex. My matrilateral cousins are cousins who are related to me through my mother; my patrilateral cousins are cousins who are related to me through my father. My bilateral cousins are related to me through both my mother and my father.

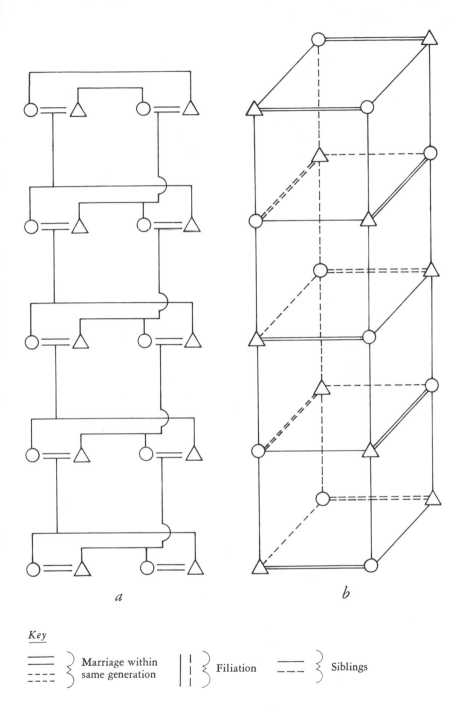

Fig. 1. *Model of bilateral cross-cousin marriage.* (a) *Bidimensional representation,* (b) *tridimensional representation*

mentions first. A Panare will begin by stipulating the preference for marrying within the local group, even though this local endogamy may entail marrying somebody who is less ideally related than a bilateral cross-cousin. Short of marrying within one's *tapatakyen*, it is still better to marry in a neighboring group than in a far-away local group. In other words, and to paraphrase Lévi-Strauss, I may write that the Panare search after "the joys, eternally denied to social man, of a world in which one might *keep to oneself*" ([1949] 1969:497, his emphasis). Actually, such local group endogamy is never achieved, for it conflicts with and contradicts a reverse tendency toward local group exogamy. In fact, the scattering of kin in different settlements makes possible the spreading out of affinity links and thus of political bonds between these settlements, something that Marquito (*unyey*-TV1) explained to me in the clearest possible way when I asked him about the marriages of his children.

In itself, such a contradiction between local endogamy and local exogamy is interesting. What really hinders the members of a local group from behaving entirely according to their conscious ideology? Why this necessity of alliances with other local groups? Actually, from a political viewpoint, such an alliance may even appear rather illusory, since local groups are not permanent entities, lasting only as long as the headman survives. Symbolically, the group's space, its locus, is destroyed, and it becomes another group. This has a direct linguistic expression, since the local group is referred to by its headman's name, as in the case of Turiba Viejo, which was said to be "Marquito's group." Socially, the headman's death entails, at worst, the scattering of the group into different bilateral extended families generally led by the brothers and sons of the deceased headman, as happened at Colorado, at best, the warping of the group composition through the splitting off of a smaller group, such as that of Ramón Gallardo (*unyey*-TR59) at Turiba Viejo. In other words, a local group has no duration other than that of its headman.

Economic cooperation between local groups, however, is minimal. For the whole duration of my fieldwork, the group at Turiba Viejo joined only twice with that of Los Pozos for a fish-poisoning expedition and went only once to barter resin for curare with a local group of the Sierra Cerbatana. At the same time, Turiba Viejo was involved in matrimonial exchanges with more than ten local groups. Such a contrast between economic and matrimonial exchanges tends to indicate that the rationality of this network is not directly economic. Furthermore, it can easily be understood that if an already large group were to behave according to its ideology, its demographic upper limit would be reached very quickly, the necessity for group exogamy thus being indirectly economic. But this does not explain the scattering of matrimonial alliances.

In fact, for a given group, this scattering represents a diversification of its social holdings, a sort of demographic insurance. The direct exchange of sisters between brothers-in-law represents more than an alliance between two residential units. Even if these exchanges abide by the model of direct exchange between bilateral cross-cousins generation after generation the groups thus involved, being themselves ephemeral, cannot be the same ones. However, these matrimonial exchanges allow a constant redistribution of the population between groups, that is, demographic regulation between groups whose members are too many or too few. What appears immediately is the exchange of women that takes place between local groups. But, beyond that, these immediate exchanges of women in the long run make possible the alternative exchanges of individuals of both sexes, that is, their circulation, their redistribution. And this is because an individual is entitled to settle in any *tapatakyen* in which he/she has at least one primary kin. Consequently, to scatter the alliances of a local group is to enter into a cycle of demographic exchanges between groups that are deprived of duration.

Such a spatialization of social relations among the Panare is reinforced in two different yet converging ways, through which the vertical aspect of time seems further suppressed while the horizontal aspect of space is reinforced. In addition to direct sister-exchange, there is among the Panare a secondary model of marriage between alternate generations which allows a man to marry his MoMo as well as his DaDa. The corollary of this is that a woman may therefore marry her DaSo as well as her MoFa (see fig. 2a), which is consistent with the tendency toward uxorilocality. This type of marriage is also consistent with the primary model of sister-exchange (see fig. 2b). Yet, it does not involve a *direct* exchange of sisters between grandparents and grandchildren, since only the husband (and definitely not the brother) of the marriageable grandmother may marry a man's sister. Conversely, only the wife (and definitely not the sister) of the marriageable grandfather may marry a woman's brother.

For the anthropologist and for the reader, this is most unfortunate, because it complicates the matter a bit. Nevertheless, let us suppose that everything is perfect among the Panare and that everybody indulges consistently in this type of marriage. If so, a man has to wait

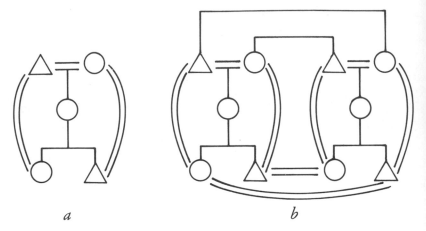

a b

Fig. 2. *Possible marriages between alternate generations*

for the death of his MoFa to marry his MoMo, because, although they practice sororal polygyny, the Panare do not know of any form of polyandry. Later, the same man may marry one or two bilateral cross-cousins and, in his old age, may marry one of his DaDa. This can be represented in a tridimensional way (see fig. 3) which should help clarify what is happening in the five generations that an individual has to know in order to enter into these types of marriage. To increase the readability of the diagram, let us omit one set of alternate generations. It can be seen now (see fig. 4) that nine generations are needed to achieve a complete spiral movement, and that there are always eight parallel spirals involved, four for any given genealogical level, and four at any adjacent level.

The diagrams represent the formal logic of the Panare marriage system, but I will hasten to say that the Panare are unconscious that their marriage system entails such a complicated scheme. They have nothing so perverted in their heads. In proposing such a model, I have only followed the logical implications of the marriages that they practice and consider perfectly acceptable. Instead of arriving at a totally incoherent picture, it can be seen that, on the contrary, the coherence of the system is perfect. But practical matters are—thank God—infinitely simpler.

First, it is quite unusual that a young male has to resort to marrying his real grandmother. At any rate, this can only be a temporary solution, since such a couple is very unlikely to have issue. The motivation for such a marriage is not sexual gratification, but economic cooperation, due to the strict sexual dichotomy of activities in Panare

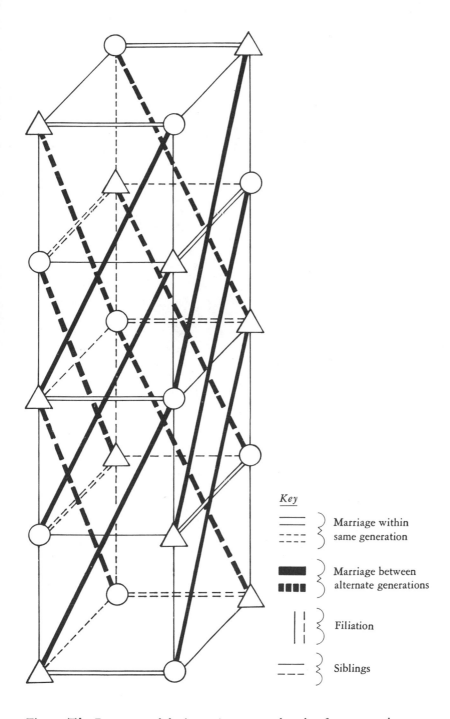

Fig. 3. *The Panare model of marriage, complete for five generations*

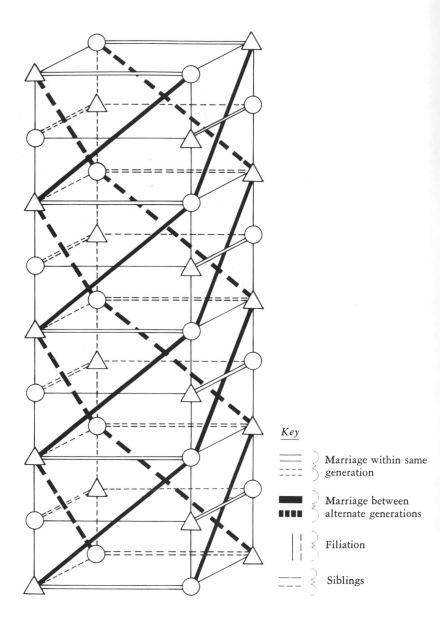

Fig. 4. *The Panare model of marriage, simplified for nine generations*

culture. On the other hand, the marriage of a grandfather with his actual DaDa occurs rather frequently. An older man has to be quite prestigious to attract a young woman, without speaking of the Oedipal situation in which such a couple has placed itself. The main reason for this type of marriage, however, seems to be sociological: namely, it reinforces local group endogamy, not only because an older man marries a close kin, but also because the granddaughter belongs to the same *tapatakyen*. I have seen no case of this type of marriage in which the intermediary parents of the bride had established a virilocal residence. In addition, this marriage is most often fertile. As we shall see later, however, this type of marriage is infinitely more frequent between individuals who are not really related in this way, but only classificatorily. In these conditions, the individuals involved are unlikely to be separated by a great age discrepancy and are apt to be approximately the same age.

This type of marriage has yet another consequence which is of capital importance. If an individual marries his DaDa, it follows that his daughter has suddenly also become his WiMo. Further, the whole kinship domain is affected, in such a way that not only are daughters and mothers-in-law structurally equivalent, but by the same token sons-in-law are transformed into fathers-in-law, sons into fathers, and mothers into daughters-in-law, both from a male and a female viewpoint. Therefore, all occurs as if the marriage system and its consequences flattened out the space of kinship.

The absence of genealogical depth is such, in fact, that two individuals are rarely capable of tracing step-by-step their relation to each other, even when they are real and not classificatory tertiary kin. In reality, kinship relations are always determined (as well as manipulated) in relation to other living relatives and never in relation to the dead. This has a linguistic expression in the naming system. At the same genealogical level, two consanguines (when they do not use a kinship term) call each other by their names alone, but two affines must add the suffix -*can* to their names. Therefore, in calling an individual by his/her name, one is always forced to make a choice, either to classify the other as consanguine or as affine. Moreover, in order to determine the relationship between two individuals, it is sufficient to pass through the intermediary of a third individual whose relationship to the former two is known. Hence, whether the link be real or classificatory, the sibling of a sibling is a sibling, the sibling-in-law of a sibling-in-law is a sibling, the sibling-in-law of a sibling is a sibling-in-law, the sibling of a sibling-in-law is a sibling-in-law.

One consequence of determining kinship relations through the living rather than through the dead is that the dead can easily be manipulated post hoc to fit the reality. Nothing is more malleable than human memory, and whenever somebody had not married "properly" —that is, had married, for instance, a classificatory sibling—it was always posable (and in most cases indeed it was done) to adjust the actual relations of the dead, so that when convenient for the present social order, some people two generations ago were said to have been siblings-in-law when in fact they had been siblings, or vice versa. These pious lies obviously resulted in great confusion, which I could not always disentangle and reconcile.

Sororal polygyny, on the other hand, further complicated the problem. A man might have married not two actual sisters but two classificatory ones, which an informant would often forget (or "forget"), therefore falsifying the step-by-step tracing of the relationship between two individuals. As a matter of fact, in this case as in the previous adjustment, this would be due less to an outright lie than to the way in which the informants reasoned, which, incidentally, showed the great confidence they placed in their own institution. It can be paraphrased in this approximate way: since this man had married that woman, any classificatory sibling of the former could not possibly be a classificatory sibling of the latter; furthermore, since this man had married two women, they had to be sisters.

Of course, I had to view such rationalization with a healthy scepticism, because it gave a picture of Panare society which was perfect, save for one major defect: it did not fit empirical reality, as I was made aware by contradicting informants. Nevertheless, it had the advantage of making explicit the Panare conscious model of marriage as well as the readjustments by which the space of kinship was flattened out.

In conclusion, it could be said that everything occurs as if the Panare constantly conceptualize themselves in relation to space but strongly distrust time, to the contingency of which they are inescapably subjected. In accentuating residence much more than descent, the Panare choose to spread out their social relations rather than root them in time. They intensify their kinship relations in one place, their residential unit, the erotic space *par excellence*. In contrast, they seem to cool history, so to speak, and time is conceived of as destructive. It is always congruent with death, that of the headman or that of the local group. Even when cyclical, as in the demographic regulations between groups, time is still a threat, since it is this thanatetic time which prevents the Panare of a given local group from living in total endogamy.

The spreading out of the network of alliances into several groups ultimately represents almost an insurance policy to protect Panare social survival. As I understand it, space for the Panare has a double sense: it is both orientation and signification.

6. The Headman's Dead, Long Live the Headman

Having crossed the threshold of Panare culture, I now had to cope with fifty-eight new "relatives" (see fig. 5) whose names I was beginning to learn and whose kinship status I was painfully trying to understand. The whole of Panare social relations deserves further examination. But it is not social relations per se, in the abstract, which will receive my attention at this point, but rather the way in which I was concerned with and directly affected by them. It was in this integrative process that my vision of anthropology was beginning to change from that of a mere collection of objective data into something infinitely more complex, something which could be called "involvement."

As I learned more about them, the Panare began to dissolve as objects of study. I found it more and more difficult to think of "the Panare," in an abstract way, and thought rather of Marquito (*unyey*-TV1) and Felipe Casanova (*naxtö*-TV17), of Domingo Barrios (*töna*-TV4) and Guzmán (*puka*-TV20), and of Domingo Flores (*manyan*-TV26), too, the five men with whom I was to develop the closest links, the five people with whom, by the end of my fieldwork, I found myself most familiar, most intimate, and altogether most relaxed. While at first it was difficult to see them as anything other than "informants," I became acutely aware that they were entering into my life in yet another way, more subtle and also more profound: I became aware that they were appearing in my dreams, side by side with my actual French kin. Progressively, but more markedly when I discovered their intrusion into my subconscious, they were turning into subjects.

This was more troublesome than anything else, and I even resented it, for it introduced a kind of "static" into my data collection. As long as a man was no more than a small triangle on a kinship diagram, and a woman no more than a small circle, this was a safe although sterile piece of information. But as soon as the same person acquired a different dimension through the thickness of our common experience, I began to feel quite uncomfortable. In many respects, I tried desperately to prevent these distortions of objective reality; at the same time I was emotionally satisfied that more than an informant-investigator relationship was developing. What on one plane was truly gratifying was, on another, utterly draining. Obviously this all came together, and I found myself simultaneously reacting in diametrically opposite ways, engaging in and refraining from a movement toward and a movement away. These were not physical forces which would have canceled each other out and left me immobile if not inert, but they were present for the duration of my fieldwork.

Obviously, my emotions were contradictory, and for the sake of comfort, if not facility, I chose to restrain from too much empathy. It is about at that time that, in this effort at compensation, I fiercely began to measure and count and tabulate. I removed myself from what was going on in the settlement, to pay more attention to the outside of it, to the gardens, their dimensions, their plants, to the composition of the other settlements, and to all sorts of ethnographic elements which were of great interest. The main function of this was, for the time being, to let me escape from my incipient involvement with the people of Turiba Viejo, from those to whom I was closest. It was a way of preventing myself from understanding our relationship and from understanding who they really were. Trying to reduce my anxiety, I was down on interpretation, down on thinking, down on feeling. I wanted facts, more facts, and only facts. The escape was total, or almost so.

Simultaneously with the "away," however, there was an equally strong "toward" taking place. It was impossible for me not to enjoy, not to savor, as an indication that I was on the right path toward rapport with the members of the settlement, the prolonged visits that were paid me in my hut whenever I stayed there. The end of the day was a favorite time for Domingo Barrios (*töna*-TV4), to whom I had to explain the principles of kinship charting as I had explained those of mapping to Felipe Casanova (*naxtö*-TV17). For them, as for Marquito (*unyey*-TV1), I was no longer a novelty in the settlement, though they were still intermittently curious about what I was doing. So they would come and sit in my hammock or squat endlessly beside me, working on an unfinished basket or preparing some dart-shafts by the light of my kerosene lamp, repeating rather patiently a term or a sentence that I did not seem to understand. After some time, I would be told: *utey*, "I am going," and my companion(s) would retire to the communal dwelling.

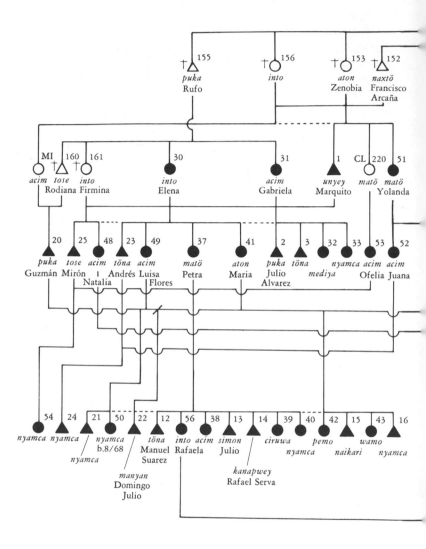

Fig. 5. *The who's who of Turiba Viejo*

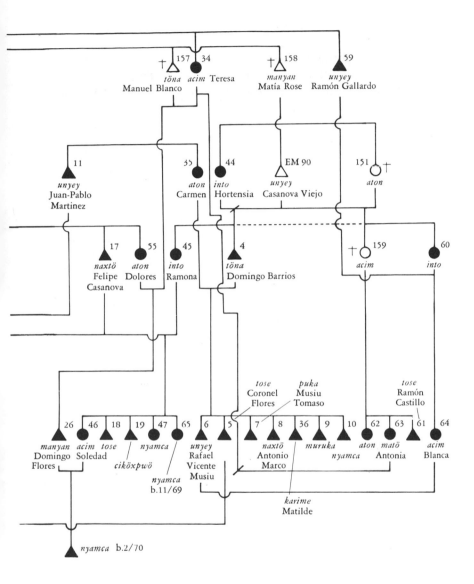

It was pure chance that Marquito had suddenly become my *yako*. The term *yako* is used as a term of reference and address for the brother of a man and for the sister of a woman; it can therefore be glossed as "sibling of same sex," while a man's sister is his *nyasu* and a woman's brother her *pin*. After all, it was not Marquito but Domingo Barrios who had called me *yim*—the term of reference and address for "father"—if not totally at random, at least on the spur of the moment. The latter's reason for choosing this relationship with me rather than another was not only a tribute to his acute sense of humor but was also probably rooted in his own subconscious; in that respect, I cannot account for it. Nevertheless, following the rules of classificatory kinship, since I was a "father" to Domingo Barrios, I was a "brother" to Marquito.

It was chance, but it was luck, too. It was Marquito who, offended one day by my doubt at one of his statements, had told me, "Brothers do not lie to each other." It was also he who had quickly added, "I am the headman, a headman does not lie." In fact, in my experience he was wholly trustworthy, and it was to him that I turned regularly for checking any information which looked suspicious. There were several reasons for his behavior toward me; his personality was as much responsible as was his status as headman. But there was yet another reason. Our huts were side by side (see map 2; his was hut I; mine, hut D), which necessarily resulted, through quasi-uninterrupted interaction with his immediate family, in what can appropriately be called a familiarity greater than that with any other family in the settlement. Progressively, he came to take our siblingship pretty seriously, and I had become to him almost more real a kin than some of his actual, classificatory kin.

Let me pause here, for I wish to advance with extreme caution onto what I consider to be the hazardous path of kinship relations. It is clear that in this domain my own countertransference reactions as a fieldworker are most likely to appear. And that which flies in the face of even the least analytically sophisticated reader would be unlikely to come to the surface of my consciousness. More specifically, when I perceive that Marquito treated me as a "real brother," am I not making a dangerous jump? Do I know this to be the case or do I merely feel it is this way? After all, Marquito was older than I, fiftyish, and he had the authority of the headman, even though by definition a headman's authority is not coercive. In deciding to enter and play this kinship game heartily, how could I not see him as an elder-brother figure, a quasi-perfect father-substitute? Because of our age difference (at the time I was in my late twenties), because Marquito was an authority figure (in a double sense: first he *had* authority as headman,

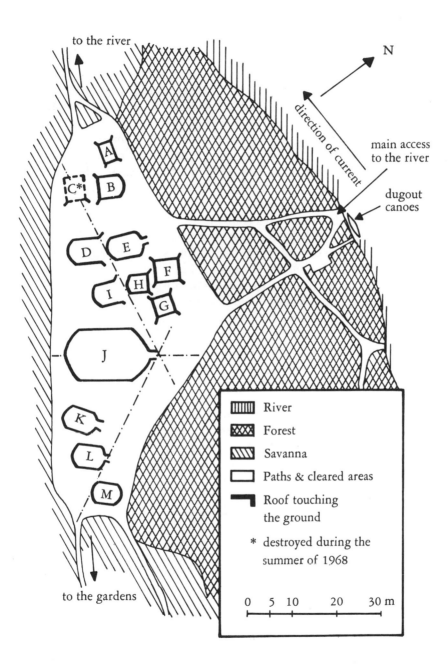

Map 2. *The settlement of Turiba Viejo*

second he *was* an authority as a trustworthy expert on Panare culture
and Turiba Viejo matters), he had to be a good father-substitute in
my fieldworking situation. At the same time, he was a reassuring land-
mark along the path of learning Panare culture. Out of the reality of
our mutual interaction, what did I introject from him, and what did I
project onto him? Beyond a "quite a good deal" answer, it would be
spurious for me to pursue these questions further, but the reader
should bear in mind what Devereux has written so appropriately:
"The anthropologist's report on a tribe and his interpretation of that
tribe's culture is, in some ways, comparable to a projective test, where
the TAT or Rorschach card is the culture studied and the anthropologist's account of the tribe the equivalent of the tested subject's re-
sponses" (1967: 43–44).

In admitting such a countertransference, I merely recognize the
necessity of its occurrence—it cannot be otherwise. Surely, the countertransferences will take different forms with different fieldworkers,
but the phenomenon itself will not be eliminated. As I have maintained so far, I am more interested in the process of production than
in the product of anthropology, because it is essential to reveal this
process if the nature of the product is to be understood. An ostrich
attitude in this matter is no solution and ultimately is extremely detri-
mental to the quality of the anthropological product. In this light, the
same question raised by Firth from a different perspective still deserves
careful consideration: "the question that has yet to be fully faced is
how far does the social structuring of experience limit communication
between the anthropologist and the people whose mode of thought he
is trying to elicit? Their different subjective apprehensions of reality
must be coincident, or at least congruent, at some points or in some
patterns for effort at understanding and interpretation to be meaningful" (1975: 9).

In my opinion, the kinship domain stands as the very locus of
this coincidence or congruency, because of the thickness of experience
that it involves. Here the hinge between text and context can best be
apprehended. Here transferences and countertransferences are best
exemplified. And it is here, finally, with a minimum of consciousness,
that I can hope to grasp reality in the least reifying way.

If Marquito was the most reliable of informants, he was by far
not the most talkative or the most cooperative. Many times when I
would come to see him and ask him some kinship information, he
would simply turn me down after a question or two with *pöröxpwö-cu*,
"I am tired," or *mancye*, "I don't want to." But when he told me

tincaa-pwi-yu, "I don't know," it was not his way of getting rid of me; he really did not know. In and of itself, this was an asset, because, while I could not get much information from him directly, I could at least check with exactitude what others had given me, so that progressively I would acquire a fairly accurate picture of the who's who of Turiba Viejo.

The death of the former headman, Manuel Blanco (*töna*-157), had not only left a power vacuum in the settlement but had also created a structural problem. Namely, as can be seen from figure 5, it introduced a cleavage between the immediate family of Ramón Gallardo (*unyey*-TR59) and the rest of the people in Turiba Viejo. So long as Manuel Blanco was alive, his brother-in-law Ramón Gallardo had been a very influential character in the local group. Now that Ramón Gallardo's sister Teresa (*acim*-TV34) was an elderly widow, the center of gravity of the group had changed, and she had lost her influence as a "headwoman." The death of her husband made her immediately lose her headwoman's position and regress, as it were, to an unmarked rank-and-file status. Ipso facto, Ramón Gallardo, though still a prestigious man, found himself "decentered," almost peripheral. He was no longer at the core of the group but was almost a new-

Pl. 7. *Ramón Gallardo (*unyey-TR59*), headman of Trapichote*

comer whose only link to the group was his siblingship with a woman whose influence had vanished. At that time, Manuel Blanco's widow had not yet remarried. Ramón Gallardo's daughters, Antonia (*matö*-TR63) and Blanca (*acim*-TR64), had not yet married, but when they did so the following year, they thus pulled their respective husbands into the orbit of Ramón Gallardo's influence. This in turn allowed him to create his own settlement at Trapichote, to clear his own garden, and to organize his own hunting parties. In brief, he became, even if relatively late in life, the dominant male of his own group and thus regained, if not increased, the influence and prestige that the demise of his brother-in-law had seriously undermined. In Trapichote he thus recovered his central position at the core of his own local group (see fig. 6).

Meanwhile, in Turiba Viejo, the problem of finding a new *iyan* was still to be solved. Manuel Blanco had two wives, now widows, Teresa (the older), whom we have just considered, and Dolores (*aton*-TV55), his BrDaDa, and therefore his classificatory granddaughter. The latter had a son, Domingo Flores (*manyan*-TV26), who did not get married until my second year of fieldwork. His bachelorhood and, more importantly, his youth (he was about twenty), as

Pl. 8. *Leaving Turiba Viejo for good . . .*

Pl. 9. . . . *on the way to Trapichote*

well as the fact that he had not yet been initiated as a shaman, disqualified him as a potential headman.

His half-brother Juan-Pablo Martinez (*unyey*-TV11), the son of Teresa, should have been in a better position. After all, he had been going through the shamanistic initiation, he had two wives, Petra (*matö*-TV37) and Maria (*aton*-TV41), and had divorced a third one (Luisa, *acim*-TV49), a sure sign of prestige for a man in his mid-thirties. He was also the former headman's son, and his twelve children gave him some pull in the affairs of the group. I would have expected him to take over, due to the patrilineal pattern of transmission of office among the Panare. Why, then, did the leadership of Turiba Viejo pass instead to Marquito?

Just by talking with Juan-Pablo Martinez, I could understand that he had no ambition toward headmanship, which he considered "too much work." By pressing him to elaborate on this topic, I learned that being an *iyan* entailed too much responsibility—economic, ritual, social, and otherwise—something he did not want to be burdened with. But I was never totally convinced by this line of explanation; it smacked too much of resigned acceptance and repressed resentment. This was hardly noticeable because of what I saw as his fair play, yet there was too much of it to be credible. Although he was in fact influential and helpful to Marquito, who consulted him frequently on

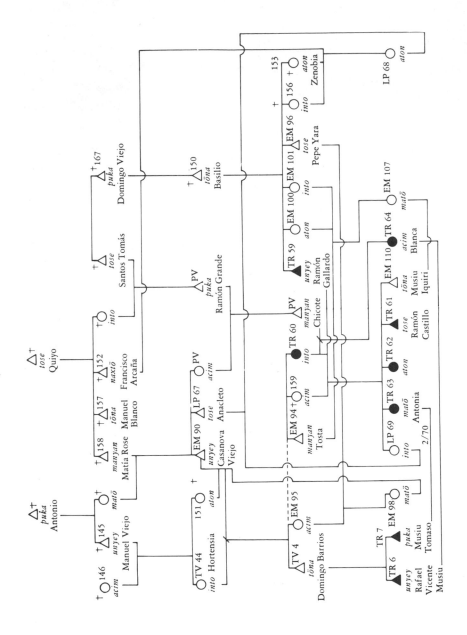

Fig. 6. *The who's who of Trapicbote*

where to conduct the next hunt or whether to pay a visit to the Creoles, he maintained a low-key political profile, always deferring to Marquito.

The ebullient behavior of Domingo Barrios (*töna*-TV4) was in sharp contrast to that of Juan-Pablo Martinez. Domingo Barrios was not only inclined to "play the headman" for the benefit of Creole visitors but also to admit his hope someday to become one in reality. In fact, Juan-Pablo Martinez himself contrasted his attitude to that of Domingo Barrios, and it is precisely this which aroused my suspicion, for it was as if he was actively contributing to reinforcement of a preexisting and actual contrast of personalities and attitudes. Without totally rejecting the value of Juan-Pablo Martinez' explanations, there is still another aspect to this, which concerns the manipulation of the model of transmission of headmanship and which, in my opinion, carries more conviction.

By the standards of age, Juan-Pablo Martinez was still relatively young to become a headman. True, I found it difficult and hazardous to estimate accurately the ages of individuals, but to approximate the age difference between Juan-Pablo Martinez and Marquito as fifteen to twenty years seems to me reasonably safe. Of these two men, Marquito, being the elder, was assumed to be the wiser, or at any rate the one with more prestige (although Juan-Pablo Martinez could still acquire more prestige in the years to come). In age, only Ramón Gallardo outranked Marquito, but the former's peripheral position in the group had ruled him out, with the results I have reported above.

As important as the age consideration may have been (and there is little doubt that it was), there was still another consideration: namely, Marquito himself had been the son of a headman, Francisco Arcaña (*naxtö*-152), who had ruled his own *tapatakyen* in the area of Colorado prior to his recent death. Not only were Marquito's and Juan-Pablo Martinez' respective fathers (Francisco Arcaña and Manuel Blanco) brothers; their respective mothers, Zenobia (*aton*-153) and Teresa (*acim*-TV34), were sisters as well (fig. 5). Both men were therefore full bilateral parallel cousins and thus classificatory brothers. Consequently, the choice of Marquito as a headman was structurally sound.

Manuel Blanco had yet another brother, Matía Rose (*manyan*-158), now deceased, who had also been a headman. His son, Casanova Viejo (*unyey*-EM90), himself already of a respectable age, could have competed with Marquito for the headmanship, since both were parallel cousins of Juan-Pablo Martinez. But by the time of Manuel Blanco's death, Casanova Viejo was already a headman in his own

right, the leader of the local group at El Muerto, so that he was truly
a stranger to the residential unit at Turiba Viejo. Structurally, then, he
was disqualified on these grounds, even if he had been interested in
heading "my" group, which is extremely doubtful.

So Marquito was the new headman of Turiba Viejo, which hap-
pily fits the model of headmanship transmission. Yet this brings about
a problem which will have struck the attention of the reader and which
ultimately shows the frailty of models vis-à-vis empirical reality.

Since Juan-Pablo Martinez and Marquito were not only first cousins but also classificatory brothers, and since I was *yako* to Marquito,
I should also have been *yako* to Juan-Pablo Martinez. With the latter's half-brother, Domingo Flores, it should have been the same. Half-
brothers are treated as brothers, and indeed I could observe Juan-Pablo
Martinez and Domingo Flores addressing each other as *yako*.

At first, I did not pay too much attention to Juan-Pablo Martinez,
who—although gracefully smiling at me with great constancy—was
continuously deferring to Marquito whenever I asked him something.
He had no hostile reaction to me. It was, rather, I who was becoming
impatient with him. He could sit forever in or in front of my hut
without saying a word, just doing his own thing. I could ask him anything and it was always the same answer: "I don't know, ask your
brother." "Marquito?" "Yes, Marquito." For months, we stayed in
this state of false intimacy. He was always there, on my back, so to
speak, but mute. There were few individuals with whom I had so
regular, yet so sterile a contact.

Nevertheless, he ended up being useful as social bait—something
I am writing with a certain feeling of vindictiveness—for other individuals would come and join him for social interaction. Of course, I
did not realize for a long time that, had I not been in the group, my
hut would have been his and his family's; because of my arrival and
Marquito's quick readiness to house me in this hut, Juan-Pablo Martinez and his family had been evicted. It is therefore quite likely that
his silence was a repressed manifestation of the grudge he could legiti-
mately hold against me.

But he was useful in another way, too. I discovered inconsisten-
cies in his use of a kin term with me, and this was all the more striking
since he spoke to me so little. For a while he addressed me as *yako*,
but then he changed and began to call me *pamo* (brother-in-law), and
finally changed once more, using the looser form of affinity: *puka-can*.
Obviously this raised some confusion in my head, for how could I one
day be his "brother" (which sounded right to me), the next day have
become his "brother-in-law," and finally end up as a vague "in-law"?

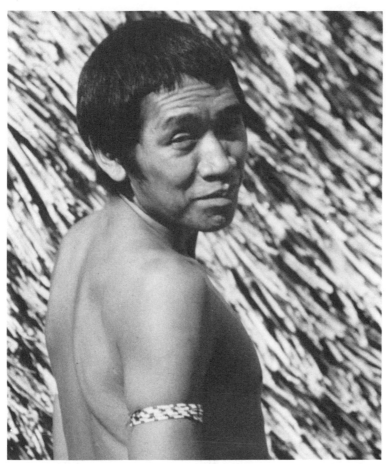

Pl. 10. *Juan-Pablo Martinez* (unyey-*TV11*)

The confusion was not entirely on my side, as I discovered from a similar hesitation on the part of his true sister, Carmen (*aton*-TV35). Apparently, the confusion was caused by their respective marriages.

Juan-Pablo Martinez had married three sisters and was still married to two of them. In each case, the marriage type involved was clearly identical. I was puzzled enough that he had married his classificatory daughters, only to discover that, by the same token, Domingo Barrios had married his own classificatory mother (see fig. 7*a*). I checked and cross-checked my information, but everything was correct. So, with logical naïveté or naïve logicality, and certainly a great lack of perceptive tact, I brought the matter to Marquito and asked him about these two cases of "incest." He readily agreed with the step-by-step

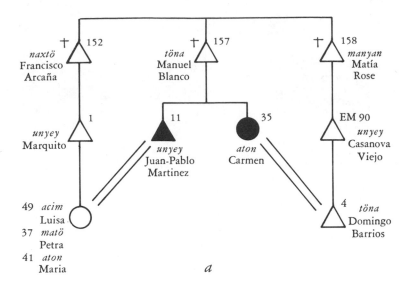

a

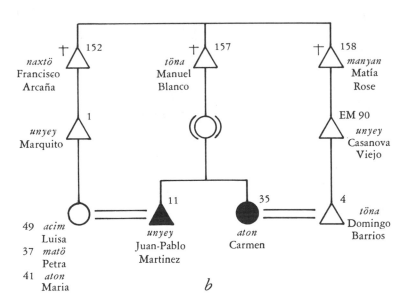

b

Fig. 7. *The marriages of Juan-Pablo Martinez* (unyey-*TV 11*) *and his sister Carmen* (aton-*TV 35*)

explication of the relation between Juan-Pablo Martinez and his wives, with the incestuous character such a relationship could have; nevertheless, it was not a case of incest, and this I simply could not understand.

The matter was soon to become much clearer. As I persisted in my inquiries, my questions were overheard and soon provoked a general charivari . . . against myself—I was obviously an idiot. The whole gamut of my aesthetic, social, and economic deficiencies was enumerated once more. The love-it-or-leave-it character of the message was clear enough, and even Marquito lost his cool on this occasion: I was not wanted any more, I asked too many questions, and so on. I subsequently retired to my hut, but, instead of the ostracizing silence which I expected in reprisal, a delegation of "wise men" was soon dispatched to see me—Marquito, Ramón Gallardo, Juan-Pablo Martinez, and Domingo Barrios, who took turns explaining at great length, if not totally convincingly, that indeed I was mistaken, and that Juan-Pablo Martinez and Marquito were absolutely not "brothers," no more than Domingo Barrios' wife and father were "siblings." It was a strong denial. To be sure, the content of their protest did not teach me anything new, but it was otherwise with its form.

On the one hand, I was absolutely wrong. Since the marriages of Juan-Pablo Martinez and his sister Carmen were recognized as such, having received a clearly positive social sanction, there was nothing incestuous about them. But, on the other hand, I was absolutely right. Not only did the step-by-step reconstruction of their kinship links to their respective spouses appear incestuous; the strong and general denial that my questions brought forth was a good indication that it was common knowledge in the local group that there was something fishy about these marriages. Otherwise, why such an emotional reaction, why such a didactic effort, which never appeared on their part with any of my other cultural blunders?

If there was something "wrong" with these marriages, it was only technically so, not socially. The technicality was what I had brought forth, indelicately, with my questions, something which had been scotomized, forgotten. The angry reaction with which I was confronted, and the lengthy explanation that followed, pointed toward the fact that incest is not a biological problem but a social one.

Furthermore, it was not a deliberate cover-up on their part, but rather a clarification directed more toward themselves than toward me, so as to reassure themselves that their social order was still intact. "He is my *pamo*," Domingo Barrios kept repeating, as if to clarify everything. That he and Juan-Pablo Martinez were brothers-in-law, fine, I had no quarrel with that, but they were not cross-cousins, unless . . . In fact, there was a loophole, an escape, an *as if* that Domingo Barrios—shrewd and perceptive as usual—discovered, telling me what we both knew to be an outrageous but truly astute lie: "Manuel Blanco is my wife's mother's father." Well, then, if so, Domingo Barrios had married a cross-cousin, and so had Juan-Pablo Martinez (see fig. 7*b*, where the "missing" connective female has been placed between parentheses). Indeed, everything was going on *as if* this had been the case.

Although to this day I do not know the psychological reason for these "normalized" marriages between adjacent generations, there is little doubt that they had three different, yet related, functions. First, an age adjustment enabled Juan-Pablo Martinez to find himself several wives, since there were none available in his settlement either at his genealogical level or any alternate one. Second, it was also a way to satisfy the tendency toward local endogamy. Third, and linked to the previous point, it had been a political move by Manuel Blanco, for this headman had no other son who had managed to survive to adulthood—Domingo Flores being still a child—and he needed to solidify the kinship web of his group.

All this points in one sociological direction. It has been well documented that an age bias at marriage, which is about five years among the Panare, is incompatible with bilateral cross-cousin marriage. As Hammel puts it, "given the existence of a bias in the attribute between mates, consistency in that bias, regardless of its direction, leads to an emphasis on matrilateral cross-cousin mating" (1967: 149). I do not find any emphasis of that sort among the Panare, but there are a number of "misfirings" in the otherwise smooth application of bilateral cross-cousin marriage. Such misfirings, which consist for a man in marrying either a "mother" or a "daughter," function as regulating compensators of the age bias so that the effect of the age bias can be canceled out and no special emphasis placed on matrilateral cross-cousin exchange. Following the distinction introduced by Lévi-Strauss ([1958] 1967: 277–281) between mechanical models and statistical models, it could be said that the misfirings stem from the latter as if to enhance the validity of the former. A similar point can be made about Juan-Pablo Martinez' sister, whose marriage was a consequence of her brother's—the latter having pushed her down one level, so to speak.

The case of Domingo Flores (*manyan*-TV26) was entirely different, however, and for several reasons. First of all, he had not been "pushed down" in the same way, because he was only a half-brother to Juan-Pablo Martinez, and his mother, Dolores (*aton*-TV55), had a

Pl. 11. *Domingo Flores* (manyan-*TV26*)

different position than that of Teresa (*acim*-TV34), although it was structurally equivalent. Second, he was about fifteen years younger than Juan-Pablo Martinez and, by the time he was of an age to marry, he was no longer the headman's son and, moreover, had no problem finding an eligible woman within the local group who fell in the proper category (see fig. 8).

In addition, there was not the same imbroglio with him as with his half-brother in respect to our kinship relation. Domingo Flores was infinitely more cooperative, more ready to chat with me or invite me to join him for fishing or working in the gardens. Quite often, he would come to see his half-brother in front of my hut, thus relieving me of the burden and anxiety of being mutely confronted with Juan-Pablo Martinez. Altogether, Domingo Flores was an outgoing young man, quite open to the outside world. He liked the goods that the Creole world could offer. After all, he owned a broken-down transistor radio and a bicycle in fair shape. I used to borrow the latter to go to

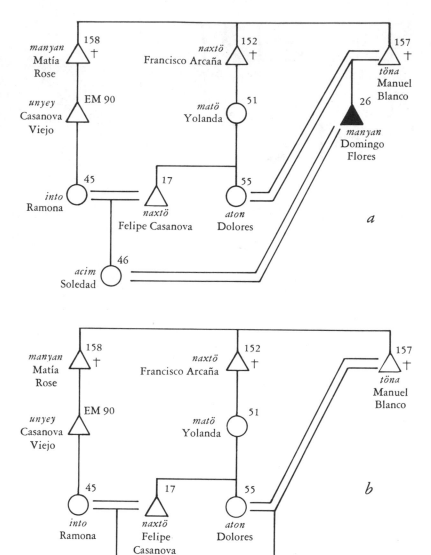

Fig. 8. *Domingo Flores* (manyan-*TV26*)

the Creole settlement at Turiba Nuevo, and he would borrow my radio
set, which he would play full blast in the *churuata* during the day,
delighted to hear, "Aquí RRRadio Barquisimeto . . ." Or he would
creep in behind me when I was listening to the B.B.C. newscast, asking me for a full report on world events which it was just impossible
to give him. Of Robert Kennedy's assassination, I had to say that a
prestigious *iyan* had been killed among the *Americano*. The May 1968
events in Paris became "the *Français* are fighting in my *pereka*." As
for the A's victory in the World Series, I could not think of anything
other than, "They have killed a lot of game and now they are going to
drink a lot of beer." Altogether, his view of the outside world was
not greatly enhanced by my performance. To the contrary—"the *Français, Americano*, Creoles, they are all bad, very bad," he commented.
How could I not acquiesce? Domingo Flores would tell me in exchange what he learned the last time he went to pay a visit to the
group of Los Pozos; or he would reveal where his mother was weaving
a loincloth in a small clearing out of sight so as not to be bothered by
my taking snapshots; or he would tell me who was preparing curare in
his hut.

Meanwhile, he was always calling me *panaxpon* (FaFa), although I had been told by Felipe Casanova and Guzmán that he was
my *yako* (Br). Despite appearances, there was no great contradiction
in this. If there was any ambiguity, it was for me in diagramming his
kinship position. Since his father and his mother were two genealogical levels apart, was I to place him one level below his father and
therefore one above his mother (as in fig. 8*a*) or one level below his
mother and therefore three levels below his father (as in fig. 8*b*)? In
the former case, I was clearly his classificatory brother, but in the latter
case, his classificatory grandfather. He thus had to make a choice,
either to trace his relation patrilaterally or to trace it matrilaterally. In
calling me *panaxpon*, he was tracing his link to Marquito, and to me
by extension, through his mother. In this way, when he married Felipe
Casanova's daughter Soledad (*acim*-TV46), he really married a bilateral cross-cousin: a matrilateral first cousin and a patrilateral second
cousin (fig. 8*b*). Of course, it is important to realize that it is structurally equivalent to marrying his FaSiSoDa, that being equivalent to
marrying his DaDa, which is really what he did if considered as immediately below his father (as in fig. 8*a*).

This example shows the confusion which results (for the anthropologist) from these alternate generational marriages, and how difficult it is most of the time to decide whether a marriage has taken place
between alternate generations or within the same genealogical level.

Consider, for instance, the case of Ramón Gallardo's marriages as represented in figures 5 and 6. At any rate, in using the term *panaxpon* to address Marquito and myself, rather than the term *yako*, Domingo Flores was manipulating the structure in order to make several points, whether these were key factors in his decision or merely incidental to it.

First, he disentangled himself from the logic of his half-brother's marriages, which could have posed a problem for him as far as finding a marriageable partner. Juan-Pablo Martinez was his *yako*, but he chose not to draw any logical consequences from that fact, which remained almost unnoticed for him. Clearly, Marquito could not be his *yako* as well. To call Marquito that would only have underscored the oddity of a situation which had been settled years ago and was not meant to be brought back to consciousness. On the other hand, Domingo Flores did not address Marquito as *uniki-can* (the *-can* form of *unyey*), the adjustment made by Juan-Pablo Martinez (thus recognizing Marquito as an affine). This is because the former had not been "pushed down"; but it left him confronted with the logical contradiction by which the brother of a brother would not be a brother. Addressing Marquito as *panaxpon* was, as I see it, a way of getting out of such a contradiction, still maintaining a "proper" genealogical level for him and leaving him the option of a perfectly "normal" marriage. Finally, an age adjustment was equally involved, according to which Domingo Flores recognized the two genealogical levels which separated him from Marquito and could implicitly state that he was of about the same age as his wife and not an old man marrying his granddaughter. In that respect at least, his case was entirely different from that of Casanova Viejo (*unyey*-EM90), who had married his actual granddaughter (*matö*-EM98) and whose case has been added for illustrative purposes to the kinship diagram of Trapichote (fig. 6). So, ultimately, the attitude of Domingo Flores was not so much culturally dictated as culturally informed, so as to allow him to express himself in a cultural idiom which could also bear the mark of his own style.

In the whirl of events that Manuel Blanco's death entailed, Domingo Barrios' position in the group was deeply affected as well. At one point, he had made a smart political move in entering into a *mwecan* relation with Manuel Blanco. The term *mwecan* is the reciprocal term of reference by which children-in-law and parents-in-law are bound together. But now, with the rise of Marquito to a position of leadership, Domingo Barrios turned out to have no direct relationship with Marquito, who was nevertheless one of his acknowledged classificatory fathers, one of the men he called *yim*. This had two complementary effects.

On the one hand, Domingo Barrios was "decentralized," if I may use the term, which gave his case some resemblance to that of Ramón Gallardo. And this in fact was expressed in the spatial arrangement of the workshop-huts in the settlement. Unfortunately I do not know what the exact pattern of occupation of the workshop-huts was before Manuel Blanco's death, but between my arrival and the departure of Ramón Gallardo, he and Domingo Barrios each had a workshop-hut on one side of the *churuata* (the former in K, the latter in L, on map 2), while the other members of the local group had theirs on the other side. Furthermore, once Ramón Gallardo left for Trapichote, Domingo Barrios stayed in hut K with his wife and his three youngest children (*karime*-TV36, *muruka*-TV9, and *nyamca*-TV10). Meanwhile, hut L was now occupied mainly by his married son, Coronel Flores (*tose*-TV5), and his wife, Rafaela (*into*-TV56), and occasionally by his three other adult and still bachelor sons (Rafael Vicente Musiu, *unyey*-TV6; Musiu Tomaso, *puka*-TV7; and Antonio Marco, *naxtö*-TV8). In addition, Domingo Barrios' mother-in-law, Teresa (*acim*-TV34), who was also, as we have seen, Ramón Gallardo's sister and Manuel Blanco's widow, resided in the same hut. At first I had overlooked that fact, because upon my arrival at Turiba Viejo Teresa was already staying with Domingo Barrios' family in hut K. But I was told that Musiu Tomaso (*puka*-TV7)—a seventeen- or eighteen-year-old—while waiting for the better days he would find in Trapichote, had married Teresa, who was already in her late sixties at least. He had thus married his MoMo, and this is the only example I have of a young man marrying his actual grandmother. Obviously, I was not in a position to check whether sexual gratification was involved in this relationship, although I am inclined to suspect that it was, but when I showed disbelief about the union, Domingo Barrios gave me the economic proof. Musiu Tomaso was bringing his fishing and hunting catches to his grandmother, who cleaned them and cooked them for him. Was she not, in addition, weaving a loincloth for him? I need not add that there was no issue from this temporary marriage, which was above all a convenient but temporary solution to the problem of the sexual dichotomy of work among the Panare. Eventually Musiu Tomaso married Ramón Gallardo's daughter (*matö*-TR63) and went with his father-in-law to Trapichote.

On the other hand, the proximity of Ramón Gallardo's and Domingo Barrios' families had created de facto a real solidarity between them, and a degree of sociality, which manifested itself quite strongly in the marriages of the two sons of Domingo Barrios to their patrilateral cross-cousins, that is, to two daughters of Ramón Gallardo.

Once this occurred, two events could be predicted. There would be very strong pressure put on Ramón Castillo (*tose*-TR61), the only bachelor son of Ramón Gallardo, to marry his matrilateral cross-cousin, Domingo Barrios' only daughter (*karime*-TV36), as soon as she reached puberty. For there was one problem with Domingo Barrios' eagerness to become a headman. He had all the credentials for this position of leadership but one: namely, he had only one daughter, which left him with very little leeway for political maneuvering. I saw him last in February 1970, but it is my understanding—admittedly from hearsay—that he has now made what was really a predictable move to Trapichote. There, he is very likely to take over at the foreseeable demise of Ramón Gallardo. I feel relatively comfortable with this speculation, less because it "makes sense" than because he was explicit with me about his ambitions and he had the ability to act in consequence.

For the time being, however, Domingo Barrios was very much part of Turiba Viejo. His good qualities and defects were quite complementary to those of Marquito. The former was an extrovert, the latter an introvert. Domingo Barrios, who (curiously) was totally at ease with the Creoles, was interested in "making it" in this world—to be sure, according to his own cultural values—and had no hesitation vis-à-vis a bit of acculturation, a bit of novelty. I could see this from his readiness to cope with me, even to initiate exchanges and conversations. In his entrepreneurial transactions with the Creoles, he was always trying, and often successfully, to stay on top in commercial exchanges which many other men tended to avoid. In brief, in a minor but real way, he was an innovator.

In strong contrast, Marquito was a much more austere traditionalist. He was not the type who would have agreed to join a Creole in a dugout-canoe trip just for the heck of it. Nor would he have experimented with the powerful *ñopo* drug brought by Piaroa Indians who in this way trip out to the supernatural world. Of the two, the personality of Domingo Barrios was the more attractive to me. Basically, he was fun. At the same time, he was the more superficial, always putting up a show. As for Marquito, he was straight, perhaps even square to a degree, but reliable and concerned. It was he who had to be generous, as a headman is supposed to be, to discover the tracks of animals to be hunted, the fish to be caught. He had social, economic, religious, and political responsibilities and, appropriately, he was the *iyan*, at the core of the *tapatakyen* of Turiba Viejo—and it is to him and his family that I will now devote my attention.

7. *My Brother the Headman*

As reserved and introverted as Marquito was, he could nonetheless be a clever and efficient manipulator, secure in his power. In that respect, he had the edge over Domingo Barrios, who was a bit too eager to push himself forward. Domingo Barrios was too transparent, no match for Marquito's poker face. Marquito's authority was well founded and deeply anchored in a solid perception of his culture. He managed to give the culturally acceptable impression of not achieving anything at all, as if everything was ascribed to him. It is true that age had been a factor in his becoming a headman. But his residence at Turiba Viejo was the result of his great knack for making the right move at the right moment. This was not something I could get out of him directly; I had to piece it together slowly.

Marquito's father, Francisco Arcaña (*naxtö*-152), had married two sisters of Rufo (*puka*-155), and the two brothers-in-law were living in the same settlement. According to Marquito, Rufo's wives (*acim*-CL207 and *matö*-CL208) were classificatory sisters of Arcaña, but not his true sisters. Despite repeated attempts, I was unable to trace the exact relationship between Rufo and his wives. At any rate, when Marquito married his first wife, Elena (*into*-TV30), he repeated his parents' marriage. It was probably, as Marquito asserted, a bilateral cross-cousin marriage, but I only know for sure that he married his MoBrDa. In addition, it was a true sister exchange, because his wives' brother, Rodiana (*tose*-160), married at least one of his sisters (*acim*-MI), still alive in a settlement of the Sierra Cerbatana.

Shortly after Marquito's marriage, and for reasons which I could not completely elicit, his mother moved away from her husband. She came to the settlement of her sister Teresa (*acim*-TV34), Manuel Blanco's wife. A year or two later, Marquito had finished his bride-service to Rufo (*puka*-155), and any further obligation was obviated by his father-in-law's opportune death. Marquito was then free to join his mother in Manuel Blanco's local group. Shortly after, his sister

Yolanda (*matö*-TV51) lost her husband, Santaria Medina (*tose*-162), and came with her children to settle in the same group.

To me, Marquito claimed that his move had only economic motivations: there was plenty of fish and game available in the area. This was true enough, but, of course, it was also a way for him to further his prestige, since that is correlated with hunting success. By that time, Marquito's prestige must already have been quite high, for he had already translated it into marriage. Nevertheless, with Manuel Blanco he was able to increase it further and thus acquire a second wife, Firmina (*into*-161), who died in childbirth after having given him four children (Mirón, *tose*-TV25, and Natalia, *acim*-TV48, now living with him; Moreno, *naxtö*-LP84, and Ursula, *aton*-LP76, now residing at Los Pozos). Afterward, Marquito married a third wife, Gabriela (*acim*-TV31). It is also quite certain that Manuel Blanco needed more hunters in his group at that time, although Marquito told me that Manuel Blanco's local group existed there before his arrival. Unfortunately, neither Marquito nor Juan-Pablo Martinez, nor anybody else for that matter, could tell me the exact original composition of Manuel Blanco's group.

Finally, there was another aspect to the problem, one which bears some resemblance to what has already been discussed in the case of Domingo Barrios. It is clear that Marquito had no compelling reason to leave the local group of his actual father, Arcaña, except for his political ambition, something that he would admit only in the most indirect manner with statements to the effect that he had been very young. Since he was so elliptic in that respect, it seems to me that such statements invite interpretation.

Marquito must have perceived that to succeed Arcaña as headman, he would have a lot of competition either from Arcaña's sons-in-law or, more likely, from Rufo's sons. At the same time, it must have seemed clear to Marquito that at Manuel Blanco's death, if Ramón Gallardo could somehow be pushed away, Juan-Pablo Martinez would be no match at all. Of course, Marquito had been there at the opportune moment. Ultimately, he had engineered everything well, even more so since it was barely obvious. I will come back later to the subtlety of Marquito's attitude vis-à-vis myself—suffice it to state at this point that my "brotherhood" with him was manipulated by both of us, each to his own benefit.

In addition to being the *iyan*, Marquito had real power, the basis of which was his children. He had attracted sons-in-law into his orbit, while at the same time retaining with him some of his married sons. It was particularly this which reinforced and confirmed Turiba Viejo's re-centering around him after Manuel Blanco's death. I have shown above how Juan-Pablo Martinez (*unyey*-TV11) had been "transformed" into Marquito's son-in-law, so as to be on a par with Felipe Casanova (*naxtö*-TV17) and Guzmán (*puka*-TV20), his other sons-in-law. Their presence in the settlement was normal, following the explicit tendency toward uxorilocality. It was more striking, however, that Marquito had only three married sons: Moreno (*naxtö*-LP84), who had married in Los Pozos, and Mirón (*tose*-TV25) and Andrés (*töna*-TV23), both of whom resided virilocally at Turiba Viejo.

My relations with Mirón and Andrés were never good, except for the first month of my stay. They remained pleasant, cooperative, and unrebellious as long as my intrusion into their settlement could still be considered news. With them more than with anybody else, I quickly tended to vanish into a sort of existential nothingness. Until the last day of my stay, everybody else was making fun of me, mocking my clumsiness in many circumstances. If I fell on a trail, that was hilarious. If I let a fish escape, that was hilarious. I was almost killed by a falling tree; that, too, was hilarious. Yet I should not have been upset by this—which does not mean that I was not—because the same incidents occurring to anybody else in the settlement would have elicited the same reaction. It is just that my clumsiness was beyond belief to them. Continuously, but more toward the beginning than toward the end of my stay, I committed cultural faults and mistakes, some of which I am sure I never even perceived, even in retrospect.

With Mirón and to a lesser extent with Andrés, I had a rougher time. There was undoubtedly hostility on their part, and even some viciousness from the former. Within six months of my arrival in Turiba Viejo, Mirón would either snub me or lie about everything just to be a nuisance. Moreover, since the very first day of my arrival, when I had found a couple of scorpions in one of my sneakers, everybody knew that I was fairly cowardly in the presence of those little beasts. One day, Mirón had captured one and dropped it alive on the notebook in which I was writing, a trick which I did not appreciate at all. Another day, he volunteered to show me how he had clubbed a wounded capybara to death. As I was totally off guard, he hit me over the head with his stick. There was not sufficient strength in his blow to hurt me seriously, but enough nevertheless for my skull to develop a huge and painful bump. Under these conditions, I find it particularly difficult, if not impossible, to give a fair and detached presentation of this "son" of mine.

In fact, I found Mirón mean and thickheaded. And I hated him with a passion that only very few of my colleagues can arouse in me.

Pl. 12. *Marquito's son Mirón (*tose-*TV25), preparing a harpoon*

To what degree this was exacerbated by the fact that he was married to a young woman, Ofelia (*acim*-TV53), whom I viewed as charming, attractive, and inaccessible, I do not know, except that my rapport with her was as good as my rapport with him was bad.

His marriage was a true bilateral cross-cousin marriage (see fig. 9). After a year of bride-service for his father-in-law, Domingo Flores[13] (*unyey*-CL210), in Colorado, he had come back to his father's settlement. It was out of the question to discuss that matter with him, but from other sources I learned that he had been homesick at his in-laws'. As the common complaint against exogamous marriages, this did not carry very much explanatory power. I also learned that, before Manuel Blanco's death, Marquito had urged him to come back. This explanation was generally supported even by Marquito, yet I was not told why, nor why his wife accepted virilocal residence. Marquito's statement was, as far as I can see, the closest to reality: Marquito needed sons with him. He would say that it was "in order to hunt," but there was more to it than that. Basically, it was to exert further

[13]Not to be confused with Domingo Flores (*manyan*-TV26) from Turiba Viejo, whose case has been discussed in the previous chapter.

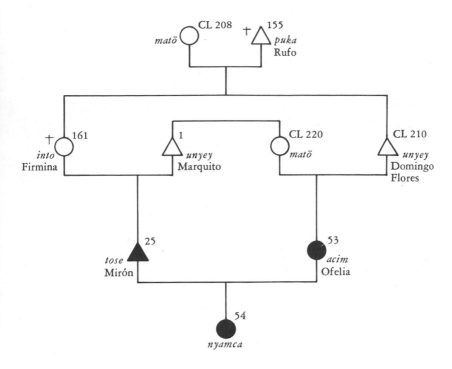

Fig. 9. *The marriage of Mirón (*tose*-TV 25)*

economic and therefore political pressure on the other members of the settlement. The return of a married son was a way to enlarge Marquito's political basis in the local group.

By comparison to Mirón, it was a joy to relate to Andrés. And yet, I found him the second most aggressive person in the settlement. This struck me fairly strongly, because of his moody character. At one minute, he would be joking or reliably discussing almost anything with me; at another, quite unpredictably, he would revert to hostile behavior. His smiling mood would disappear—he would frown at me as if to frighten me and then refuse to speak to me at all or just come to me to complain about my medical incompetency. It is true that I had been unlucky with his child, a one-year-old son whose head had been covered with skin sores. Antibiotics and mercurochrome remained relatively ineffective, because the child kept scratching with dirty hands, and the infection lasted for over six months. Andrés blamed it on me. Sometimes he would accuse me of being a bad *panaxpon* to the child, of being powerful, but not delivering the proper medication. At other times, I was so miserable and ignorant that I fell

Pl. 13. *Marquito's son Andrés (*töna-*TV23), during the* waxpoto *ritual*

not only below my kinship status but below humanity. His greatest insult was to call me a howler monkey. Once in a while he would just bring his child in his arms, point at the sores, and ostensibly remain silent. The child, who had seen me so many times armed with a syringe, would cry immediately, and to the father this was a sure indication of my nastiness.

This child was the fruit of Andrés' marriage with Juana (*acim*-TV52), a first patrilateral cross-cousin and a second matrilateral cross-cousin (see fig. 10). In addition, this marriage was a sister-exchange, since Juana's brother, Felipe Casanova (*naxtö*-TV17), had married Natalia (*acim*-TV48), Andrés' half-sister and Mirón's full sister. The marriage was endogamous, since Juana had joined Turiba Viejo with her mother, Yolanda (*matö*-TV51), under circumstances related above. Since Andrés' father-in-law, Santaria Medina (*tose*-162), had long been dead by the time of the marriage, there was no bride-service involved. Furthermore, since the marriage was endogamous, residence, properly speaking, was both uxorilocal and virilocal. However, at least an appearance of bride-service and uxorilocality was maintained, as indicated by the fact that Andrés' family occupied hut E in the settlement (see map 2) not only with his wife and son but also with his

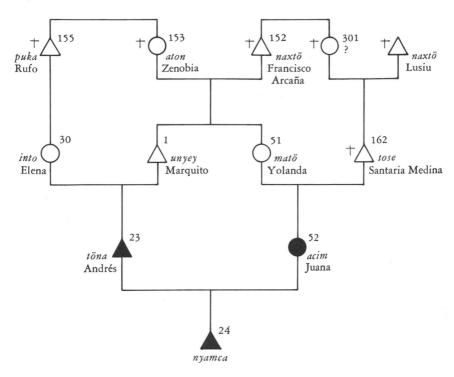

Fig. 10. *The marriage of Andrés (*töna-TV23*)*

mother-in-law. In addition, his wife's sister, Dolores (*aton*-TV55), and her son, Domingo Flores (*manyan*-TV26), also stayed in the same workshop-hut from the time of my arrival until the latter's marriage.

There was no problem for the anthropologist with Andrés' marriage, and yet Marquito had retained another of his married sons with him, increasing the stability of his political situation. When I saw Marquito last, I mentioned to him that so far only one of his children had married outside of his *tapatakyen*. He looked very optimistic, saying that he still had four more unmarried children: two sons (*puka*-TV2 and *töna*-TV3) and two daughters (*mediya*-TV32 and *nyamca*-TV33). He planned on more. "Nineteen," he said, which was striking, because the numeral *asatnan-axptakatoito* was not frequently used. When I showed my surprise, he pointed at his wife Gabriela's (*acim*-TV31) belly and then joined his fingers and his toes to indicate "twenty," which was the maximal numeral used by the Panare. So he would have more children, and his precision was mainly rhetorical.

Meanwhile, his two married sons in the settlement indicated the prosperity of his affairs within the group. My fictive brotherhood with their father did not make them less aggressive toward me; in fact, the situation was quite the contrary. I wondered for a long time why this occurred. At first, I blamed it upon Andrés' and Mirón's individual characters, upon their personalities. Very quickly, I could see my error just by observing their loving attitude with their immediate family and their respectful behavior toward their father. Respect and familiarity were mixed together, for it was to Marquito that they would often turn for goods and services, to borrow tobacco, kerosene, or anything else they were short of. This demand for protection, love, help, and the like from their father was greater with them than with any other Panare adult man I have known, including their unmarried brothers. It was as if there was something slightly infantile about their behavior vis-à-vis their father, who was so positively valued that any negative aspect to the relationship had been entirely repressed. Since they also recognized my fictive kinship status, I could have expected them to behave *mutatis mutandis* in a roughly equivalent manner with me. But it was exactly the other way around. Most of the time they would call me *yim* as expected, but they would seemingly make every effort possible to manifest opposite feelings toward their actual father and toward their fictive one.

Their attitude with me can be interpreted in two different ways. The more I was integrated into the settlement, the more their hostility manifested itself. This tends to mark their sensitivity to my marginality to both their *pyaka* and their *tapatakyen*. It indicates their jealousy of me, the alien who had intruded into their family and their residential group. In other words, from their viewpoint, I received too much attention from Marquito. Far from being negligible, this aspect of the problem may be complemented by a more directly Freudian interpretation. Namely, if anything, it was not that they overemphasized the fictitiousness of my brotherhood with their father, but that, to the contrary, they took the link too seriously. Indeed, I was figuratively their father's brother. It followed that structurally I was at least a father figure and, moreover, a double of their father. Clearly enough, when they interacted with a classificatory brother of their father, such as Casanova Viejo (*unyey*-EM90), the headman of El Muerto, or Anacleto (*tose*-LP67), the headman of Los Pozos, they acted "normally" with these *yim*. They did not either overplay the positive aspect of the relationship as they did with their actual father or underplay it as they did with me. With my intrusion into their physical as well as mental environment, the figure of Laius—Oedipus' much maligned father—could be split into two components: the positive one imposed upon Marquito, the negative one imposed upon me. Thus, whatever hostile feelings they held against their actual father, which are normally repressed among the Panare, could now be expressed openly. Thanks to the extreme ambiguity of my kinship status, I was both fictive and fatherly, therefore perfectly instrumental in letting them express the ambiguity of their Oedipal feelings.

In a truly penetrating analysis, Paul writes: "Since Freud argued that the primitive feeling by a junior male to his 'father' is one of ambivalence, that is both love and hate, it is easy to see that in human society, the institution having both a father and a mother's brother, separated out from each other, is an excellent structural solution to a possible source of conflict, since one can serve as the recipient of love and friendship, and the other as the object of hatred and rivalry" (1976: 346).

In the same paper, Paul points out correctly, after Lévi-Strauss, that "if a man is close and friendly with his wife, he is likely to be distant, formal, or hostile with his sister, and vice versa; and the same holds true between a man and his father on the one hand and his mother's brother on the other" (1976: 344). Because of the absence of a unilineal rule of descent and of a strictly enforced rule of residence, there are particular variations to this among the Panare. In general, however, a Panare man is closer and friendlier with his wife and his father, and therefore more distant with his sister and his mother's brother. Interestingly enough, in the settlement of Turiba Viejo, Mirón and Andrés had no mother's brother to whom they could show reserve (see fig. 5). The dichotomy of their attitude vis-à-vis different "fathers," Marquito and myself, then appears as a structural transformation of the opposition between positive father and negative mother's brother.

Characteristically, the instrumentality of my position in the local group appears even more vividly when attention is given to Marquito's sons-in-law: Guzmán (*puka*-TV20) and Felipe Casanova (*naxtö*-TV17). Structurally, their situation is reversed. Their father-in-law is in the same group as they are, but they have no father in the group. It will therefore come as no surprise that these two were my best informants and that, conversely, they were more reserved with Marquito in comparison to other Panare son-in-law/father-in-law relations in which I had no part.

I could readily satisfy Guzmán's curiosity about me, for my hut (hut D on map 2) opened almost directly on the front of his (hut F). He could watch what I was doing at all times, just as I could con-

Pl. 14. *Guzmán (puka-TV20), bringing back electric eels to the settlement*

stantly see what was going on in his hut. Given such spatial proximity,
it would have been difficult for us not to interact frequently. The
whistle of my teakettle, in particular, had the power of attracting him
to pay a visit. It was almost comic to see him always arrive when this
whistle signaled to him the imminent prospect of some hot chocolate
he would never have dared ask for.

From my hut, I could see his wife, Luisa (*acim*-TV49), seated
Guzmán was a young man in his twenties, extremely soft-spoken
and always smiling. I got along fine with him from the beginning. I
would have liked to talk with him more fluently, but at first I had to
satisfy myself with very simple linguistic exchanges. I had elicited my
first rudiments of Panare vocabulary from him. His willingness to talk,
to repeat his utterances into my tape recorder, was certainly very helpful
in learning the language. But even more importantly, it was through
him that I began to understand social relations in the settlement.

From my hut, I could see his wife, Luisa (*acim*-TV49), seated
on a mat for long hours spinning cotton or grating manioc and cooking it into cassava bread. She was a rather heavy woman who for some
reason, in contrast to most other women in the settlement, had no
reluctance to talk with me. I would often reciprocate Guzmán's visits,
sitting on a tortoiseshell under their thatched roof. On such occasions,
I would be given a snack of smoked fish. More importantly, in these

informal interviews, I was learning the who's who of Turiba Viejo. Through my daily visits, I also got a chronicle of what was happening in the settlement from this family's viewpoint.

They had a little two-year-old son (*nyamca*-TV21), who at first was terribly frightened by my "ugly" face, but soon became less reluctant to come to my hut with his father when it was evident that I was about to prepare some hot chocolate. As time passed, I became a more and more familiar character in the settlement. The child obviously lost his fear of me. When I squatted talking with his parents, his favorite game, much to the amusement of his parents and to my legitimate concern, was to pick up cockroaches and send them crawling down my back, thus creating between us a degree of intimacy which I felt was a bit excessive.

It is through this intimacy with Guzmán's family, however, that I began to make headway in the Panare social organization. In marrying Luisa, Guzmán had practiced local exogamy and was therefore an outsider to the settlement, almost a stranger. He was nevertheless addressing (and addressed by) the other members of the *tapatakyen* with a kinship term. Since he could not remember who his real *panaxpon* (FaFa) was, a fortiori he could hardly retrace step by step his relationship with anybody in the settlement. So how did he know, or

Pl. 15. *Guzmán's wife, Luisa* (acim-TV49), *about to boil tapir meat*

rather how did he determine, that Felipe Casanova (*naxtö*-TV17) was his *yako* (sibling of same sex) and Domingo Barrios (*töna*-TV4) his *pamo* (brother-in-law), given that they were not really close relatives of his, but only classificatory ones?

Felipe Casanova was Guzmán's FaFaSiDaSo, and Domingo Barrios, his FaFaSiHuBrSoSo. After having painfully worked this out over a period of several months, I told Guzmán about my deductions from what looked like a kinship puzzle. Foolishly, I was hoping he or someone else could confirm them. It certainly amused him and the others, without actually convincing anybody. It was about as absurd to him as for me to try to figure out who is the half-brother of the ex-husband of the sister-in-law of my thirty-second cousin twice removed.

The truth of the matter was infinitely more simple. Felipe Casanova and Guzmán were classificatory brothers because both of them had married daughters of Marquito and hence stood in the same structural relation to him. "What about Domingo Barrios?" I asked Guzmán, anxious to find out how he would get out of this tricky problem. By that time, his patience with me had worn out, as I could tell from his exasperated, "you already know," but he still gave me a whole array of explanations. Domingo Barrios was Marquito's classificatory son. Domingo Barrios' sister was married to Felipe Casanova. Domingo Barrios was therefore a classificatory brother of Guzmán's wife. From an anthropological viewpoint, Guzmán's marriage was almost flawless, a textbook case, since he had married a true bilateral cross-cousin (see fig. 11). My perception of it as quasi perfection was largely enhanced by this couple's willingness to provide me with much information that Marquito could confirm.

Guzmán's wife was some eight years older than her husband, and although it was his first marriage, it was her second. Less than three years before my arrival, she had divorced her former husband, Juan-Pablo Martinez (*unyey*-TV11), with whom she had a son, Domingo Julio (*manyan*-TV22), now in his early teens. From time to time, I could see him spending the whole day at his mother's. But, in general, he was too preoccupied by hunting and thus getting prestige to want to spend much time with me.

Despite the close link which existed between Guzmán and his wife, he was still a newcomer to the settlement, where he had come to perform the customary bride-service for Marquito (*unyey*-TV1). The bride-service, by which a son-in-law renders some labor to his father-in-law, such as helping him in slashing the gardens and making occasional gifts of food, lasts for about a year. After this initial stage in which a newly married couple must reside uxorilocally, they have much

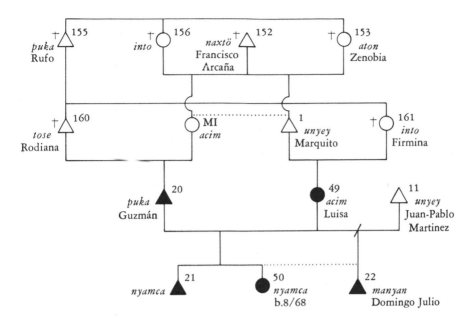

Fig. 11. *The marriage of Guzmán* (puka-TV 20)

liberty in their choice of a more or less permanent residence. Undoubtedly, there is a tendency toward uxorilocality among the Panare, but it is no more than a tendency, and I prefer to refrain from too sweeping a generalization in this respect. For the time being, Guzmán was still in his father-in-law's settlement, the last in-marrying man at Turiba Viejo. But after nearly three years of marriage, the discontinuation of such bride-service was definitely in order.

One of its last manifestations was his present of smoked fish and ripe bananas to me one day in April 1968. When he gave it to me, I did not understand his unexpected display of generosity—it did not make sense to me at all. I usually ate at the common male meal and, when I wanted extra food, bartered for it. The only exception to this was with Marquito, but Domingo Barrios had made it clear to me that since Marquito was the headman, he had to be generous. I usually reciprocated Marquito's gifts with rice, salt, or canned sardines. Once more, the scandalized "you know nothing" of Domingo Barrios, who seemed to enjoy my ignorance, enlightened me, although much too late, about the way in which I had grossly misbehaved with Guzmán. It had been as "brother" of his father-in-law that I had received such a gift, and it had been bad of me to suspect that Guzmán was trying to initiate some barter with me. It had also been a blunder to reciprocate his gift with a counter-gift of some kerosene, since his was already a counter-gift of sorts for my "daughter."

Furthermore, rather than calling me by my male name, *puka*, Guzmán was calling me *puka-can*, by which he was drawing a rather important distinction. Although Guzmán did not call me *yawon*, a term he reserved for Marquito, his actual father-in-law—as he reserved the term *waninye* for Marquito's wives—I still entered in the category of his *mwecan*. This term of reference designates, as we have seen, an affinal relationship, more precisely the real or classificatory parents of one's spouse(s) and the real or classificatory spouses of one's children. The terms *yawon* and *waninye* are used for both address and reference; they are mainly used for actual parents-in-law, and to a much lesser extent for children-in-law. The terms *tamu* (husband, but also MoFa), *pwi* (wife), and *pamo* (sibling-in-law of same sex) are also terms of both address and reference. The more distant (in all meanings of the word) the relations between two individuals, the less likely these individuals are to use a kinship term with each other. However, short of a kinship term, the proper way of addressing one's affine is to suffix his/her name with the particle *-can* which "connotes the idea of return, of reciprocity with an idea of positive value" (Dumont 1976: 87). As I have indicated elsewhere, "in a naming context, the use of this particle connotes an affinal relationship between two individuals, while its absence connotes a consanguineal relationship. Before addressing somebody with his (her) name, the speaker therefore has to know what kind of relationship already exists between himself and the person named. Of course, one can also manipulate an existing relationship by the use of a *can*-modified name that would not normally be used" (1977: 94).

In presenting his gift, Guzmán had called me *puka-can* because I was structurally equivalent to his actual father-in-law. The relation being symmetric, I was supposed to call him *puka-can* too and to call his wife (my "daughter") *acim*, and not *acim-ican*.

From the viewpoint of the conscious Panare model of the kinship system, Guzmán's marriage was not absolutely perfect, because he had not conformed to the ideal of residential endogamy, which meant that most members of his *pyaka* (kindred) lived in other settlements. Of course, he was a true member of the settlement of Turiba Viejo, because everyone settled there by definition belonged to the same *tapatakyen* (local group) and to the same *pereka* (settlement). Yet, he had left behind most of his kin in his settlement of origin in the Sierra Cerbatana, at the *pereka* of José Medina (*manyan*-JM), in order to marry Luisa. Evidently, there is never complete coincidence between one's *pyaka* and one's *tapatakyen*, but if one marries within one's own settlement, the overlapping between the two is much greater than if one marries without. As a consequence of being *ticasaptu* (literally "one very much," i.e., "all by himself") at Turiba Viejo, as he phrased it, Guzmán still enjoyed relatively little prestige in this settlement. To be sure, his marriage and its issue, as well as his hunting abilities, indicated that he was nevertheless doing well. But his status could not yet be on a par either with that of men who had in-married for a longer time or with that of core members of the group, i.e., those who had managed to acquire a spouse within the settlement. And what I saw as shyness and reserve on his part was merely an expression of his still peripheral status in the group.

In this respect, Felipe Casanova (*naxtö*-TV17) was in a better position, because he had resided at Turiba Viejo for a much longer time. In other words, he was part of the "establishment" to a greater extent. He was some six to seven years older than Guzmán, too. With this headstart on his classificatory brother, his prestige had accrued, and he had a solid hunting reputation in the settlement. He taught me how to identify tracks with a patience that I cannot but admire. Domingo Barrios and he were undoubtedly the two most successful hunters in the settlement. To be sure, Marquito, and Ramón Gallardo before his departure, had more prestige, but they were benefiting from accumulated past successes. Now they had nothing to prove anymore, and their current accomplishments were somehow less spectacular, mainly (but not only) because they invested less time than Felipe Casanova or Domingo Barrios in predatory activities.

When I wanted to learn how to hunt with a blowgun, Marquito turned me over to Felipe Casanova who, undoubtedly flattered, was taking my instruction very seriously. I was never good at spotting animals in the forest, but his comments, such as "*puka-can*, we are all going to be very hungry," were always infinitely more affectionate than critical. At first, he had me shoot darts into a papaya as a practice target. Extreme luck and not skill made me hit the bull's-eye the first day. He was stunned. So was I. In exchange, Felipe Casanova needed no lesson to use my shotgun, only cartridges. So we exchanged weapons frequently. One day, in an exploit I was never able to duplicate, I killed a monkey with his blowgun. This, of course, did not match my reputation for clumsiness, and the more Felipe Casanova repeated that it was I, not he, who had killed the monkey, the more he was disbelieved by everybody else in the settlement, since nobody else had witnessed the event.

The lesson from this incident was drawn by Domingo Barrios, whose manipulation is revealing. He had watched the skinning of the animal and had seen that there was only one dart wound in its body. Nevertheless, when the monkey was served, boiled, at the male common meal, Domingo Barrios managed to "find" in its flesh a lead pellet, which he produced out of his mouth with incredible gesticulation. The point of this act was not so much to discredit Felipe Casanova's story—in fact, everybody knew that it was one of Domingo Barrios' tricks—but primarily to discredit my achievement, because it did not fit the context of my "clumsy" interaction with them. It was a little bit as if I had suddenly been able to speak and behave grammatically, in an idiomatic way and without the slightest accent, if only for a brief moment. The second reason for Domingo Barrios' behavior followed from the first. It was a brake applied to the possibility, more than the reality, of my acquisition of prestige in a culturally meaningful way. By becoming a successful hunter, I was, potentially at least, a threat. If I could secure game, then I could also acquire prestige and therefore women. Hence Domingo Barrios' reaction, which was placing a check on pushing my integration into their group too far, putting a halt to my "going native." The point of the incident was to secure the limits of my position in the group and to bind me to my marginality.

In this sense, it would have been preferable if Felipe Casanova had killed the monkey himself. In fact, he never would have let me kill the monkey if he had not already cashed in on his hunting success by marrying two women: Ramona (*into*-TV45), with whom he had four children (*acim*-TV46, *tose*-TV18, *ciköxpwö*-TV19, *nyamca*-TV 47), and, more recently, Natalia (*acim*-TV48), who was still childless (see fig. 12).

My interaction with Felipe Casanova was less spontaneous than with Guzmán, because our huts were separated by that of Mirón, but I spent a considerable amount of time with Felipe Casanova and his two sons (*tose*-TV18 and *ciköxpwö*-TV19). Both boys regularly brought to their fictive *tamu* all sorts of local gossip, after which I had to hand them pencils and paper on which they could draw or imitate my handwriting, to our mutual delight. Their sister, Soledad (*acim*-TV46), however, was more than cold with me until her marriage with Domingo Flores (*manyan*-TV26). This was candidly explained to me by her brothers. She would have to call me *tamu* as they did, but when a female is speaking, this term means "husband," and she was afraid of me. To leave no doubt, the two giggling brothers vividly mimicked sexual intercourse.

Pl. 16. *Felipe Casanova's daughter Soledad* (acim-TV46), *who later married Domingo Flores* (manyan-TV26)

With his two marriages, Felipe Casanova had certainly played it safe. His two wives were not actual sisters, only classificatory ones. His first wife, Ramona (*into*-TV45), was a second bilateral cross-cousin. The second, Natalia (*acim*-TV48), was his first matrilateral cross-cousin and his second patrilateral cross-cousin. The former was Domingo Barrios' sister, the latter Marquito's daughter. This suggests that he had readjusted his political alignment, in conformity with the history of Turiba Viejo. Even before Manuel Blanco's death, when it became clear that Marquito would become the next headman, he had taken Marquito's daughter for his second wife. Both marriages, in addition, were locally endogamous, and Felipe Casanova had never had to move. Meanwhile, from a political viewpoint, he had covered all his options. It would be interesting to know which one he would choose if and when Domingo Barrios decided to leave Turiba Viejo. He could either decide to stay with his father-in-law Marquito or join his brother-in-law Domingo Barrios. To choose between these two possibilities would be his problem, and I will not venture to make any prediction here. However, it is safe to assume that he would probably maximize his family's economic interests and his own political ones. Furthermore, Domingo Barrios would try to attract him, while Marquito would most certainly attempt to retain him.

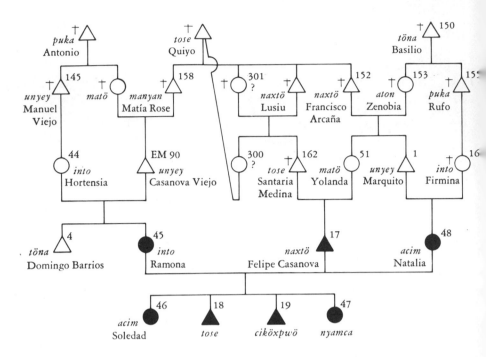

Fig. 12. *The marriages of Felipe Casanova (*naxtö-*TV 17)*

As this review of Marquito's sons-in-law has shown, as far as the ethnographic present is concerned, Marquito's core position in the group remained obvious. It was equally evident to everybody that my fictive consanguinity with him was a powerful symbol. Even though its power was limited to the duration of my fieldwork, as long as it lasted, it was manipulated as much by Marquito as by me. Each of us could obtain something out of this relationship, although not necessarily what we both expected. And this will be examined next.

8. *A Divided Duty*

The fiction of my kinship links with the people of Turiba Viejo had started as a joke. Yet, from its inception, I was aware that as a heuristic device it would be a useful fiction, which is why I jumped at the opportunity with confidence and optimism—not knowing, of course, or even foreseeing what it would entail. I knew something was to be gained, but I did not know what. At the same time, it was truly manipulative, and it neatly fitted my objective as well as objectionable view of the Panare at the time. Yet I was only reacting to a joke that, after all, I had not initiated. When I thought that I could take advantage of the situation—that is, that I could ultimately control it—I greatly underestimated the capacity of the Panare to outfox me. I overlooked the ability of the "objects" to remind me that they were "subjects" indeed and that I had no manipulative monopoly. A few examples will help clarify this intense period of my interaction with the people of Turiba Viejo.

Although my acquisition of a kinship status had not been initiated by Marquito, he knew full well how to turn the situation to his advantage. It was obviously not just "to please me" that everybody—some with more determination than others—let me enter into the relationship. Actually, Marquito had done nothing at all, for he was too much of a conservative to joke about an institution as grave as kinship. The initiative had come from somebody who certainly felt less secure about his situation in the local group: Domingo Barrios. Because of this very insecurity, he was compelled to act out his dominance, to take initiative, in brief, to show off. The weakness of his position was that he constantly had to make a point. Marquito was beyond asserting himself in that way. His place in the group was clear to everybody, his position unthreatened, and his self-confidence total. The strength of his position was that he did not need to do anything; he just had to wait, to observe, to listen. And that is what happened with my "adoption."

That Domingo Barrios was my fictive *inkin* (child) was as amus-

ing to me as to anybody else in the settlement. Yet, in the family relationship of the Panare, linguistic distinctions are rarely made between
sons (*nawan*) and daughters (*yinsön*), two terms of reference to
which the more general term *inkin* is overwhelmingly preferred. But
this relative sexual neutralization in the language contrasts rather
strongly with the differences displayed in behavior. Even nursing children will be given different ornaments depending upon their sex (see
Dumont 1976: 31–32). As soon as a child is weaned, he or she so-
cializes with and is encultured by members of his or her own sex
group. In fact, jurisdiction over a weaned child falls entirely to the
parent of the same sex. This, in turn, receives linguistic recognition; a
son is referred to as his father's child (e.g., *puka-nkin*, the child of
puka), and a daughter as her mother's child (e.g., *acim-kin*, the child
of *acim*). In calling me "his father," then, Domingo Barrios was placing himself under my jurisdiction, fictively and jokingly in many respects, but actually in others.

As he explained to me, I was rich. He did not fail to point to my
camera, tape recorder, metal tools, and books, asking me their price in
Venezuelan currency. My survival instinct prompted me to divide the
value of everything by a hundred to minimize my apparent wealth. He
would also pinch my skin over my ribs, thus squeezing a bulge of fat
between his fingers, the method he used to evaluate the eagerly sought
after fatness of a killed tapir. Next, he would do the same operation
on himself. And then came the unflattering comparison: he was *mu-
kurupe* ("slim"), at least more so than I, whom he declared to be
tökaxse ("fat"). There is no doubt that in his opinion I was what in
the U.S. would be called a fat cat. I could give goods away, therefore
I should. There was indeed a Kantian flavor in his opinion.

His constant and somewhat childish demands, always articulated
in a kinship idiom, truly exasperated me. Whenever I undertook a
quick round trip to Turiba Nuevo on Domingo Flores' bicycle, he
would welcome me back to the settlement with the same question:
"What has my father brought me back from the Creoles?" I even
learned rapidly from him a simple sentence construction—he would
request day after day: *yukwa akinyuya kawa ikwasenya*, "give your son
tobacco to smoke." Trapped as I was in this situation, I stood as firm
as possible, miserly as ever, but that did not discourage his requests.

For Domingo Barrios to call me *yim* had been, as far as I could
tell, more an impulse than a calculation. At first it was only an expression of what my beard had made him judge to be a respectable age difference between us. However, he was quick to perceive that since I was
ready to take his impulse seriously, he could go one step further. Be-

tween parent and child of the same sex who live in the same settlement, the relation is not only affectionate; the child, even upon reaching adulthood, can constantly request goods and services from the
parent. I have shown previously how Andrés and Mirón overused this
option with Marquito. Domingo Barrios was Marquito's classificatory,
not actual, son and therefore could not act likewise with him. His demands for tobacco would have been within the norm for a father-son
relation. In turning to me, Domingo Barrios was evidently after cigarettes, not chewing tobacco, which the Panare grew themselves in their
gardens.

In contrast to Mirón and Andrés, Domingo Barrios was never
hostile. He just kept asking. When I began to understand Panare kinship relations, I pointed out to him that he should direct his requests
to his true father, Casanova Viejo. What did he acquire from him?
Evidently nothing, since Casanova Viejo lived at El Muerto. Altogether, Domingo Barrios was not getting much out of me: just enough
cartridges, hooks, fishing lines, and cigarettes to maintain a friendly
relationship. I did not satisfy most of his demands, but he was generally a good informant and a pleasant companion, so I tried to be fair
in my payments. However, from his viewpoint, it was not enough, and
he would never take no for an answer, knowing all too well what he
would end up with. As a matter of fact, what he was really doing was
testing me constantly and relentlessly, which was part of his political
maneuvering. Even though he was not obtaining what he was request-
ing—for otherwise I would have had to give him everything I owned
—he was still winning a power game which, with his usual loquacity,
he could easily amplify. To me, he could complain that I was a "miser"; to the other men of the settlement, that he had obtained "very
much" from me, which of course greatly impressed those of his listen-
ers who believed him.

I did not deny most of Domingo Barrios' requests simply because
in my opinion they were unreasonable. Except for direct payment for
an individual service, I much preferred to give away knives, machetes,
matches, and so on, through Marquito. Initially—and for once it had
been the right intuition—I had thought the proper way to shelter myself behind local authority would be to make transactions through the
headman. Almost immediately, I was encouraged in this attitude by
the fact that Marquito had redistributed all my initial gifts. But as I
progressively discovered, there was yet another aspect to this redistribution. Suffice it to say here that it quite strongly reinforced Marquito's prestige. In many respects, while I believed I had given to
everybody through Marquito, I was wrong. Although the people of

Turiba Viejo knew that I, not Marquito, had brought metal tools to
the settlement, they also saw Marquito as the prestigious man who had
managed to snatch them from me for their benefit. No wonder that
Marquito encouraged me to go through him for such gift distribution!
In doing so, I was losing the benefit of making a direct impact on the
others of the settlement, but ultimately all the parties concerned were
satisfied: the individuals who received metal tools at no cost; Marquito, who increased his prestige; and I, who was thus developing
excellent rapport with my "brother."

Similarly, Marquito was quick to understand the benefit of his
brotherhood with me. Because he had not initiated it, he could discreetly use it to enhance his authority as a headman—whatever goods
and medical services I could provide were always made to appear as if
he had provided them. This, of course, was done with my complicity.
As I understand his behavior, his greatest skill was twofold. First, he
never asked anything at all from me, and this was in sharp contrast to
Domingo Barrios' repetitive demands. Second, he kept scrupulously
all the forms of brotherly behavior, which required a minimum of
solidarity and assistance. In this way, I could always turn to him for all
sorts of help: my roof was leaking, my pocketknife had disappeared,
and so on. In addition, all my gifts were, one way or the other, reciprocated with fruit, yams, cassava bread, or smoked fish. Occasionally, he
would present me with an unexpected gift of food just because "you
are my brother." We were indeed dutiful to each other in that respect.

Smooth as this interaction may have been and integrative as it
was for me, I was "used" in ways which I did not always suspect. An
incident which took place one day late in the rainy season, almost a
year after my arrival, is revealing in this respect; its interpretation will
require a lengthy commentary. When it occurred, I naïvely assumed
that I was allowed to savor one of those too rare instances of sweet
fieldworking success. But, as will be seen, there was much more to it
than that.

Fresh tapir tracks had been spotted in the vicinity of the settlement, and the whole group of initiated men was going to hunt for the
day. I had learned this from Felipe Casanova, who had come earlier to
borrow my shotgun. He had come with Domingo Flores and Musiu
Tomaso (*puka*-TV7). The three of them were all in a jolly good
mood, animatedly anticipating the excitement of the hunt and the
amount of meat that success would provide. There was one track for
sure, maybe a second one, according to Domingo Flores.

As Musiu Tomaso watched Felipe Casanova helping himself to
my supply of cartridges, he commented, both teasing and serious, "You

have to go to Ciudad Bolivar, *panaxpon* (FaFa), and buy more cartridges." This brought up the ambiguity of my status, as well as its ambivalence in their eyes. It was a sort of reminder concerning my liminality. I was both stranger but kin *and* kin but stranger, at times simultaneously, at times alternately. Already in, I could be addressed by an affectionate kinship term; still out, my acceptability depended upon my economic contributions. Both were real and faked, a compromise which left a large margin for maneuverability by both parties.

"Are you coming with us?" Domingo Flores asked. I was welcome to do so, yet this was not a question that a man would ask either his brother or his grandfather. I had participated in perhaps half a dozen of these day-long hunting expeditions but, except on one occasion, I had not been able to keep up with the pace of the hunt in its final phase. And when I had finally caught up with the hunters, either they had already lost their prey or its butchering was well under way. I thus declined the invitation and asked who, meaning by this which initiated adult male, was going to stay within the settlement. The three men consulted each other in a conversation too animated for me to follow and then declared that they did not know. This ignorance, real or pretended, should have caught my attention immediately, but on the spur of the moment I overlooked its unusual aspect.

Hunting big game such as tapirs or wild pigs was always a collective enterprise which required the participation of the whole group of initiated men for the day. Tapir hunting was fun and exciting for all participants; in fact, it was the epitome of challenging enjoyment, even if a bit exhausting. In addition, as I have mentioned, prestige was bestowed upon the successful hunters. Yet, each time a hunting expedition of this sort was undertaken, there had been at least one adult man who, for one reason or another, did not participate in the venture. Why then would anyone withdraw from such a festive and glorified activity? In some settlements, a man might have been too old to display the physical stamina required. Such was the case at Pavichima with Ramón Grande (*puka*-PV), who satisfied himself and his companions by putting in an occasional pro forma appearance with the hunting party at the moment of its departure. But nobody in Turiba Viejo was old enough to be in such poor shape.

Here, in general it was a physical impairment that prevented one man from hunting—a sprained ankle, a bad cut, a toothache, or some other reason that he was ready to admit. Sometimes, it looked to me like a fabricated excuse, as when Coronel Flores (*tose*-TV5) pretended to suffer from a charley horse, although he had been under no physical strain whatsoever in the past two days, having spent most of that time in his hammock making a basket. For whatever reason a man stayed in the settlement, the reason offered was his poor physical condition. Yet, no matter how prompt a man was to offer this explanation, it always differed from that presented by the hunters. Repeatedly, they offered me a less immediate cause for their companion's absence. And this was all the more striking because it was independently formulated by different individuals in pretty much the same way. Someone had to keep an eye on the women; not that they were intrinsically bad, but one could never be absolutely sure with them. This was all but the post hoc rationalization of a male sexist fantasy.

More to the point, but never volunteered at first as an explanation, a man was needed to keep the settlement safe against possible intruders. Although the latter may appear at first as no more than a watered-down version of the former, there was some measure of reality in this defensive strategy. There was no danger from a raiding attack, but a Panare, Piaroa, or Creole visitor might arrive impromptu. Not only would the women not have anything to do with him in the absence of a man, but it also would leave them defenseless and fearful of sexual abuse. Therefore, the man staying in the settlement was less keeping an eye on women than keeping a security check, as it were, on a feared visitor. As far as I can tell, women endorsed that position to a certain extent, but not wholly.

It took me a long time as a male anthropologist to get their viewpoint. Adopted or not, I still had a tough time speaking with women, and a fortiori with women alone, who would ignore my questions rather pointedly. There were two exceptions to that situation: Marquito's elder wife, Elena (*into*-TV30), and—as I have indicated earlier—her daughter Luisa (*acim*-TV49), Guzmán's wife. Both were not only friendly with me, but less reserved than any other women. From both of them I learned that men were only fools and that there was no real need to keep an eye on women. Still, from their viewpoint, it was not a bad idea to have one man around in case some stranger came unannounced. But it was hardly a real defense, as they were prompt to point out, since that defender was often sick or injured. When I remarked to them that, in my opinion, some men pretended to be sick, both women laughed, and Marquito's wife, softening the volume of her voice even more than usual, said, "Don't you know? It is because of you." Laughing again, her daughter added, "They keep an eye on you." And this was so obvious that it deserved little more commentary. But she added a final remark, "men are fools," which brought the approval of her female companions. No man was around to react to this.

At this point, it can be seen that these incidents reveal the latent antagonism between the two sexes, which is disguised under the pretext of the protection of women. But at the same time, what is asserted is the solidarity of each sex group. On the one hand, men pretend to control women by leaving behind one of their number whose physical disability they deny. As an individual, this man must forego the pleasure of hunting and its rewards because of his sickness, but the group of men construe this disability as a sacrifice which is made for their sake so as to watch and protect the women. Or he denies himself the same pleasure by pretending to be sick, undertaking the same task of protecting women (against me) and of watching them (against themselves). In both cases, he actually sacrifices his pleasure, that is to say ultimately himself, for the good of the whole group of men. From a male viewpoint, he is the symbolic victim of women, and at the same time his sacrifice reaffirms male solidarity.

Meanwhile, the group of women is not duped. And in this process female solidarity can also be reasserted by considering the foolishness of men, about which the women can be very explicit. Yet, this antagonism of sex roles is dialectically solved, at least partially. For the man who stays not only expresses both male and female solidarities but, by the same token, negates them and establishes the solidarity of the whole local group. In staying, he stands for the whole male group, and figuratively the settlement remains complete with both a male and females. He is the keystone of the dynamics of this antagonism. Ultimately, his staying is a symbolic statement, an expression of the dominant ideology. And it is a contradictory statement. It states the male solidarity and it implies the female solidarity. It states the control of women, but it is a fictive control. Finally, it states the solidarity of the members of the settlement. Obviously, this synthesis is unbalanced and remains imperfect, since it is a man who stays with the female group and not the reverse—for instance, one woman accompanying the whole group of hunters. Men may be foolish, but they remain in control: their ideology is imposed on the group; they retain political control over women; they can manipulate the ideology, while the female group has to be content with merely being aware of it.

In all of this, I was the pretext, since the men claimed to be protecting the women from me. Under these conditions, it is little wonder that I was properly stunned when Marquito came and asked me to keep an eye on the women for that day. This struck me at first as a totally unexpected move, for I had never, absolutely never, been asked such a thing in the past. I truly disbelieved him, and in fact was even suspicious and alarmed by what I thought could only be a trick. Had it been Domingo Barrios asking me this, I would have gotten the pun right away, for his outgoing, extrovert personality made him prone to tease. But Marquito had a more tranquil personality. His statements were straightforward and largely unambiguous.

For the moment, however, I was utterly puzzled by Marquito's request, which he probably read on my face, for he added, "I am not lying, you know that." I knew that indeed, and I could also see his irritation with me. But when he offered "nobody is sick and nobody is tired" as a casual explanation before retiring to the *churuata*, it left me in a state of even greater perplexity. Actually, although I did not know what to do with Marquito's statement, I knew about the hunting project for that day.

His remarks had been made rather matter-of-factly. He left me to my reflections, even more so after the whole group of men departed from the settlement to track the elusive tapir. That was it; I was stuck keeping an eye on the women, supposedly watching and defending them. I was so totally panicked that anything might go wrong—that any move, if not any movement, of mine might be misinterpreted— that instead of taking advantage of this opportunity to observe and talk with the women, I blinded myself, sitting in my hut and trying to keep my eyes on a book upon which I was utterly unable to concentrate. I could hear the conversations and the noises of manioc grating and squeezing in the surrounding huts. I could even see this activity being performed. But I was unable to look and unable to listen that day. I welcomed with the greatest relief the early return of the hunters with their load of meat. Success had put them in a joking mood. Two tapirs, a female and her young, was indeed a success. My shotgun had been returned without a word when Marquito asked me, "Everything fine with the women, brother?" Everything was fine.

Marquito's move had been both integrative and manipulative. I had been entrusted with a symbolically important role. And from then on, I was to be entrusted with it more and more frequently, without any need for panicky reaction on my part. In many respects, it was a great success. It was integrative in that I was trusted and I was ascribed a role that no total stranger, but only kin, could ever take. But, on the other hand, it was a manipulation on the part of the male group, since it made it unnecessary for anyone to play sick just for the sake of keeping an eye on the women. Also, it reversed my position in the group from watched to watching. It was now I who was, so to speak, sacrificed to a nonhunting role. And this was so true that from then on, I no longer saw anybody pretending to be sick when a collective hunting party was organized. Either somebody was really sick or

I was asked to stay in the settlement. Superficially, and yet really, it was the ultimate display of trust. At a deeper level, however, they efficiently prevented me from joining the hunters. Finally, despite the obvious progress of my integration, I was still being kept at a safe distance; my marginality was reinforced, since I was *made* disabled so that somebody else in the group might participate in the hunt and gain prestige. More precisely, I was indeed encouraged, if not forced, to play a role that assured the others that I could not gain prestige within their value system. In other words, my collaboration was sought, while the very possibility of my becoming competitive was prevented. It goes without saying that it was not the actuality of my prestige acquisition which was at stake, but only its possibility. Except for the monkey killed in "training," I never killed any game when I participated in a collective hunt, for which I generally took my camera as my only weapon. And it looked as dubious to me as to my companions that I would ever increase my hunting skills.

This double aspect of my ambiguous status in the group deserves to be further illustrated by another incident that took place a few months later, which is equally eloquent as to the contradictory manipulation involved. On the one hand, it tended to push my integration into the group one step forward, but on the other, it prevented it even more vigorously. By then, I had been hosting a French friend for about a month. Thank God, he not only had a beard, but a red one like mine, and to introduce him as my "brother-in-law" presented no problem. When he left, however, Marquito began to be more persistent in his questioning about my marital status. "Where are your wives? Bring them here." Since I could not do that, for good reason, I replied that they were keeping the children and taking care of the gardens.

Time passed, and more and more frequently there were comments to the effect that having no woman was bad for me. How could I not agree with that? Then came this flabbergasting proposition from Marquito: "Do you want a wife?" My virtuous resolutions of yesteryear became blunted for a while, but, wisely cautious, I gave a faint no for an answer. Whatever sexual fantasies I might have had, they were given a tough check by the sudden apparition of Hortensia (*into*-TV 44), whom Domingo Barrios and Marquito were almost pushing in front of me. The venerable but decrepit ancestress squatted, apparently impassively, while the two men were exhorting me to take her for a third wife. They detailed the advantages of such a marriage: she could cook, weave, and so on, and I could provide her with meat by buying it from the Creoles. They must have been serious enough in their intention, for they brought me inside the *churuata*. There I could see that, unknown to me, my hammock had been relocated in a "married" position, as will be explained later, close to Hortensia's. Altogether, from my viewpoint at least, the situation was more comic than tragic, but it took me the rest of the day to talk the two men out of this generous yet unpalatable plan for my immediate future.

Concerning the meaning of this minidrama, several remarks may be made. I have shown on several occasions the ambiguity of my status. Apparently, my marriage to Hortensia would have integrated me further into the group, and the fictive aspect of my kinship relation would have been not only diminished but even suppressed, since I would become an *actual* affine. Also, this marriage was in conformity with my kinship status. As a "father" to Domingo Barrios, I was a proper "husband" to Hortensia, who indeed was Domingo Barrios' own mother. Appropriately, she used to call me *tamu*, and I called her *pwi*. Seen from Marquito's standpoint, she was the ex-wife of Casanova Viejo (*unyey*-EM90), his FaBrDa. Thus, from a structural viewpoint, and if the fake aspect of my brotherhood with Marquito is forgotten for a moment, it would have been a sound marriage.

In addition, since I appeared to the Panare much older than I actually was, it is certain that Hortensia and I were perceived as approximately coeval. Now, this lack of age difference is in itself instructive, for no Panare man in, let us say, his sixties would ever marry a coeval woman. And this, of course, is because she would not be able to bear children anymore, while his DaDa could. In this respect, Hortensia was decidedly past the age. As I have indicated in a previous chapter, an old woman may still marry a daughter's son, as a temporary measure. And this is expressed in the language, since the reference term for MoMo is *wacon*, which mainly means old, while the term for FaMo is *ano*, which to my knowledge has no other meaning.[14]

Marquito and Domingo Barrios did not "offer" me a young woman as a potential spouse. Rather, they confined me within the limits, so to speak, of a necessarily sterile marriage. Furthermore, this was not considered as a temporary measure—it was to be my fate to be locked forever in this barren situation. This was not randomly done. Quite evidently, my insertion in the local group was greater than that of any other individual foreign to their culture, because I was not passing by but staying with them almost indefinitely. Yet, I was not one of them and could not be allowed to be fully integrated by repro-

---

[14]I assume here that another word which I also transcribed as *ano* that refers to a solitary, gigantic, and dangerous, but unidentified, ant is a case of homonymy and not a case of polysemy.

ducing in their group. On the one hand, they had to do something with me; on the other hand, it had to be limited and limiting.

In fact, there was a striking parallel between my keeping an eye on women and my being married to an old woman. In both cases, Marquito's initiative had been a concrete attempt to solve the logical scandal of my presence, patching up our cultural differences and using them at the same time. For there was more to this proposed marriage than I had thought at first. After all, Hortensia did not need "to obey" Marquito or Domingo Barrios. When I wrote that she was "almost pushed" by them, it must be understood that her acceptance was only halfhearted. Nevertheless, as consenting victim of the ideology we are going to examine, she was accepting their maneuver. Although I meant no prestige or status for her at all, I—being rich—could give her goods which eventually would be redistributed within the local group. The whole idea behind this marriage project was to force me into giving more, to place Hortensia under my economic protection, so that everybody in the group would benefit from it.

Marquito's initiative had been manipulative vis-à-vis myself, but it was so vis-à-vis her as well. In fact, I can state without exaggeration that she was ultimately a pawn in the bargain through which Marquito, and all the men who backed him in this, reasserted their ideology. This appears more clearly as soon as the ideology of sex roles among the Panare is brought to the foreground. A complete examination of this problem is beyond the scope of the present work, and only a rapid sketch is presented here. Moreover, as far as I can judge, although women were accomplices in this view, it tends to represent an essentially male standpoint. This ideology finds concrete expression in the way in which the hammocks are slung in the *churuata*, where the members of the settlement come back to sleep at night.

The hammocks of the initiated but still single men are all clustered at the center of the *churuata*, close to the central pillar, which is the *axis mundi* of the Panare. All the other hammocks are slung at the periphery of the construction, with the two groups of hammocks separated by an imaginary corridor. The center of the building, although not strictly separated from the rest, thus represents a sort of "men's house." During the day, the hammocks are stretched above head level, and yet women always follow the imaginary corridor to go from place to place in the communal dwelling, even if it forces them to make a detour. It is said that a woman who entered this space would be raped. Characteristically, it is only at the time of rituals that women enter it and are then surrounded by men. This central group of hammocks is quite large for at least two reasons. First, a boy's initiation takes place between the ages of seven and ten, that is, relatively early. Second, men marry in their late teens or early twenties, that is, relatively late.

All the other hammocks are located at the periphery of the *churuata*. Women's hammocks are parallel to the siding of the building, while men's hammocks are perpendicular to it. The latter are fastened to the thatched siding at one end and point in the direction of the central pillar, from which they are separated by the corridor and the "men's house." The two cowives of a man sling their hammocks on either side of their husband's. Nursing children share their mother's. As has been mentioned, from conception to weaning, an individual is a *nyamca*, after which he/she becomes a *tikon* until initiation for boys and first menses for girls. The youngest of the *tikon* sling their hammocks above that of their parent of the same sex. The oldest ones use the third side of the triangle formed by their parents' hammocks, a space which is sexually neutralized. Such a position can also be occupied by a pubescent single girl, a woman still sexually inactive.

From the entrance tunnel to the back end of the *churuata*, the order of the hammocks for married men is such that a man will tend to have "brothers-in-law" for neighbors. Walking along the corridor, one encounters successively the hammocks of all the married men. The location of each married man also indicates the location of his family (families) of procreation. There is no special place for unwed nubile women, who not only remain with their family of orientation but tend to marry early. Neither is there a special space for widowers. A widower would have to be very young and/or enjoy very little prestige to be sent back to the "men's house." Finally, a young woman who delayed her marriage or a widow who remained in that state would sling her hammock at the back end of the *churuata*.

Except for adultery, which takes place in the lover's garden, premarital and conjugal sexual relations always involve the man's movement toward the woman's hammock. Women give birth in their own hammocks. Each individual thus begins biological and social life in the female space. Only boys will leave it in growing up—girls will be confined there all their lives. At marriage, if a woman moves at all, she slips, as it were, along the thatching to settle in her new residence. Whether postmarital residence is virilocal or uxorilocal changes nothing in this pattern. Ultimately, the displacement of hammocks remains the only absolute indication that a couple got married.

This relatively static female state can be contrasted with a relatively dynamic male state. A boy, conceived and born in female space, leaves it when weaned to make a move toward the center, ultimately toward the father. Of course, he is not displacing the father, since he is either above him or beside him in the sexually neutralized space. Although the boy is not yet in the male space, nevertheless he is no longer in the female one. When initiated—that is, socially if not biologically adult—he crosses the corridor and enters the "men's house." In getting married, he returns toward women, but stays perpendicular to them; he is now opposed both to a female space and a bachelor space. During their lives, women revolve along the thatching of the *churuata* and remain equidistant from its central pillar; the movement of men is perpendicular to that of women: back and forth from the circumference to the center, it describes the radius of the *churuata*.

In the workshop-hut, the hammock of a married man is slung along the axis of the building, that is, at the center, while that of a married woman is along the thatching, that is, on the side. Although the absolute positions are different, the relations are similar, and the spatio-sexual relations remain invariant. By opposition, it is noteworthy that women rarely go outside the perimeter delimited by the settlement, the gardens, and the point where they fetch water, while men leave constantly for predatory or trading activities or just *paseando* (taking a walk). From a conceptual viewpoint, women are almost wedged in between men, right in the middle. On the one hand, women are regulated, almost exiled, to the periphery of the *churuata*; on the other hand, women are almost confined within the rather narrow limits of the settlement.

This suggests the conceptual mediation that women exert between two contradictory types of men: one coping with nature outside the settlement, the other, with the supernatural world represented by the *axis mundi* inside the *churuata*. The place of women is thus medial in relation to men. Spatial relations between individuals are the material representation of the exogamous ideology and become its symbol: the arrangement of hammocks is a formulation of the Panare intentionality. A woman in her roles of sister and wife is the mediator between "us here" and "them elsewhere," that is, between different local groups. Since the reverse ideology exists too and, as we have seen, ultimately has more bearing on reality, this is not merely the mediocre representation of an ideal behavior through which a man from here and a man from there become affines through an exchanged woman. The position of hammocks is thus the graphic representation of the ideal alliance among the Panare.

Women are not only mediators between men but mediators between the natural and the supernatural worlds as well (see Dumont 1976). In fact, the basis for such an ideology is to be found in the economic system, more specifically in some aspects of the sexual dichotomy of work and of the process of consumption. Altogether, the role of women is contradictory. On the one hand, women are indispensable economic partners. Men never produce food, but only a raw product which requires further elaboration by the women in order to become consumable food. For instance, men indeed kill game, but never cook it. On the other hand, the role of women is secondary, and men have precedence over them. With very few exceptions, women have no direct access to the resources of the territory, but their activities always intervene after those of men. For instance, during the gathering of mangoes and palm fruits, women collect the fallen fruit after the men have knocked or cut it off. Examples of that sort could be multiplied almost infinitely. Generally speaking, women's activities consist in transforming the raw product of men into a finished product (see Dumont 1976: 41–76).

Similar remarks can be made about the process of food consumption. Not only do men and women eat separately, but men eat before women. Furthermore, men eat more and better, according to Panare taste (see Dumont 1976: 142–158). Since women already have the role of mediators in the techno-economic infrastructure, it is no wonder that they are perfect mediators in the ideology. Consequently, the spatial organization of hammocks in the *churuata* is but the ideological negation of an actual contradiction: between the complementarity and the supplementarity of women. Women are mediators indeed, but wedged in between two male spaces. In this way, Panare men make two contradictory statements, as they assert their distrust of women, upon whom their survival depends but whose role they intend to minimize. Ultimately, women are manipulated, since ideologically the value of their mediation is recognized, while actually a constant check upon them can be maintained by men.

Coming back to my nearly enforced marriage with Hortensia, Marquito and everybody else in the settlement who was involved in that frustrated transaction had been "using" her in an interesting way, even though it is quite sexist to Western eyes. From a social viewpoint, she was basically useless. Her daughter's son, *tose*-TV18, was still a child unsuitable for marriage, and her sister's daughter's son, Ramón Castillo (*tose*-TR61), had already left Turiba Viejo with Ramón Gallardo. Consequently, from an economic viewpoint, she was a burden, mainly to Felipe Casanova, in whose hut she resided. Ideologically, by "forcing" her, or rather by putting pressure upon her, to marry me, Marquito and the other men were reminding her that she was worthless to the local group. In fact, she did not need that reminder; she knew, and everybody knew that she knew. But it did serve as a male power display, suggesting the control that men may and do exert over women. Furthermore, it was not only an ideological statement but had a very concrete side to it, since I was involved too. As Domingo Barrios had put it candidly to me, I would bring a lot of money and a lot of Creole goods which would circulate within the group for the benefit of all its members.

Ultimately, Marquito had acted as a good and wise headman as well as a good and wise fictive brother, even though I had a different opinion when confronted with the concrete situation. My marriage would have been an opening toward the outside world, its abundance and also its fantasies. So, once more, I was located at the hinge between colliding worlds: the Panare world and the vast world beyond them. By marrying in the group, I too could "at last" be productive and beneficial to its members, since I would no doubt bring about the golden age. More than Marquito, who was more shrewd in keeping his usual reserved attitude, Domingo Barrios could be explicit on that point. "You marry her, you bring beef meat; I will never be tired anymore," he said, although he was only half-convinced that it would really happen. I remained pensive, but silent.

So, in the end, after all these efforts on my part to distinguish myself from the outside world of the Creoles, I had failed. I was somehow worse than a Creole. I was the ultimate innovator in Panare culture, a role that I had tried so hard not to play. I was the gate to the Creole world. And it is this outside world and the relations it maintains with the Panare world that must be examined next.

Part III:

Cross-Ethnic Transactions

9. A Little Less than Kin

Few foreign visitors ever came to Turiba Viejo, and nobody with such insistence as myself. Yet, for Marquito and his companions, the outside world is close by. It is also closing in upon them rapidly.

South of Turiba Viejo and Trapichote, the Piaroa territory begins, but the Panare have little contact nowadays with this ethnic group. Its encroachment on the southern bank of the Suapure River is receding. Only once, in early September of 1968, did I see a party of twelve Piaroa men reach Marquito's settlement. Their arrival had been so quiet that I had not noticed it until Guzmán brought it to my attention. The twelve men, squatting and silent, stayed in front of the *churuata* for an hour or so before Domingo Barrios invited them to drink manioc beer and to hang their hammocks inside the "men's house." They had brought resin[15] and wanted to barter it for tobacco and curare. "Where did they come from?" I asked Domingo Barrios, who extended his arm in a vaguely southern direction.

This brief encounter is all I saw of the Piaroa. That evening, they shared the Panare male common meal. They slept overnight and disappeared the following day toward other Panare settlements in the Sierra Cerbatana to barter for blowguns and more curare. To any student of the Piaroa, such as Monod (1972) or Kaplan (1975), this trading venture will seem bizarre, since these Indians are known for their curare and blowguns. But I could learn little else about them and their trading expedition. Domingo Barrios, Felipe Casanova, and Domingo Flores were the only Panare who talked at all with them, and the conversation, carried on in trade-Spanish, was short and directly related to the economic exchanges. In general, the Piaroa territory was receding toward the south. While a few years ago there had been at least one Piaroa settlement on the right bank of the middle Suapure, there was none now. This withdrawal was indeed one of the reasons

---

[15]The resin called *maköya* by the Panare is known in Venezuela as *peramán*. It is extracted from the tree of the same name (*Morronobea* sp.); see Roth (1924: 82–83) and Alvarado ([1945] 1956: 150).

that Ramón Gallardo established the first Panare settlement ever on the left bank of the Suapure, soon to be followed by a second one, that of Pepe Yara (*tose*-EM96).

While the Piaroa were progressively becoming more and more remote neighbors, the Panare of Turiba Viejo were confronted on the north by the ever-expanding territory of a more formidable neighbor: the Creoles. In contrast with the concentrated habitat of the Panare, the Creole encroachment in the savanna is dispersed. Nuclear or matrifocal Creole families live in scattered mud houses, the closest of which were no further than an hour's walking distance away from Marquito's settlement. A more remote Panare settlement may be, at most, a half-day's walking distance from the nearest Creole *rancho*, but close proximity between the two is a recurrent pattern. Under these conditions, it is not surprising that frequent and regular relations are maintained between the two cultures. Acculturation for the Panare results partially from the exchanges which have been carried out with the Creoles.

Indeed, the Panare have changed. This manifests itself mainly in the domain of technology. The Panare now have metal tools such as machetes, knives, and so on. The occurrence of such changes could be expected. But what is truly astonishing is the limited aspect of these changes. Unlike other Carib peoples of Venezuelan Guiana, the Panare have been able to maintain, to an unexpected extent, their traditional way of life. Unlike the Makiritare, they have not turned to an intensive trading relationship with the Creoles; unlike the Cariña, they have not (yet) turned to wage laboring for the Creoles; and above all, they have maintained, almost intact, their ritual life. In brief, the situation of contact has not yet meant—at least, had not meant at the time of my investigation—cultural collapse, as too often has been the case.

Cultural change is taking place, but at a slow pace. The reason for this now needs to be examined if further light is to be shed on the acculturative role that I as ethnographer played among the Panare. Two points are easily made. First, the relations between Creoles and Panare are codified and not left to the whim of the individuals involved; in other words, there is a proper and generally accepted way of coping with a member of the other group. Second, my intrusion was disruptive because, given my ignorance as well as my anthropological aims, the text of my interaction with the Panare did not entirely fit the context of proper relations between Panare and Creole.

The theory of communication expressed by Lévi-Strauss can be used as a working hypothesis: "In any society, communication operates on three different levels: communication of women, communication of goods and services, communication of messages" ([1958] 1967: 289). To the best of my knowledge, no society lives in total isolation. The border between two adjacent societies is the zone of minimal communication. In discovering the structures of communication between Creoles and Panare, some understanding of the slow pace of acculturation for the Panare and of their apparent cultural resistance can be gained. Let me now review successively the linguistic, economic, and matrimonial exchanges between Creoles and Panare.

Strikingly, nobody in the area could be employed as an interpreter, as I have noted earlier. With the exception of Servando Vitriaga, no Creole spoke Panare; with the exception of Pedro Castro, no Panare spoke Creole Spanish. However, there exists a pidgin Spanish which is used almost exclusively as a trade language and can also be used, as we have seen, between Panare and Piaroa. Yet, this trade-Spanish has not evolved into a *lengoa geral* used between Venezuelans and all other Indians. It must be understood in the specific context of the relationship between the Creoles and Panare. In itself, this language is already a contradiction. Undoubtedly, it creates a code of verbal communication between the two societies, but due to its grammar and vocabulary, it places very narrow constraints on the way it can be used. Actually, it is the vocabulary which is altered, because there are phonological incompatibilities between the two mother tongues, similar to those that Weinreich (1953) has described so well in another context. The words in use generally have a concrete and simple referent, for the most part, objects that can be traded. Panare products are sometimes referred to by their Panare names, but most words are borrowed from Spanish. Only verbs can convey abstract ideas. As already noted by Riley (1952, 1959), verbs often have a wider extension in the trade language than in Spanish. For instance, *vendiendo* not only means "to sell," but also "to barter," sometimes even "to buy," although in the latter meaning the use of *comprando* is more frequent. From a grammatical viewpoint, the gerundive form of the Spanish verb becomes the unmarked verbal form in the trade language, in which times, modes, persons, and numbers are neutralized. Altogether, Spanish morphology is abandoned, since only the unmarked form of nouns and adjectives is used. The progressive structure (subject-predicate-complement) of Spanish syntax is favored over the regressive structure (complement-predicate-subject) of Panare syntax. Finally, except for completive clauses introduced by *que*, all the clauses are independent from each other and their relation, by mere juxtaposition, depends entirely upon the context.

Sketchy as this description is, it indicates that the code of verbal communication, not to mention the messages, is a compromise, resulting from a series of relatively balanced exchanges. The Panare and the Creoles each use their own phonological structure and borrow elements of vocabulary from each other. Verbs are Spanish, but at the price of the extension of their meaning. The basic syntactic structure is Spanish, but at the price of an extreme reduction of the morphology and a quasi suppression of phrase articulations. Such pidgin secures the means of exchanging verbal messages, and these messages are almost entirely concerned with economic transactions. But in so doing, this pidgin restricts the possibilities of exchange tremendously, since there are narrow boundaries to the types of messages which can be exchanged. The language is geared entirely toward practical matters.

When economic exchanges are examined, a similar situation occurs. These exchanges seem to be submitted to a code which limits their applicability. In this way, no pressure can be put upon the Panare which would threaten them with acculturation. The Panare supply the Creoles with two types of goods: horticultural surplus and handicrafts. Bananas, manioc, and yams are the most common produce traded by the Panare; their handicrafts are either means of production such as manioc squeezers and cheese sieves or curios such as baskets or toucan skins which have been used ritually and would otherwise be discarded.

Horticultural products are used in daily barter with neighboring Creoles, while baskets are more often sold in target-marketing expeditions. Horticultural products are bartered for consumption goods (salt, sugar, matches, etc.) while handicrafts are sold for cash with which tools (axes, machetes, knives, hooks), cloth (blankets, mosquito nets, etc.), beads and so on can be obtained.

Horticultural goods are not specifically produced for these exchanges but come from the production of a surplus which the Panare conceive of as insurance against the possibility of a bad harvest or hard times with fishing and hunting. Indeed, except for tobacco, the whole surplus is not used for bartering, and part of it is left to rot in the incompletely harvested gardens. Tobacco and the skins of wildcats and some rodents are bartered directly for pups in a third sphere of exchanges. Actually, the Panare barter these skins only because otherwise they would throw them away. It is noteworthy that no other hunting, fishing, or gathering product is ever traded, because their production grants prestige and thus cannot be actualized as surplus.

Since part of the goods acquired by the Panare are metal tools, and since these tools increase the productivity of their economic system, I expected their economic production to be deeply affected. Such does not seem to be the case. A greater productivity gives the Panare more free time, but this time is not reinvested to increase the output. Rather it is enjoyed as more leisure, in a way which is reminiscent of the situation described by Salisbury (1962) for the Siane of New Guinea.

Since there is hardly any exchange of economic services in the area of Turiba Viejo, it is noteworthy that economic exchanges are quantitatively and qualitatively limited. Quantitatively, only a few products are traded. Qualitatively, the means of production bought from the Creoles do not bring about an increase in production. As for consumption goods, they are traded in such minute quantity that their effect on the system is minimal.

Therefore, the structure of economic exchanges seems balanced, too. The code of economic exchanges creates the possibility of exchanging but at the same time limits its practical range. This is due partly to the fact that the Creoles have no superior technology to offer to the Panare except for the metal tools which can be obtained without changing anything essential in the existing economic structures. Finally, the limits of the two value systems prevent the Panare from increasing their output and discourage them from entrepreneurial efforts.

Passing now to the exchange of women, am I going to discover what I should expect, namely a code allowing these exchanges but limiting them at the same time? At first glance, such is not the case. I have never seen or heard of any mixed marriage between Panare and Creoles. In fact, in both societies, the mere idea of having an affair with or marrying a man of the other social group provoked fear and horror in women. The only exception to this is the meritorious resignation of Hortensia described in the previous chapter. However, it may have been a different story in the past, since Wavrin reports (1937: 172) that sexual relations between Panare men and Creole women as well as between Panare women and Creole men were frequent in his time. But the evidence for these ideally reciprocated exchanges came from hearsay, undoubtedly rich in fantasy, rather than from direct observation. At any rate, the historical events of the past forty years, such as collecting of rubber and chicle as well as *sarrapia* gathering, most certainly have brought about change in this domain.

The two latex products were gathered during the rainy season and the *sarrapia* during the dry season. *Sarrapiar*, in Venezuelan Spanish, means to look for tonka beans, the seeds of the trees *Dipteryx odorata* and *Dipteryx oppositifolia*. The fragrant coumarin ($C_9H_6O_2$) found in these seeds was used as a perfuming agent in soaps and tobaccos. The close of World War II brought an end to the use of the two latex products, while *sarrapia* gathering lasted until 1967, until the industrial synthesizing of coumarin eliminated the market for the natural product. Thus, until recently, Creole men combed Panare territory in search of these precious goods. Unfortunately, they were organized in parties of men without women, and an account of the sexual abuses suffered by Panare women would be an endless litany. The Panare reacted to this excessive communication by shying away from any sexual relations with the Creoles, who became less demanding anyway once the *sarrapia* lost its value. This was the situation I found upon my arrival at Turiba Viejo. Hence the warning given to me repeatedly, wherever I was, concerning the unavailability of women.

Nowadays, sexual and a fortiori matrimonial exchanges are "forbidden" between Creoles and Panare. Nevertheless, it is worthwhile investigating whether there might be something else which occurs in lieu of these exchanges at a symbolic level. This something else, occurring instead of marriage but in the same structural relation to the other exchanges, is still to be discovered. In order to do so, I will begin by examining the case of marginals who have abandoned their culture and society to join the other one. In the system of communication, their position is reversed in relation to the norm. In addition, their sexual position is marked. This tends to indicate that everything holds together and that, in the case of normal individuals, sexual exchanges should be marked, despite the empirical absence of matrimonial exchanges.

At Turiba Viejo, I was confronted off and on during my stay with a small mystery. A Creole in his thirties, whose name and identity I have never learned, appeared in the local group for periods of two to three weeks and disappeared as he had arrived, surreptitiously. He used to sling his hammock either in the "men's house" or at the rear end of the *churuata*. At first, he wanted me to believe that he was a Panare, pretending that he did not understand Spanish. His disguise was to no avail because his physical aspect, his stature, taller than any Panare, and above all his golden teeth had betrayed him from the very first day. Although he wore a loincloth and followed the Panare way of life, he was far from being assimilated into the group. Indeed, the Panare have no socialization process for adults who have not been encultured from their birth. On the contrary, he was perceived as a potential threat to the group. So far, from the Panare viewpoint, this does not make him very different from me. But several factors made the Panare distinguish between the two cases. I stayed and he did not, and he had apparently been coming and going like this for the past few years. He never brought any goods or medicine with him, pretending to be Panare even to the Panare, which amused more than irked them. On his part, it was an all-out attempt to go native. Although the regularity of his visits had ended up making him a familiar apparition, his status remained ambiguous. After all these years of "playing the Panare game," he still did not speak the language with any fluency. He was referred to and addressed as *tatto*, the most neutral of all possible appellations. In fact, Panare individuals manifested no strong emotion toward him: none of the hostility that Mirón displayed toward me and none of the affection that Guzmán showed me either.

Despite this apparent indifference, the men of the settlement were prone to boss him around. He was required to perform tasks that they were loath to do themselves, and it was made clear to him that this was the condition of their "hospitality." Clearly, this was a way for the Panare to reinforce their social cohesion at his expense. He was asked to go and fetch water, to carry heavy loads of dead wood, and so on, that is, to perform the most menial of women's daily chores. It seemed as if he had not only been socially neutered but reduced to the role of a woman-object, used entirely as a means of production. Constantly blackmailed and ridiculed by the Panare men in the settlement, he was explicitly and repeatedly denied access to women. The sexual prohibition which struck him was total. In preventing his integration and thus rejecting him on the side of marginality, the Panare manifested their opposition to his position in the communication system and prevented its transgression.

Of course, the differences which existed between his "project" and mine were of no relevance to the Panare. We were, however, treated differently, and I would like to think, if not to believe, that it was partly due to a better grasp of the situation on my part. But it would be ludicrous for me to perceive there a qualitative difference between him and me where, in reality, there was a quantitative one. I too represented a transgression of the mode of communication between Creole and Panare; I too had an economic use; I too was prohibited access to women. Eventually, Marquito and his people had a choice; they could treat the two of us equally or differently and, if differently, then in a wide range of possible ways. In fact, it was striking that the other man and myself were never compared to each other. No logic of classes bound us together. To the concreteness of each situation, the Panare reacted altogether differently. They could not or did not want to get rid of either of us, but they excluded him and integrated me further than any Creole.

This became strikingly apparent to me a few weeks after I had dissuaded Marquito from marrying me to Hortensia, when the Creole man appeared once more in the settlement. He planned to stay for a couple of weeks. On his second day, however, after a good ten hours of hard work weeding several gardens, he was told that he could not be fed because there was nothing to eat. This was an outright lie, since I was invited to gorge myself at the male common meal. There was no dispute involved, but he was notified indirectly of his "deportation." Guilt overcoming my reluctance to be involved in this, I fed him that night and—to my relief—the following morning he disappeared once more. I never saw him again but learned that he had come back to Turiba Viejo in the fall of 1969, that is, after my departure.

The fate of this man can be correlated with that of Pedro Castro, for whom symmetric and reverse causes had similar consequences. As I have shown in a previous chapter, this Panare man had been excluded from his local group because he worked too often for the Creoles, among whom he had not been integrated despite his efforts. His social life, the process of his socialization into the Creole world, was thus confined to the sleek and sleazy pleasures of cheap drinks and women in Caicara. His individual behavior had been perceived as a social sign by his kin and coresidents, to whom he had appeared as a threat to the communication system between Panare and Creoles. With the excesses of his innovating wage laboring, his deviancy had been revealed, and he had been chased away from his *tapatakyen*. Clearly, this case is the reverse of the previous one. In the case of the anonymous Creole, which was also mine, the threat could be controlled, thus tolerated and above all manipulated.

With the anonymous Creole and with Pedro Castro, the linguistic norm was reversed. The former did not speak Panare fluently but instead would mumble it rather than use trade-Spanish, which was also avoided by Pedro Castro, who preferred to use his halting Spanish. Similarly, the economic practices of the two marginals reversed the norm, since both had become dependent upon their respective group of adoption. One had become a factotum, the other a wage laborer, when neither should have done so. Finally, the sexual practices of the two men were strongly marked either by an imposed chastity or by a venal promiscuity. In both cases, and in an opposed but symmetric way, the Panare and the Creole models of marriage were reversed. Therefore, whether permissible or forbidden, sexual exchanges are marked; otherwise, the sexual behavior of the two deviants would be indifferent, which was not the case.

Consequently, the problem of the exchange of women in the system of communication between Panare and Creoles rises again. If marginal behavior is the reverse of normal behavior, and if sexual behavior is marked for marginals, then such sexual behavior must be the reverse of something marked in the norm. Neither of the two marginals spoke the language of the other group fluently. Yet, they spoke it more than anybody else, that is, too much. In addition, their economic behavior—one as a barterer, the other as a wage laborer—reversed the norm of their group of origin and aimed, however unsuccessfully, at the normal economic behavior of their group of destination. Finally, they both reversed the sexual and matrimonial norms of the two groups.

Since linguistic, economic, and sexual behavior visibly forms a coherent whole for marginals, it is impossible to dissociate sexual exchanges from linguistic and economic ones, at least within the norm. But the empirical difficulty remains: there is no mixed marriage. Yet, if this is a structured ensemble, as I believe I have shown it to be, this type of exchange is bound to take place one way or another. It remains to be discovered, and to do so will require a detour through the ideology of this communication.

The Panare call themselves *ötnyepa*, but the meaning of this term has a greater extension than a mere self-designation, since it refers to any other Indian group as well. The word *tatto*, used to designate anybody who is not Indian, means "human being," but in addition it has a derogatory connotation. In fact, its equivalent *sotto* in Makiritare derives from or has the same origin as the Carib root *itoto*, which has the meaning "slave" (Acosta-Saignes [1954] 1961: 55–76).

The Creoles refer to themselves as *criollos, racionales,* or *patriotas*. I will not enter into the historical origin of these terms here. Suffice it to say that each one refers to a different semantic dimension. They are *criollos* because they are peasants of mixed blood. It makes them different from the Indians and from the ruling bourgeoisie of Venezuela, but puts them on a par with the Colombian peasants, for instance. They are *racionales* because, in opposition to the Indians sometimes referred to as *irracionales*, they consider themselves capable of rational thought. Finally, they are *patriotas* because their ancestors have fought against Spain for political independence. The Creoles thus identify themselves either with other Latin American peasants (*criollos*), or with other classes of Venezuelan society (*patriotas*), or with both (*racionales*), but never with the Indians. On all these accounts, the Panare are "excluded," and this would also be true of any other tribal group.

All of the Creoles whom I have known picture themselves in an intermediary position in terms of social hierarchy within complex

Venezuelan society. They see themselves halfway between the *doc-tores*, members of the bourgeois class, with a higher social status, and the *Indios*, with a lower one. The false consciousness that this reflects is striking, at least as far as the Indians are concerned. It is evident that the Creoles have great ambiguity of feeling vis-à-vis the two groups. The *doctores* are admired, envied, despised, and feared, all at the same time, while the Indians are also despised and feared but treated with a great display of paternalism.

The Creoles and the Panare are both locked in their own ethno-centrism and consider each other inferior. As I believe I have shown previously, the Panare do not miss any occasion for scoffing at the Creoles' incompetence in predatory activities, by which prestige is acquired in Panare culture. Conversely, the Creoles either express their feelings explicitly, complaining that the Panare behave *como puercos* ("like pigs"), or, more often, implicitly, lamenting that they are *pobrecitos* ("poor little ones"). Therefore, the ideology of interaction between Panare and Creoles is such that each group "condescends" to entertain relations with the other. This ideological imbalance is symmetric and limited, and, as I have shown, the very practice of exchanges rebalances the situation. But, in fact, even at the level of ideology, a process of rebalancing does occur, thanks to a ritualization of the actual relationship. This is performed through the *compadrazgo* institution, the social result of Catholic baptism, which tends to normalize the relations between the individuals of each group.

Several factors intervene in determining in each group who may enter into contact with whom. Geographical proximity between the individuals is important; two individuals have to be in the same vicinity to perform exchanges. In addition, once an exchange has occurred, the two partners tend to maintain this relationship. Even more importantly, the mobility of the individuals has to be considered. Since men among the Creoles as well as among the Panare are freer in their movements, it follows that culture contact is established through men more than through women. The bonds between *compadres* are thus stronger than between *comadres*. In this context, these bonds, rather than those between godparents and godchildren, are the only ones of significance, except in one important respect.

The ritual through which *compadrazgo* relations are established is a form of baptism. The Spanish word *bautismo* becomes, in pidgin, *patimo* for the Panare and *batimo* for the Creoles. The administration of the Christian sacrament is performed without the intervention of a priest, and the Creoles make a distinction between *bautizar*, which a priest would do, and *echar el agua* ("to throw water at"), which the

Creole does. The initiative for this ceremony can be taken either by the Creole man or by the Panare father of a small child. I observed it for the first time in Turiba Nuevo at the house of a Creole called Manuel Suarez. I had accompanied Guzmán, his pregnant wife, and their young son to the Creole settlement. They were on their way to the Panare settlement of El Muerto. As frequently happens in similar circumstances, Guzmán's wife and child stayed outside the Creole's, sitting on the ground. Guzmán had gone into Manuel Suarez' home with me, but he remained silent and visibly uneasy while I spoke with the Creole man. The conversation was in Spanish, and he could not follow it. Shortly after, as I was about to depart, Guzmán said just one word, *patimo*, at which Manuel Suarez asked me if I had ever seen such a ritual. My answer was irrelevant, for I believe he would have "thrown the water" anyway.

Manuel Suarez called his wife for his book of prayers, and Guzmán called his wife and child. In this unfamiliar setting, the boy, being held by his mother, began to panic. But a taste of "the salt of the earth" must have been a great trauma or a real delight, for it quieted him down. *En el nombre del Padre, del Hijo y del Espíritu Santo*, concluded Manuel Suarez. The Catholic part of the ritual was over, but the ritual then took a different turn. The Creole's wife was dispatched to the kitchen corner of the house. She soon came back with three cups of coffee for the three men present, a secondhand shirt for the child, and a small container of kerosene and several matchboxes for Guzmán, who swallowed his cup of coffee in one gulp. He took a few plantains from his basket and almost threw them on the table. *Nya mayi*, "Let us go," said Guzmán. *Que te vayas bien*, "Have a good trip," replied Manuel Suarez. Exit the Panare family.

This ritual deserves some commentary. The performance of the baptism itself is followed by an economic exchange. The Creoles may give tools or consumption goods such as canned food and sometimes cloth. I have always seen this gift reciprocated by the Panare men who has now become the Creole man's *compadre*. On this occasion, a basket, some tobacco, or other horticultural products are proper counter-gifts. In and of itself, such an exchange of gifts and counter-gifts is remarkable, because it is the modality of exchange between the Panare, while bartering and buying and selling are more characteristic of the exchanges between Panare and Creoles.

For the Creoles, the ceremony has two aspects. The first is to *bautizar* an Indian child, the second to *regalar su nombre* to the child. This means "to make a gift of one's name." It is indeed a gift and not a mere attribution, for the Creoles use the verb *regalar* and not the more neutral *dar*. One of the reasons for this behavior is that the Creoles do not know Panare personal names and assume that the Indians have no names, a half-truth in the case of a *nyamca*. In the few cases where the baptized child is a girl, she will receive the name of the Creole's wife. However, in the course of her life, she will have very little to do with the Creoles except in the company of a Panare man, so that her Creole name will very soon be forgotten. In contrast, in growing up, a boy will be more and more frequently in direct contact with the Creoles, and in this situation he will refer to himself by this name and so, too, will the Creoles address and refer to him.

Furthermore, not only is the Creole's first name transmitted through this ritual, but also his last name. Guzmán's son was still undifferentiated among the Panare as *nyamca*; yet, among both Creoles and Panare, he would be known from now on as Manuel Suarez, that is, by the name of the Creole who had "thrown water" upon him. The giving of the name establishes a congruency if not a continuity between the Creole baptist and the baptized Panare. It represents a sort of phonic hyphen between the two individuals considered as metonyms of their respective cultures. Although the Creoles consciously transmit to the Panare child a full identity made up of a first and a last name, the practical use of these names varies. I have shown examples of complete names, such as Felipe Casanova or Domingo Barrios. More often, however, the last name alone is remembered (Rodiana, Casanova Viejo), or the first name alone (Julio, Ramón), or its diminutive form (Marquito, Ramoncito). Sometimes, a Creole is better known locally by a nickname than by first and last names, so that the nickname will be transmitted to the Panare child. To mention only the most extravagant but picturesque case, there were a Creole man and a Panare teenager in the same area called Bigote Caldo Frío, which translates literally as "Cold-Brothed Moustache."

The Creole and Panare motivations for entering into this type of exchange are simple to understand. The baptism of a pagan child satisfies the religious obligations of the nominally Catholic Creole as well as paternalistic feelings. As for the Panare, the baptism creates a precedent, and the house of the baptizing Creole becomes a place to obtain food and shelter when on the move. The two adult individuals, the Panare whose child has been baptized and the Creole who gave the sacrament, have not only become *compadres*, but privileged partners in commercial exchanges. On occasion, exchanges may involve somebody else, but the two *compadres* exchange more and more frequently with each other rather than with members of the other culture who do not stand in the same relation.

In this process, the ideology of communication seems, at long last, to be rebalanced. In becoming a *compadre*, the Panare man has been "Creolized." In giving and receiving gifts and counter-gifts, the Creole man has been "Panarized," since normally gifts and counter-gifts remain an Indian affair, not a modality of relationship between Panare and Creoles. Needless to say, the first viewpoint is the Creole; the second, the Panare.

In their now classic study of *compadrazgo*, Mintz and Wolf have recognized two main functions in ritual coparenthood in European feudalism. The first "was to structure . . . individuals or family relationships vertically between members of different classes" and the second "was to solidify social relations horizontally among members of the same rural neighborhood" (1950: 347, 348). In the present case, in which social stratification and geographical proximity are determinants of the ideology of the communication system, the two functions fuse.

From a structural standpoint, the *compadrazgo* between Panare and Creoles is a transformation of the other types of *compadrazgo* in which the Panare play no role. There the two functions remain separate, for there are two possibilities. The Creoles either emphasize "horizontal relations" and choose Creole neighbors for *compadres*, or emphasize "vertical relations" and choose *doctores*, that is, individuals who are not neighbors but city-dwellers and members of a higher social class. With their Panare neighbors, who are perceived as members of a lower social class, the Creoles integrate the two functions. This can be interpreted as the entirely ideological revenge that the Creoles take upon their actual situation within the complex Venezuelan society.

At any rate, the ritual of baptism initiates an authentic alliance between the parties involved, and this leads me back, now at a symbolic level, to the initial problem of matrimonial exchanges. Indeed, in counter-giving to their Creole *compadres*, the Panare actually reciprocate two gifts: the material gift of goods and the linguistic gift of names. Accepting the Creole names is a way for the Panare "to incorporate" the Creoles into their culture—that is, ultimately to contract an alliance with nature, since the Creoles are the barely human inhabitants of the profane savanna (Dumont 1976: 14–15).

Furthermore, the baptism creates a relation of fictive kinship, more precisely of fictive consanguinity, since the *compadres* are "parents together," as the term indicates. Of course, the *compadrazgo* is a Creole institution which involves the Panare by extension only. Yet, in the trade language, the Panare do call the individual who baptized the child *compadre*, and this man's wife *comadre*, and vice versa. Manuel Suarez the Creole and Guzmán the Panare addressed each other in this way. In addition, Guzmán knew as well as any other Panare that the *compadrazgo* prohibits any sexual and a fortiori matrimonial relation between *compadres* and *comadres* as well as between godparents and godchildren. Therefore, in entering into this relationship, a Panare man has—or believes he has—protected his daughter and his daughter's mother against Creole sexuality. But Guzmán gave me a further explanation. Due to the classificatory aspect of Panare kinship terminology, he believed that he had "protected" all the classificatory sisters of his wife, that is, exactly one-half of the Panare women. Moreover, he thought that "the other half"—his own sisters and potential daughters-in-law—were protected by other *patimo*, because he imputed basically the same kinship system as his own to the Creoles. Verification of this projection emerges clearly from the readiness of the Panare "to translate" their kinship terms into Spanish ones, even though the two systems are incompatible.

Consequently, baptism can be considered the reverse of marriage, which is another way of avoiding the latter while still placing the focus on it. In fact, baptism may seem paradoxical, because it is both alliance and nonalliance. It creates a political alliance, but it is also the reverse of marriage, which by definition is alliance. The relationship between baptism and marriage is not only an interpretation on my part but also has an empirical expression. When a Panare man and a Creole man who are not *compadres* meet, they often call each other *cuñado*, "brother-in-law." This is a pun indeed, the sexual connotation of which amuses the Panare as well as the Creoles. Sexual communication stops here, at the linguistic level, for this jokingly sexualized speech does not lead to any sexual act.

Yet, in the case of the pun as well as in the case of the *compadrazgo*, sexual or matrimonial exchange remains the point of reference. And both are tropes of marriage. With the pun, the exchange is potential but does not become actualized. With the *compadrazgo*, the exchange is indeed actualized but consists in transforming potential affines into fictive consanguines. Ultimately, in this communication system, although the exchange of women is not part of the praxis for either Creoles or Panare, it is constantly, almost obsessively, on their minds. What was empirically absent at first sight now seems present, although disguised. In this context, women are objects of exchange, and the problem for men is less to keep them for themselves than to exchange them as consanguines, albeit fictive ones. It is noteworthy that the male viewpoint is not reversible with the female, because, again, it is men and not women who are in contact with each other in both societies.

The existence of this system of communication suggests that the two cultures are compatible with each other, or rather establishes a rapport of compatibility between the two. In addition, the system is self-regulated, as shown by the example of the marginals. Such a system establishes the possibility of exchanging, thanks to the code that it implies. At the same time, the same system controls the practices of these exchanges and limits them, with the effect of slowing down the rate of Panare acculturation.

But here again, as I have maintained all along in this work, the dialectics of context and text, of structure and event, must now be reintroduced, for obviously the very practice of these exchanges is a constant challenge to the balance of this system. However, such a challenge never threatens the system of communication itself, within which a process of rebalancing takes place under the impact of each individual practice.

Having mentioned this, it is time to recognize and identify what has been left out of this presentation of the communication between Creoles and Panare. I am referring to the processes which are grafted onto this structural ensemble. At least two different orders of processes are involved here. On the one hand, there is the actual, concrete, active, individual behavior of Guzmán, Marquito, Felipe Casanova, and others, when they deal and cope with neighboring Creoles. Each of them, including the marginal cases mentioned above, fits the described model. However, I must hasten to return to my own situation in that model and thus immediately soften the strength of my assertion. As I have pointed out, I did fit the system as a marginal who, by definition, pushed things a bit too far. To an even greater extent than the other two marginals whose cases have been reviewed, I as ethnographer represented a limit to the extension of the system. But it is not too difficult to perceive equally well that this limit was a hinge whereby I was located simultaneously within and without the system. In comparison to the Creole man who ended up "chased away" from Turiba Viejo, I was much more integrated into the Panare settlement. I have pointed out some similarities and discrepancies between our respective cases. While my linguistic and economic role in the *tapatakyen* of Turiba Viejo offers no difficulty in interpretation, my "marriage" involves something else. What does this apparent transgression mean, even though it did not occur in the end? Did I fit the model or not?

I have no simple answer to these questions and can only point to the paradoxical and ambiguous status I enjoyed. The consideration of my marriage with Hortensia had been a day-long event, thus very brief. It had also been a serious project, serious enough to have been proposed to my unpredictable self. Neither Marquito nor anybody else could have anticipated my refusal, and Hortensia's resignation suggested the seriousness of the situation. Once it is recognized that it was neither a joke nor a trick, it must be indicated that it was the most formidable put-down I have ever been subjected to. It had certainly been an integrative success, but an incredible denial, too. Moreover, it fit the image of the defects and excesses of my linguistic and economic role. Fluency in Panare did not make me a native speaker any more than my goods and services made me a Creole. The "too much" or "not enough" aspect of my situation was obvious to everybody: the Panare, the Creoles, and myself. It was as if the mask of familiarity had fallen off, revealing my true identity underneath: a reluctant innovator who could only behave erratically. Whether I begrudged or welcomed my position and my relation to the communication system between Creoles and Panare, I was playing both within and without the system.

This will appear with greater clarity when the second order of processes is brought to the foreground. In reality, I have mentioned only in passing that the Creoles were part of a so-called complex Venezuelan society. Because of this, the problem of the relationship between Panare and Creoles cannot be limited to this context. Actually, the Creoles are but a stratified segment of this complex society. The impact of the Venezuelan nation-state upon the Panare is different from that of the Creoles and infinitely more dangerous to their cultural and physical survival. For the compatible compromise between Creoles and Panare can be balanced, unbalanced, and rebalanced constantly in the praxis because in this process the system is subject only to its inner dialectic and can absorb the events which take place within the limits of its invariance.

But the problem becomes entirely different with the intervention of individuals such as the missionaries and the promoters of forced integration whose relentless aim is culture change. In this case, it is no longer the balance of the system which is threatened, but its very existence. It is no longer a problem of inner contradiction between structure and process, but the problem of incompatibilities between two entirely different systems. Consciously or unconsciously, in good faith or in bad, with a generous ideological rationalization or with a hypocritical one, the purpose of the intervention is to replace the existing relationship of compatibility between Creoles and Panare with a relationship of domination whereby the Panare are confronted with a drastic choice, between assimilation to the nation-state on the one hand and ethnocide on the other.

10. *At Play in the Fields of Semantics*

The system of communication established between Creoles and Panare is not the only relationship existing between this Indian group and non-Indians in Venezuela. I have explained in the previous chapter how two cultures, the Panare and the Creole, have developed a system of communication which regulates change and slows down the pace of acculturation. I have also indicated how, beyond the inner dialectic inherent to the functioning of the system, outsiders could introduce a disruption that affects less the equilibrium of the system than the system itself. Such outsiders, who will soon be identified, manipulate another system, incompatible with the first one, which it attempts to replace. The object of the present chapter is to examine some of these disruptive attempts and interpret their failures and successes. It also represents an effort to get the most out of the few historical data which I can rely upon.

Before understanding how communication succeeds or fails, it will be necessary to consider who the agents of communication are in the present case. The Panare are on one side of a border. The newscast I could listen to on the radio left me with no doubts on that account. The frequency of use of words like *desarrollo* ("development") and *conquista del Sur* ("conquest of the South") sufficiently indicated that there was another side of the border: complex Venezuelan society, which regarded Panare "independence" as a regrettable obstacle in the path of its expansion. The intervention of the complex society as a whole in the frontier zone is the affair of a few of its representatives at this point. Government agents and missionaries clearly represent the interests of the ruling segment of the bourgeoisie which retains the political power in Caracas. The government agents, who execute given policies, represent these interests directly; the missionaries, Catholic or Protestant, indirectly. Catholicism is the state religion in Venezuela, and the whole area south of the Orinoco was subjected to Mission Law at the time of my fieldwork. The collusion between politics and religion needs no further comment. The Protestant missionaries may seem to be in a slightly different situation; they are considered intruders in a territory in which the Catholics have legal exclusivity. Moreover, they are not Venezuelans, but U.S. citizens. Their actions, however, have always been approved by the government—at least tacitly—and in spite of their illegal presence, they have never been evicted. Although not Venezuelan nationals, their interests are compatible, if not identical, to those of the Venezuelan "integrationists."

Therefore, it is not the entire complex society which interacts with Panare culture, but the representatives of its ruling segment. This relationship is asymmetrical. The agents of communication on the Venezuelan side belong to and represent the establishment, whose values they try to impose on the Panare. As intruders in a territory which they want to control and dominate, their action is essentially political; it results from a political decision of the ruling bourgeoisie. These actions are not a matter of establishing links between neighbors and thus become entirely different from the communication existing between Panare and Creoles.

This policy of integration has its ideological rationale. The ruling segment of Venezuela and its representatives start from a set of prejudicial assumptions about Indians in general and the Panare in particular. These must be explained. Since the borders of Latin American countries have been delineated with total disregard for the original inhabitants of these territories, it follows that some Indian groups still "occupy" parts of Venezuelan territory. In particular, the Panare, who are now in a contact situation with the Creoles, are perceived as a hindrance to the southward expansion of the "frontier," as an obstacle to economic development. Their territory is considered sparsely settled, and it is believed that the land could be more profitably exploited. Because the economic rationality of the Panare is different from that of the Creoles, they are accused of being irrational. Indeed, Panare behavior is perceived by Venezuelans as a set of individual peculiarities which does not fit the norms of the established order. The Panare are therefore viewed as deviants: primitive and infantile. It is thus the "mission" of Venezuela to help them pass from their present half-humanity to the full standing as accomplished humanity they would reach once they have been pressed into the mold of Venezuelan "civilization." This perception of the Panare holds true for other tribal groups as well, but the Panare have the burden of being directly in the frontier zone, while the more remote Yanomami, for instance, are relatively safer (see Chagnon 1968, 1974, and Lizot 1976).

Such a view transforms cultural differences into a relation of dominance. First, the Panare are different from "us" the Venezuelans. Second, they are within "our" territory and they are "our" Indians. Third, they must be made like us. This is sufficient justification for interfering in the world of the Panare. Of course, if it were just a case of a contiguous relationship like that between Creoles and Panare, this ideological perception of the situation would be nothing more than another instance of ethnocentrism manifested by one culture vis-à-vis another. But here, because the complex society and its members who hold that view have the coercive power to enforce their ethnocentrism, a relation of dominance is involved. The Panare do not take the initiative in contacts with government agents or missionaries any more than they do with the anthropologist. However, their cultural survival is endangered, since the dominant ideology is conducive to forced integration.

This aspect of Venezuelan middle- and upper-class ideology represents an interesting departure from the political reality of the situation. While the Panare must become part of Venezuela, they are not meant to become members of the ruling segment of Venezuelan bourgeoisie. Instead, as was clear to any of my Venezuelan informants, the Panare are to become Creoles, and their full Venezuelan status is correlative with their Creolization. Not only is acculturation mistaken for enculturation, but the claimed enculturation is to take place at the lowest possible level of the complex society's stratification. This viewpoint clearly indicates how Venezuelans perceive their society's social stratification: bourgeoisie at the top, then Creoles, and finally, at the lowest level, the Panare and other tribal groups.

However, the Venezuelan viewpoint and that of the Panare imply distortions of reality, although the warping is different in each case. For the Venezuelan bourgeoisie, the Panare are part of their nation, but marginal to it; therefore, they must be integrated, assimilated, absorbed. For the Panare, the relationship is exclusive, and the complex society is viewed as the intruder. Undoubtedly, each group perceives the other in terms of social stratification as well as in terms of spatial distancing. Yet, the Venezuelans emphasize the social-stratification aspect of the problem to a greater degree than the Panare, who place the accent on spatial distance. To be sure, the latter have their own ethnocentrism. Yet, even though outsiders are perceived as inferior, the *doctores* stand further away than the Creoles.

In both cases, the Creoles occupy a middle position between the Panare and the Venezuelan bourgeoisie. Consequently, the Creoles become cultural brokers, and culture change passes through them. The Panare interpret any effort at culture change within the framework of their relationships with the Creoles. The missionaries and government agents are little aware of this framework. Yet, whatever their feelings about it, the agents of acculturation set up communication through the preexisting channels of a balanced system. Thus, the impact of the missionaries and of the government agents is preceded, historically as well as structurally, by the system which exists between Creoles and Panare. This impact results in a disruption of the system to the extent that it uses the familiar forms of a preexisting code.

Before I call upon a few historical examples which will help illustrate this point, it is noteworthy to remember that I was as much an outsider as the government agents and missionaries were. At best, my difference from them was ideological, in that I had no intention of introducing any change among the Panare. And yet, no matter how reluctant I am to perceive similarities where I had hoped for radical differences, the introduction of these historical events represents a detour that will shed light on my involvement with the Panare of Turiba Viejo.

The first official intervention of the Venezuelan government into Panare life originates in a decree of December 12, 1958 (no. 472), which created a Commission for the Administration of Tonka Beans (C.A.S.),[16] in order to organize the collection of the seeds. Turiba Nuevo, the Creole settlement, was selected as the geo-economical center of the Middle Orinoco Basin for the installation of a C.A.S. branch: this is the "Station" to which I have alluded in a previous chapter.

An official publication reports that a government program was initiated in 1960 for the "transculturation and incorporation of the natives of Venezuelan Guiana to national welfare" (Hurtado Izquierdo 1961, front cover). This publication deals only with Turiba Nuevo, but similar events took place simultaneously in Candelaria, a Creole settlement on the east bank of the middle Cuchivero. The Station had been built and was used as an official warehouse and purchasing center for tonka beans; it was also a general store for the Creoles who tended to cluster around it. Indeed, even as late as 1970, it was the only cluster of Creoles on the right bank of the Orinoco River between the Suapure and the Cuchivero except for the town of La Urbana and the administrative center at Caicara. Around its Station, Turiba had become a marketplace, where staple food such as rice, coffee, sugar, and salt, tools like machetes, knives, and axes, and other

[16]The C.A.S. is a member organization of the National Agrarian Institute (I.A.N.), which in turn is an autonomous organization within the framework of the Department of Agriculture (M.A.C.).

important products like kerosene, mosquito nets, and so on could be acquired.

The Panare of Turiba Viejo, who were then settled at Guamure, understood that it was easier to obtain metal tools from the Station than to go as far as La Urbana or Caicara and, above all, that prices were better in the official shop at Turiba Nuevo than in private shops at the two other places. Their best way to obtain cash was to bring some tonka beans to the Station. This was also understood by the government as a manifestation of goodwill on the path to "civilization."

So a program was designed in order to develop a "rational economic behavior" among the Panare by which they would understand the use of credit and become profit maximizers. This was aimed at increasing tonka-bean production, but, in reality, the amount the Panare produced fluctuated according to their own needs. Of course the rationale of Panare economic behavior was totally overlooked. In teaching "our native compatriots" (Hurtado Izquierdo 1961: 11) capitalistic rationality, the object was to convince them of the merits of Venezuelan culture, which would be embraced following the acquisition of "our" economic rationality. As stated in the official document, "teaching the natives how to buy and to sell is a way of integrating them into the economic life of the nation" (Hurtado Izquierdo 1961: 39). But this could not be undertaken without proving "our" good faith, which was done by distributing gifts to the Panare.

"On a special occasion, and with the necessary wisdom in order not to create habits, . . . [the Station] undertakes free distribution of food, clothes, and medicines" (Hurtado Izquierdo 1961: 40–41). Apart from those goods, a shotgun and some metal goods were also distributed, as can be inferred from several comments in the same publication. Characteristically enough, much less emphasis is placed on the latter gifts, which are especially significant for the Panare, since they provided them with what they really wanted. Actually, the former gifts were much more significant to the government than to the Panare. In using these goods, the Panare could be seen as participating in Venezuelan culture in a small way. Such a distribution of gifts requires further examination.

Although it is not specified in the publication under consideration, the distribution of gifts clearly had to take place sometime during the dry season. Heavy supplies had to be brought by truck, and trucks cannot travel in this area during the rainy season. This supposition is confirmed by the photographs published by Hurtado Izquierdo. The dry season is the period of abundance for the Panare (see Dumont 1976:61), so that distribution of food (consisting of rice, cans of sardines, and sugar) was superfluous at this time. Ironically, rice is the Venezuelan staple, but at this time of year, yams, manioc, and bananas are plentiful in Panare gardens. To eat canned food is, of course, to eat Venezuelan food, but the distribution took place when the Panare fish supply was at its peak. Finally, whereas the Panare truly love sugar, they produce it themselves in abundance, for the main part of the dry season in the form of sugarcane and at the very end of it with honey.

Clothes are another consumptive good which the Panare used at the time of my fieldwork whenever they were in the presence of outsiders. As I became a familiar figure in Turiba Viejo, this behavior was abandoned in my presence. Clothing has recently been adopted because of the constant pressure which has been exerted upon them by the outside world. This pressure has taken two forms: gifts and mockery. This distribution completely contradicts the statement that "the natives may go half-naked. . . . But this represents . . . the rational adaptation—without vain prejudices—to the weather conditions with which they are confronted" (Hurtado Izquierdo 1961: 33). Of course, it proves that the government, despite its claims, was itself not immune to those "vain prejudices." In fact, not only do the Indians have no need for clothes—clothing is actually harmful to them, and an ethnocentric conception of decency results in gifts which are really poisoned apples. Clothes get dirty and soon become the vehicle for diseases when people do not use soap. Furthermore, the Panare sweat in their clothes, wear them wet, and catch colds, which often worsen into fatal respiratory diseases.

Medicine distribution may seem different but in fact is not less dangerous. At first, the medicines, mainly aspirin and penicillin, appeared quasi-miraculous to the Panare, and even when they did not cure at least did not harm them. Yet, at the time of my fieldwork, most adults in Turiba Viejo were addicted to aspirin because the commercial brand, *cafenol*, contains caffeine. The average consumption of *cafenol* was over 15 pills a week per adult, one pill containing half a milligram of acetylsalicylic acid. Still worse, penicillin was self-injected in quantity by the Indians under almost any pretext. Since needles were not sterilized, I am still puzzled by the absence of infections. When I arrived, any infectious disease was resistant to penicillin treatment, and I had to turn to other antibiotics.

Although these gifts were either irrelevant or harmful to the Panare, metal goods were an entirely different matter, since otherwise they could only be acquired by going to the peripheral marketplace. Since native pottery had already disappeared from the area, metal pots and plates were used year-round in the preparation, conservation, and consumption of food. Machetes were used, together with axes, in the clearing of the gardens, and worn-out machetes were recycled for making spear and harpoon heads.

At least one gun was also presented, which the adult sons of Domingo Barrios still had in their possession when I arrived. With this gun Manuel Blanco had acquired personal prestige in the eyes of the other members of his local group, but it was certainly not the "most promising symptom of advance in the process of transculturation and adaptation of a Panare Indian to a progressist way of life," as has been claimed (Hurtado Izquierdo 1961: 20). This gun could have been the beginning of a shift in hunting techniques affecting the Panare mode of production, thus their economic system and finally their whole culture. Such was not the case. In most local groups, there is generally one antiquated shotgun, but the new weapon has not replaced more traditional weapons such as blowguns and spears. The main reason for this is that the gun requires costly cartridges to which the Panare have little access. Of course, the case was different with my own shotgun, since they could use it at no cost at all.

The very same day that this distribution took place, the Panare were "initiated" into the practice of official barter and trade. Two lots of goods stood by the Station: the first, for barter with the Panare in exchange for basketry; the second, for sale to the Creoles and the Panare. But the results of this operation did not fully meet the expectations of the government. In fact, the Panare did not undergo the drastic culture change that had been hoped for. While the Panare got used to barter and trade at the official Station, their tonka-bean production remained as unpredictable as ever. The Panare continued to exchange with their *compadres*, who were in fact competing with the Station and had greater flexibility than the Station in terms of exchange rates, but the official barter provided a kind of guarantee for the Panare output. Besides, the Station was not perceived by the Panare as a shop per se, because the civil servant in charge of it was a Creole from Turiba Nuevo whom the Panare quickly saw as a sort of super-*compadre*, the one who had the best choice of products in the area. The change that was ultimately introduced was only a tendency toward centralization and a better rate of exchange for the Panare, but it did not result in any increase in the Panare's output. Trade was nothing new, any more than barter was. Trade indeed is viewed by the Panare as an indirect form of barter; money is not perceived as a general equivalent, but only as the equivalent of certain goods. Everything remained fixed in the context of the system of communication between Creoles and Panare.

Predictably, within a year or two, the official barter collapsed, and the program which had encouraged steady tonka-bean production by the Panare failed. The production of tonka beans was not increased, because the Panare used the Station only as a convenient place for target marketing. Since the Panare could use surplus horticultural products from their gardens, they did not need to harvest tonka beans, and they did not. In fact, the Panare did not depend entirely upon the Station for obtaining cash, because they could go to sell their baskets in Caicara. Agricultural products are heavy to carry and can be bartered locally, whereas basketry may be bulky to carry but is rather light. For what one individual can carry, the profit realized with basketry sold at Caicara is about 100 times the profit realized from horticultural products sold or bartered at Turiba Nuevo. Therefore, practically all the baskets are reserved for the distant market. Neither is there any need to increase basket production for the local market, since the local *compadre* is unlikely to buy baskets, and agricultural products are at hand to be exchanged at practically no labor cost.

To sum up, trade and barter were developed at the Station because it was convenient within the preestablished frame of communication between Panare and Creoles but did not disrupt the trade and barter with individual, local Creoles. Nor did it halt journeys to peripheral marketplaces at which the Panare could obtain goods unavailable at the Station. From the government viewpoint, the program was a failure. Not only had tonka-bean production *not* been increased, but their whole attempt at stimulating culture change had been absorbed into the pattern of the preexisting system of communication between Creoles and Panare. Apparently, in this case, the event had been unable to disrupt the structure, and yet one question remains unanswered.

The gifts were distributed by the government and were apparently not reciprocated. Some goods were introduced that previously had been unknown among the Panare. While it was difficult to conceptualize these goods within the preexisting system, it was by no means impossible. I have indicated that the Station was ruled by a Creole and that it was not perceived as an official Station but rather as the house of a super-*compadre*. In a similar way, the gifts were not distributed by the *doctores* themselves but by the Creoles, and not by just any Creole but by the leaders of the Peasants' Union (S.A.), whose head was "Coronel" Domingo Flores, one of the two founders of the Creole settlement. The Panare of the area recognized in him not a *doctor* at all, but a Creole with special status as *cacique* of the Creoles. In fact, they still referred to him as a *tatto iyan* (headman of the Creoles) at the time of my fieldwork. The distinction may appear subtle, but is quite important, for the giver was at the same time Creole and *iyan*. As the Panare understand the situation, Creoles do not give away, but headmen do. Indeed, headmen do not give but redistribute, which is exactly what the "Coronel" was doing. He had received gifts from the *doctores*, and the Creoles who in turn were passing them to the Panare were obeying the *cacique*. For the Panare receivers, the giver was not the distant *doctores*, but the headman of the Creoles, thus the Creole mediator between the Panare and the government agents. At the same time, the distribution was confined to a homogeneous circle, for the gifts were not made to the Panare in general but were made specifically to Manuel Blanco, the Panare headman, who in turn redistributed them to the members of his *tapatakyen*. Therefore, the hook of the gifts was totally unbaited; the gifts were not really from the *doctores*, but an exchange between Manuel Blanco and his *compadre* the "Coronel" which had only been catalyzed by the presence of the *doctores*. In Manuel Blanco's opinion, the cycle of exchange with them was closed the following day by the visit paid to the Panare settlement by the same *doctores*. Strictly speaking, from the Panare viewpoint, the *doctores* had given nothing at all.

In brief, the Panare had been able to co-opt the intervention of the government and to play out the event in their own structural terms. Such intervention had failed because it remained compatible with the communication system established between Creoles and Panare and had been interpreted in these terms. Failure had resulted from the fact that the government had been neither forceful in its attempt at cultural change nor convincing to the Panare, who remained culturally safe.

The last convulsion of officialdom in Turiba came about with the presidential visit of 1965 which had allowed Marquito and Felipe Casanova to visit Caracas, and Domingo Barrios to fantasize about it. Brief as it had been, this action in a way had a greater impact than the earlier gift distribution. It was an interpersonal contact. The late headman of Turiba Viejo had also made the trip to Caracas and, according to Marquito, considered the president his *compadre*, although no baptism had been performed. Hence I, too, was a relative of the president. My arrival with the gendarme stood as proof of this connection because, after all, was not the Presidential Palace in Caracas guarded by uniformed men?

The electoral shift of power to President Caldera in March 1969, of which Domingo Barrios had learned from the Creoles, made the matter simple. However, in reporting the news to the other members of his local group, he had already reinterpreted it. According to him, my father—the big headman of the Creoles—had died, and his brother-in-law was taking over, because I was but a miserly little headman and did not belong to the same *tapatakyen*. In reality, of course, Raúl Leoni had not died; his party had only lost the elections to Rafael Caldera; and both men were unrelated not only to me but also to each other. The incident, however, was revealing, because I had never before been so specifically and explicitly linked to the government by anybody else in the settlement. Nor did I ever get closer to real power than by having, albeit in Panare fantasy, a former Venezuelan president for "father" and a present one for "father-in-law." I never learned whether my "son" had made that story up or had misunderstood what the Creoles told him. It was probably a combination of both, and given the idiom in which it was expressed, it immediately made sense to everyone in the settlement.

In fact, the ability of Domingo Barrios to relate to the unfamiliar, to reformulate his experience in a culturally meaningful idiom, was his proper genius. He could "explain" everything, and it made him the person in the settlement who was closest to being an innovator. After all, he always took the most care of outsiders. He also had brought back a *cuatro*—a four-stringed, guitar-like Creole instrument —to the settlement and mercilessly scraped it for hours on end in a way that was most unpleasing to my ears. It was he, too, who had introduced the cross as a motif in a Panare ritual. Although he had certainly seen such a cross at the *Americano*'s as he said at first, he had witnessed earlier a much more dramatic display of the Catholic paraphernalia on another occasion which he narrated to me with humorous accuracy.

As far as I know, there had been no regular contacts between the Panare and missionaries prior to World War II. The first missionary report comes from a priest (Antolínez 1944). Despite the abundance —a superficial one at that—of his later papers (1946*a*, 1946*b*, 1947*a*, 1947*b*, 1952*a*, 1952*b*), Antolínez gives no indication of any attempt on his part to convert the Panare. Missionary activity on the Catholic side has been, in fact, a one-man affair conducted by the archbishop of Ciudad Bolivar (who appeared in a previous chapter). No Panare came to his see, which is too remote from their territory, until the archbishop became interested in their souls. He began touring different Panare settlements, but another event definitely crystallized his missionary project.

In the spring of 1966, a suspended bridge over the Orinoco, a very short distance upstream from Ciudad Bolivar, was inaugurated. It was the first bridge over the Orinoco and is still unique. It was quite a technical achievement, and the Venezuelan government was rightly proud of this infrastructural investment. This called for a celebration, and the "First Great Fair of the Orinoco" was programmed simultaneously with the inauguration of the bridge. In due time Ciudad Bolivar became a gigantic exhibition city. The Indians of Bolivar State were invited to participate in the exhibition—as objects rather than subjects. The architect of the Indian meeting was the archbishop. "The basic idea . . . was to have each tribe build their house and in there, in front of the visitors, have the Indians produce their respective crafts" (Armellada 1967: 93). With the collaboration of the Venezuelan Air Force, a few Panare as well as other native representatives of Bolivar State were brought to be exhibited in Ciudad Bolivar. I do not know exactly how many Panare were gathered on that occasion, but there were at least several individuals from the Turiba area, Domingo Barrios and his immediate family among them. Each Indian group danced, and a missionary reported, "They [the visitors] dashed shouting 'The Indians!' in the same way that the colonists ran away to hide in their houses at the arrival of the redskins. But what was most important, the extraordinary cultural value which they beheld, this nobody saw" (Arribas 1967: 100–101). The event was still remembered in Turiba Viejo by Felipe Casanova as the craziest thing he had ever seen; Domingo Barrios, of course, had seen it as a lot of fun. A few machetes and knives and the thrilling pleasure of a ride in a plane had convinced him.

This event, which at first glance had little impact on Panare life, turned out to be the occasion for the prelate to obtain more, and in fact, decisive, support from the government to install a mission not in the area of Turiba as originally planned but in the area of Candelaria. This took place during the winter of 1969. To my distress, I discovered that the great plan was "to concentrate" the Panare, which sounded to me too reminiscent of concentration camps. I shall not dwell upon this intervention not only because I have reported it in detail elsewhere (Dumont 1972) but also because, disastrous as its effects were, this first mission among the Panare was too remotely located from Turiba Viejo to have any direct impact upon its people.

The Protestant couple in Caicara were remote from Turiba Viejo too, and yet they played an important role in the lives of Marquito and his people. Their situation is distinct from that of their Catholic counterparts, because in addition to religious differences, their social and ethnic background, their culture, their training, and their techniques are all different. Their target, however, is identical: the Christianization of the Indians. Unless one considers primitive religion as a mere cultural epiphenomenon, which no serious anthropologist would do, this amounts to total destruction of the culture, since the fundamentalist tradition is particularly loath to tolerate any other religious expression. Conversion, however, had not yet taken place with the Panare.

Protestant penetration was initiated by the New Tribes Mission from Colombia after World War II. A good sense of organization and serious financial backing from the United States helped them disperse widely in Venezuelan Guiana. For twenty years, Don Carlos and his wife had made little or no effort at converting the Panare. They had concentrated their efforts, although with little success, upon the Creoles of Caicara. In fact, following the recurrent pattern of Protestant proselytism, no conversions could be undertaken without prior knowledge of the language, which Don Carlos and his wife had not yet mastered. They were obviously preparing the terrain for others who would follow them, and a few years after my departure, a Protestant mission with different personnel settled north of Turiba Viejo in the area of Colorado. Slower to start, better planned and executed, the Protestant intervention is far more efficient than the Catholic one, which does not mean it is less dangerous to the Panare.

In Caicara, Don Carlos and his wife welcomed the visiting Panare, attempting in this way to learn the Indian language gradually. Their role, however, cannot be understood without examining the long-range trading expeditions of the Panare to market centers like Caicara, for it was in this context that the missionaries managed to have their impact upon the Indians. Their skill consisted in making themselves useful, if not indispensable, to the Panare so as to become more efficiently involved in their culture.

As far as my Creole informants could remember, there had always been such Panare expeditions, although the nature of these journeys had been considerably altered during the recent past. Fifteen years earlier, it was most unusual to see women reaching Caicara and even more rare to see them dressed in anything other than their miniloincloth. At the time of my fieldwork, however, it was unusual to be in Caicara without meeting at least one Panare. There were still few women who came to town, but when they did, they always dressed the Creole way. The existence of a truck path from Caicara to La Urbana provided the opportunity for easier and more frequent trips to this Creole center. During the dry season, the only time of the year when motorized traffic was possible, an average of two trucks (or jeeps) per week undertook the Caicara–Turiba round trip. When the Panare were not pressed by an emergency, they usually waited along the track and hitchhiked in the truck of a Creole *compadre*. The attitudes of truck and jeep drivers varied greatly, some asking payment for the service, some refusing to carry any Panare. In any case, these rides were often the source of trouble. The Creoles gave priority to Creole riders who, if they were not relatives (blood kin, fictive kin, or affines), were supposed to pay cash for the fare. As for the Panare, they did not understand why some empty vehicles would pass by without picking them up, while others would stop even if they were overloaded and would add a few Panare to the heterogeneity of their cargo for free.

In Turiba Viejo, each family head made one trip each year to Caicara, while adult bachelors made two. They did not always obtain a ride and sometimes had to walk the 180 km which separate Caicara from Turiba, a three-day walking distance. By late May, all motor traffic was halted by the rainfall, but some individuals still undertook the trip at that time, forfeiting their chance of getting a ride. After completing the planting of the gardens, it was a good time to go to Caicara in order to sell baskets and obtain supplies for the whole rainy season during which the Station would be short of almost everything. The "need" for blankets and mosquito nets would soon be at its peak: nights were cooler, and mosquitoes, regaining new vigor in the inundated savannas, became ferocious.

There was some additional motivation for such trips to Caicara, somewhat equivalent to a reversal of touristic eagerness for exoticism. In the clumsy local movie theatre, Marquito and the other members of his settlement could watch colorful "redskin" massacres for free. Bars offered the permanent spectacle of turbulent Creoles drowning in the artificial paradises of alcohol, nicotine, caffeine, and penny gambling. The activities of an odoriferous river port which flourished at cotton-picking time had its attractions, too. But Caicara was also a place where a Panare could meet people from other local groups, where news and gossip were exchanged, and where one could possibly meet a sexy classificatory cross-cousin. It was a place offering topsy-turvy images and sensations.

Caicara may be characterized as the "peripheral market" (Bohannan and Dalton [1962] 1965: 1–32) of the Panare who come to sell products (essentially basketry) for cash to Creole merchants (trade intermediaries) or individuals (buying for themselves without intention of reselling), for whom, in turn, such a market is not peripheral. In this sense, the Panare can be recognized as "target-marketers [who] engage in marketing sporadically to acquire a specific amount of cash income for a specific expenditure" (Bohannan and Dalton 1965: 11).

In this respect, Don Carlos played a privileged role. All the Panare marketing activities focused around his backyard, and he encouraged, albeit indirectly, their target marketing.

On their way to Caicara, the Panare were able to rely upon Creole households for food and shelter. But this pattern of rural hospitality stopped once the city limits were crossed. Thirty years ago, Caicara was probably much less important than it was in the late sixties, and the rural model of hospitality could still be followed. At the time of my fieldwork, however, this problem was greatly eased, if not totally solved, by Don Carlos. His partly roofed backyard was used by the Panare to sling their hammocks, and each visitor was fed during his stay. Obviously the security of obtaining food and shelter was a factor which favored Panare movements to the marketplace.

Don Carlos' backyard had turned into a center of marketing activity, which was different from the interaction that was taking place between the other inhabitants of Caicara and the visiting Panare. There were two different spheres of exchange. The first, taking place in the Creole town and motivating Panare movements, involved goods that men bought and sold for cash. Because the Panare were target marketing, prices fluctuated greatly. Usually, in the trading of basketry, both sides anticipated bargaining, but the flexibility of the Panare's final price was affected by the "target," the price being higher if he needed more cash. When he had fulfilled his expectations, if he had baskets left over, he would sell them at lower prices so as not to have to carry them back home.

The other sphere of exchange resulted from the existence of the first; it did not occur in the same place and did not involve the same participants or the same goods. The second market was not a determining reason for going to Caicara but was still a target marketing operation, though based upon a principle of reciprocation where cash was not normally involved. The marketing place was the backyard of Don Carlos, and the transactions involved only the Panare, mostly men. The main difference from other exchanges between Panare is that they were not based upon kinship links but essentially upon economic "needs." In the absence of kinship bonds, that is, of social obligations to exchange, an individual exchanged goods only for the product he desired. Finally, it was a way of exchanging Panare products as well as excess goods acquired from other Indians. For instance, from the Piaroa, the people of Turiba Viejo had acquired resin in larger amounts than they needed, which they then retraded with Panare individuals who had no direct access to the Piaroa goods but could offer products, such as curare, unavailable in Turiba.

The backyard of Don Carlos was essentially the place where goods were traded between partners who otherwise would not have been in contact with each other, because their settlements were too far apart and their kinship links no longer activated. The Panare of Turiba Viejo no longer have any contact with the Panare of Candelaria except in this backyard. So far, we have seen Don Carlos in the role of a double catalyst who mediated exchanges both between Panare and Panare and between the Panare and the Creoles of Caicara. This already important role of Don Carlos was further enhanced for the Panare by the fact that at the time he was their unique source of an essential means of production: blowguns. The acquisition of these blowguns was not the only, but certainly the main, motivation for Panare target marketing.

Blowguns are used by every initiated male for hunting birds and monkeys. The blowgun is a very frail weapon of which the Panare take the greatest care; it may crack, warp, or break, and after two or three years of use must be replaced; thus the demand for blowguns is quite important throughout the Panare territory. The Panare prepare their own darts and hunting poison but they do not manufacture their blowguns, for they lack the necessary reeds (*Arundinaria* sp.) in their environment.

The Panare used to trade for blowguns with their neighbors. Prior to the arrival of Don Carlos, in the Sierra Cerbatana–Turiba area they were bartered from the Piaroa, while in the Candelaria– middle Cuchivero area they were bartered from the Shikano (also known as the Hoti). At the time of my fieldwork, barter with the former had almost disappeared, while barter with the latter was still active. As a consequence, the Panare of the Candelaria–middle Cuchivero area had little reason to buy blowguns from Don Carlos. Whether as a cause or consequence, they had no baskets to sell, and Caicara is very far from where they are located. However—this did inspire a few trips to the Creole town—the blowguns obtained from the Shikano area were considered to be of lower quality than those Don Carlos sold, which were manufactured by the Ye'cuana (also known as Makiritare), a fact which requires some explanation.

In her well-documented monograph on the Ye'cuana, Arvelo-Jimenez reports that "the two [Catholic] mission centers, Santa Maria de Erebato and Canaracuni, are highly attractive places for acquiring industrial goods. . . . Some upstream [Ye'cuana] obtain on credit out-

board motors, gas, radios and record-players at the mission centers"
(1974: 30). Among the crafts sold to the missionaries are blowguns.
She also notes that "the Baptist missionaries have no trading center"
(1974: 30, footnote). Yet, as I have witnessed, the Catholic missionaries resell blowguns to the Protestant post in Ciudad Bolivar, which
ships them on to Don Carlos in Caicara (see map 3).

Among the Ye'cuana, price fluctuations were not a function of
target marketing, which tended to moderate their range. In Caicara,
the price of a blowgun in 1967 varied from 30 to 45 Bs, according to
its quality. As a service to the Panare, Don Carlos resold the weapons
at their buying price. According to him, not only did he make no profit
at all, but he incurred a net loss, because some blowguns would never
be bought by the Panare. A Panare did not buy just any blowgun, but
chose carefully from among Don Carlos' stock. In his selection, the
Panare always unwaxed the mouthpiece to pull out the inner tube, in
order to examine it thoroughly, rejecting most of them for technical
defects which totally escaped the layman's eye. The selection of the
desired item did not automatically mean the immediate completion of

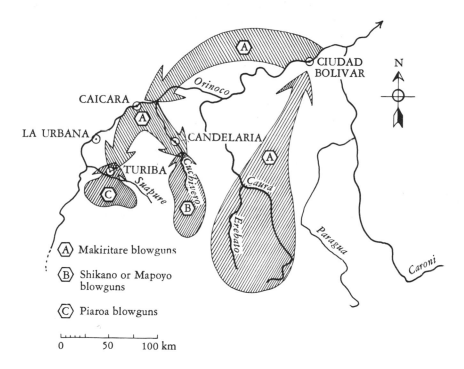

Map 3. *Blowgun circulation*

the transaction. Very often, a man made a first trip to Caicara to select and reserve a blowgun and inquire about its price. Then, he returned to his settlement and made enough baskets to acquire, on a second trip to Caicara, enough cash to conclude the blowgun transaction.

In providing blowguns to the Panare, Don Carlos added a new dimension to his already important role, since he focused on himself an intertribal trade between two Indian groups which otherwise were no longer in contact: the Panare and the Ye'cuana. The dynamics of such mediation are important, because at the same time it affected two other Indian groups, the Shikano and the Piaroa, without as yet annihilating trade with these groups. The Panare of the Candelaria–middle Cuchivero area still relied greatly upon Shikano blowguns. In addition, in the absence of Don Carlos, who went back to the United States for a year, blowgun trade with the Piaroa was temporarily resumed, although initially it had been the unreliability of the Piaroa providers which had created the market for Don Carlos' blowguns.

The striking role of Don Carlos takes on a linguistic expression. In the eyes of the Panare of Turiba Viejo at least, he is considered neither completely a Creole nor a *doctor-iyan*, but participates in both. The fact that Domingo Barrios and Marquito always referred to him as *Americano*, rather than as *tatto* or Don Carlos, is a reflection of his in-between position. This was reinforced by his ability to utter a few Panare sentences and to deal with something other than Spanish, in this case English. Although he is not a *compadre* and Creole hospitality has disappeared in Caicara, Don Carlos' house is ironically like that of a Creole *compadre* where one is fed and sheltered. His backyard is the locus of mediation between local groups which undertake exchanges there, but in his absence. His backyard is also a Panare enclave in a town which is peripheral to their territory; it remains off limits to the Creoles and yet determines access to cash for the Panare. His house, finally, is the locus of an intertribal exchange, indirect and mediated by Don Carlos himself. Through this impressive series of mediations, the Panare have the illusion of acting within their own cultural frame at the very moment when they are most endangered by the setting through means which, though antithetical to those set by both the government and the Catholic missionaries, tend toward an equally disruptive end.

At first sight, of course, nothing in the actions of Don Carlos seems disruptive. On the contrary, his action is not forced upon the Panare; it is they who come to him. Yet this is but an illusion, for two reasons. First, the actions of Don Carlos must be understood in their larger frame, which involves the conversion—that is, the cultural destruction—of the Panare. His hospitality in Caicara, Christian as it may look, was not purely disinterested philanthropy but clearly a bait to make the Panare dependent upon him, so that they could be evangelized. The establishment of a full-fledged Protestant mission in the Colorado area after my departure stands as proof of this in-depth penetration attempt. Second, luring the Panare to Caicara and facilitating their accommodation in the Creole town had another result. Much more efficiently than the government had been able to, it introduced them to a truly mercantile behavior. This was a subtle change indeed, which had not yet fulfilled all its promises, but it was a real one. The more the Panare came to Caicara, the more they learned about buying and selling. Even though they had not yet gone beyond target marketing, they experienced, if not understood, the economic laws of supply and demand.

To sum up, the Protestant intervention was subtle, where the Catholic one had been brutal and the government one ignorant. But, in all the cases examined, the aim was strikingly similar: to enforce culture change upon the Panare. Short of sheer violence, the efficacy of any intervention depends on its being meaningful to the Panare, and this is where the Protestant action succeeded most. The Panare do not perceive qualitative differences between Creoles, missionaries, and *doctores*. Ultimately, all are varieties of Creole, even though, for the Panare, Don Carlos could embody more singularities than anybody else. As a result, the elaboration of a new system of communication between Panare and Venezuelans, oriented toward the acculturation of the former, necessarily passes through the imperative of compatibility with the system set for dealing with the Creoles. Nevertheless, as the Creole-Panare system is a regulator of change and the system that the Venezuelans want and tend to impose is an innovator, as such, they are contradictory.

However, the contradiction is purely analytical insofar as it is not transformed into the incompatibility of the two systems. As long as Venezuelan action is compatible with the previous system, it either has no effect at all or provokes an inner restructuring of elements of the system—within the system itself—and thus does not bring about the hoped-for change. But, as I have shown, whoever the agents of communication were, they all attempted to control, in one way or another, the economy and/or the language of the Panare. It is precisely at this point that the limits of structural invariance of both systems of communication are located. So far, the government action has failed: it has been totally neutralized by the Panare, since it fell completely within their old system. But the action of the missionaries is far more efficient in the attempt to control the Panare way of life: the Catholic trying very quickly to seduce the Panare, which had the effect of abusing them; the Protestant, with more subtlety, making himself indispensable so as to penetrate slowly but more deeply the culture upon which he wants to act.

In either case, the semantic abuse is complete. Messages are transmitted in a familiar code. But the messages involve a double entendre. They refer to a double code—one is familiar, through which the Panare decipher, the other is ultimately the reference code of the missionaries and leads, whatever the intentions of the latter, to the destruction of Panare cultural identity. Whether it takes the form of an economic or a spiritual imperialism, every action oriented toward the cultural change of the Panare has to start within the preexisting system of communication between Creoles and Panare. In this way, Panare culture will be destroyed and replaced by a system which the Panare are forced into but which satisfies the Venezuelan agents and, beyond them, Western civilization. In confusing acculturation and enculturation, all these cultural innovators remain, consciously or unconsciously, at play in the fields of semantics.

11. *On Effect and Affect*

The historical events I have just related were not perceived as a totality by the Panare. Indeed, they could not be, because the self-consciousness of this tribal group is not expressed in any institution which would be pan-tribal. The experience of the encroachment and aggression of the West against the Panare is seen by individuals as something fragmented. The totalizing—to borrow a Sartrian term—is effected by me in the domain of the logos. To this logos corresponds not a single, unified Panare praxis, but many different ones. At worst, it is that of each individual Panare; at best, that of the different local groups, if the headman is interpreted as the focal point of the local group, as its active consciousness. Clearly I am the Panaro*logist*—the one who is reflective—while they were and remained themselves, coping in various ways with the diversity of their sociocultural experience. To put it in different terms, the aggression of the West did not produce a unified Panare response. Quite to the contrary, it generated a whole array of effects and affects on which I would like to focus now.

Nobody in Turiba Viejo had realized yet that the southern expansion of Venezuela was a direct threat to Panare life. So far (and indeed with some justification) even Marquito, poised and concerned as he was, believed that in each contact situation, the Creoles, the Venezuelans, the missionaries—not to mention the anthropologist—had all been largely outsmarted. The common experience in the local group had been to comply with practically any formality which was requested of them to obtain whatever they wanted. On that, my "brother" was explicit. "When in Caicara at the house of the *Americano*, you do not fart or belch, you do not smoke, you do not drink. You wait until he is asleep. This way, you can sleep [in his backyard] and eat his food." But then, he could also draw a parallel which I found unflattering, yet evident. "We talk a lot with you; you are crazy writing, taking pictures, and we get your fishing line, rice, kerosene, a lot."

Such pragmatism was striking enough, but on another occasion he expressed a rather different opinion, which indirectly showed that he could perceive the Venezuelan encroachment upon his people. "It is no good for the *muchachos*," as he often called the young unmarried men of his settlement, "to work for the Creoles." This comment was made when the Creole in charge of the Station had asked him for some labor to open up a stretch of jeep path in the bush. From the Creole viewpoint, this job should be done by the Panare, because the subsequent possibility of motor traffic traveling to Turiba Viejo would allow a sick Panare to be evacuated to the Caicara hospital. This was a sneaky argument, for the advantages were more evident for the Creoles. They would be able to ride jeeps and trucks between Turiba Nuevo and Pijiguao during the dry season. Ultimately, Marquito's opinion did not prevail in his group, and the jeep path was opened, but he let the man at the Station know that he did not want any *tatto* to come to Turiba Viejo with his truck.

Marquito was occasionally nostalgic about the past, when the Panare lived deeper in the forest and further away from the Creoles. Did he refer to the time of his childhood or to a more remote time? I do not know, but there were then very few head of cattle in the savanna, no landing strip for small airplanes in the vicinity, no hitchhiking rides to Caicara. However, nostalgic or not, the *conquista del Sur* had not yet shrunk his territory. In his experience, the Panare could still expand, their groups fission, their hunting and fishing remain excellent. In fact, even though Marquito did not want to see any more *tatto* hanging around his settlement—one *tansipoto* was enough—it was he who had pushed for maintaining his *pereka* conveniently close to the Station.

Marquito was occasionally nostalgic about the past, when the Panare's viewpoint about the outside world. In many respects, he was torn by two contradictory tendencies. A certain cultural conservatism made him consider any more acculturation as a danger which he could only perceive in part. But simultaneously, his curiosity attracted him to the outside world as long as he could maintain the initiative in these contacts. He was not the last to go and pay a visit to a Creole *compadre* just for the fun of it. His trips to Caicara indeed had economic motivations, but he also viewed them as a touristic endeavor, something basically pleasurable.

The opinions and attitudes of the other members of his settlement expressed the same paradox. Some individuals were impatient *with* change, others were impatient *for* change. But, wherever one placed the emphasis, the other aspect was there too. Women had by far the most conservative attitude. This is understandable since they, unlike the men, had little occasion to deal with the outside world. But, as much in their case as in that of men, reactions to the pressure of the outside world were not uniformly mixed and balanced as they were for Marquito. Age was of course a factor, too, although not as much as I had first expected. For instance, Hortensia, who was indeed an elderly woman, was conservative in almost all respects. She had refused to talk to me for a long time and she never draped a blanket over her loincloth in the presence of Creoles or slipped into a dress when in Caicara. And in the end, she had resigned herself to marrying me under male pressure. To be sure, it was an emotional relief to her that the marriage did not occur, even though it did not help her economic situation.

In contrast, Felipe Casanova's younger wife, Natalia (*acim*-TV 48), who was still in her teens, was infinitely more open. Undoubtedly this was a matter of personality, but at the same time I could see in her an altogether different attitude vis-à-vis the outside world. It did not take long for her to change the fear of me that she was expected

Pl. 17. *Domingo Barrios' mother, Hortensia (into-TV 44)*

to display into a game. She displayed her fear with a good sense of theatricality and more and more joyfully played at being afraid of me, as the children sometimes did. While Hortensia was extremely devious about asking me for aspirin or other things, Natalia would come straight to the point and, for example, borrow my can opener, systematically "forgetting" to give it back. I could talk more readily and more seriously with Luisa (*acim*-TV49) and with Elena (*into*-TV30), but they would never borrow a can opener from me. With Natalia, not only was there a flirtatious playfulness, but she was attracted more than any other woman in the settlement by my "toys." Anybody else would open sardine cans with a knife, but she would not. Sometimes she came to borrow my multibladed Swiss knife or to look through my camera. At one point, she wanted a taste of all my medicines! In brief, she was daring, and her curiosity constantly overcame her fear, so that she appeared at times to act in an "un-Panare" way.

When she accompanied Felipe Casanova to Turiba Nuevo, she entered the Station instead of staying outside as women usually did and would then ask me what all those products in the store were. One day, while Felipe Casanova was bartering with a Creole outside the latter's home, she entered and inspected the kitchen corner, startling the Creole's wife. By Panare standards, her behavior was extreme in its uninhibitedness, but she was considered neither a "libber" nor a "lost woman." In fact, she did not step out of her expected role despite appearances. She was just going further than any other woman had in following her curiosity and her attraction to novelty, and yet staying within the boundaries of her sexual role. It is not that her curiosity was greater than that of any other woman, but that her willingness to follow it was. And yet, she "played" exclusively with female toys or sexually unmarked ones; she wanted to light my kerosene stove and lamp, to use my whistling kettle, and so on. Similarly, my camera, radio, tape recorder, books, and pens could be manipulated because they were too exterior to the Panare culture to be anything other than sexually neutral. But under no conditions would she ever touch my shotgun, a weapon and therefore a male object. Look at it, yes; touch it, no. Therefore she still had a number of cultural inhibitions. The curiosity, the attraction, the appeal of the outside were all there in her, but the fear of going too far was also there, even though it was minimized in her behavior.

In the continuum bounded by the shyness of Hortensia and the daringness of Natalia, all possible intermediary positions could be found in the settlement. Neither of these two women was a good informant. One was too withdrawn; the other, too playful. But Elena,

Marquito's wife, and Luisa, Guzmán's wife, were different. They also had to struggle with the same contradictory tendencies. But their position was more balanced, midway between fear and attraction, experiencing both at the same time. While Natalia would demand anything peremptorily, though never seriously, the other two women alluded to what they wanted and in this way disguised their desire. Moreover, it was more the fantasy of desire than true desire. When Elena told me that she enjoyed the music from the radio and that she would like to have one, I lent it to her for the day. Interestingly, she refused to borrow it, and when I left my set with her for the day, she did not play it at all. However, she came to me several times after this incident, asking me to put on the radio, which she could easily listen to from her own hut. My coffee and cigarettes were an even better indicator of these attitudes. The offer of a cigarette or a cup of coffee to Hortensia or, for that matter, to Teresa (*acim*-TV 34) was met with total disre-

Pl. 18. *Marquito's elder wife, Elena (into-TV 30)*

gard. They would not even acknowledge my offer. But Natalia would ask for both. As for Elena and Luisa, they would take one or the other if offered, but they would save the cigarettes for their husbands.

Even in this brief review of women's attitudes, it appears that it was much more than myself as an individual which was at stake in these dealings. It was I as a social being who was involved, for I was the embodiment of the outside world made present in their daily life. This came from my physical presence in Turiba Viejo, but it also came from the goods that I had brought with me, which were, conceptually at least, inseparable from me as a person. Such goods, just like my beard, were the signs of my otherness. And the women's reactions to these goods were largely identical with their reactions to me. Because women had little occasion to cope with outsiders, except when accompanied by men, I was the pretext and the instrument of their transaction with the Western world. To the extent that, in a real if limited sense, I had "forced" my stay in Marquito's group, I could be considered as a cultural broker, a sociocultural link between the Panare and the Western world. Even though I was different from the missionaries and civil servants who wanted to enforce cultural change, I was part of the same equation, but closer to the level of temptation than the level of enforcement.

In this sense, I was infinitely more than myself; I was a figure of the Western world, of its attractions and of its dangers. This was much more so for the group of women, largely confined to their settlement, than for men who had not had to wait for me to acquire a thorough experience of the West. Yet, for them, too, I was also a symbol of otherness, and their reactions to me paralleled their reactions to Western civilization. Marquito's relationship with me represented a middle ground, similar to that of his wife. He knew our respective positions, the ambiguity of our "brotherhood," its seriousness and its limitations. I also knew of his ambivalence about the world of the *tatto*. In fact, he could be fairly explicit about this sort of love-hate relation and the uneasiness of his situation. Although he was not as colorful as Domingo Barrios in his mimicry, he could mock the Creoles, the *doctores*, and the Protestant missionaries, and in so doing display an exceptionally acute sense of observation. The *benedicite* of the missionaries, the pretentiousness and arrogance of the *doctores*, the prudery of the Creoles: of all these Domingo Barrios could give a fierce parody. Marquito used them merely as illustrations of *tatto* foolishness. But he was also too confident of the values of his own culture to fear them as harbingers of Panare acculturation. At the same time, he clearly enjoyed the world outside, more to observe than to participate in. And yet, the story of

Pedro Castro remained unbelievable to him, properly un-understand-able, as it was to the marginal man's relatives who had expelled him from their settlement.

The Western world had already made its impact on some men in Turiba Viejo. For instance, this same story of Pedro Castro made in-finitely more sense to the adult sons of Domingo Barrios. In fact, it was largely under their influence that the truck-path clearing had been undertaken. It had been a first for them in terms of wage laboring. Ultimately, for a whole day of work, what had they gained? Material-ly, they had not been paid any money, but they had been given some canned goods and sugared water. However, as all of them readily pointed out, it had been great fun as a social event.

For Coronel Flores (*tose*-TV5), working for the Creoles was a way to get money, even though his experience had been decidedly to the contrary. With money, he hoped to buy a shotgun, and that was his way to justify wage laboring. But at the same time, save for the jeep path mentioned, he never did undertake any wage labor for the Cre-oles nor did he even seriously try to. The shotgun was his castle in the air.

Most of his talk was fantasy. The reality of wage laboring had much less appeal. Instead, and like most other men in the settlement, he was making baskets for target marketing. When he saw that I had bought several baskets from Marquito, he tried the hard sell on me, for the maximum price, and of course he became angry when I refused to buy any. He had quickly seen in me an easy opportunity and had made terrible baskets which he would not even have tried to sell in Caicara. In this case, his scheme did not work, but this tends to indi-cate that he had already internalized the profit-maximizing mechanism. Thus, although his modernism was fantasized, the Western model of economic rationality had already had an impact on him.

Actually, their father, Domingo Barrios, was much more of a modernist than Coronel Flores or any of his brothers. At first, this may seem paradoxical, because Domingo Barrios was all talk against the outside. There was not the least possible doubt left that he despised the Creoles, the *doctores*, and the missionaries. But at the same time, he was more influenced by them than anybody else in the settlement. In great contrast to any Panare man I have known, he was at ease with all of them and remained unthreatened by them. It was he who bor-rowed cultural trait after cultural trait and introduced them into the settlement.

Clothing or cosmetic items were his delights. There was also the *cuatro* he played mercilessly, the motif of the cross he had introduced in the Panare ritual, the piece of soap he cherished, the bottle of rum, the packs of cigarettes, and so on.

Curiously, all these items had come into his hands because of his sense of observation. These were the paraphernalia he liked to exhibit in order to put on an act against the *tatto*. At the same time, and even though they were pointers to mark his ridicule, they were also new items introduced into the Panare way of life. To him, the *tatto*—and that of course included me—were a spectacle he observed minutely, found extravagantly ridiculous, and used as a model for a derisive show at the time of the male common meal. So, he would go often— if not regularly—*paseando*, taking a walk to the Creoles, or sitting beside me for hours, observing, questioning, and avidly carrying out his own ethnographic investigations. I could see in him a distorted mirror image of myself, struggling between empathy and detachment.

With Domingo Flores, the problem was different. At first sight, he could have passed for the most modern of all the Panare men of Turiba Viejo. After all, the one bicycle in the settlement was his, and he also had a radio set, albeit defunct. These items, along with a fancy straw hat which I saw him wear on few occasions, constituted "his" Western world. Of these three goods, only the first had a use value, and even its value was limited, circumscribed to an occasional round trip to the Station. It could be used only in the savanna, and even then not without a good deal of struggling, because the gramineous vegetation got caught in the chain in a most unpleasant way. But Domingo Flores treasured his little-used bicycle, his broken-down radio, and his spiffy-looking straw hat, which he displayed proudly and regularly to me.

These treasured paraphernalia were put to different uses than those of Domingo Barrios. For Domingo Flores, their only function was not to be displayed within the settlement, except to me, but to the *tatto*. In fact, he was even proud to have been to Caicara once and to have visited the *Americano* with his bicycle. Yet, long-distance riding was not his forte, so he rode only to Turiba Nuevo and in Caicara and hitched a truck ride in between. For the occasion, and to my dismay, he once "borrowed" my glasses—through which he must have had a blurred vision of the Creole market town—exclusively to show off to the Creoles, and obviously not to the occasional Panare visitor, who was never thus favored with an exhibition of his *tatto* goods. In fact, since he could not carry the bicycle and baskets at the same time, the whole point of that trip to Caicara had been only to display these Western goods, mainly for Don Carlos' benefit. And yet, although he had gone to all this trouble to convince the outside world of his worthy modernity, it had not been undertaken to please anybody but himself. It was his version of the famous "when in Rome," so that no Creole would make fun of him. It is hardly necessary to add that his visibility had been increased rather than reduced by the bicycle and spectacles and that the result had been rather contrary to his expectations.

Upon his return to Turiba Viejo, he admitted that his trip had fallen short of its desired effect and complained bitterly at the insensitivity of the Creoles who "behave like dogs anyway." Only Don Carlos, who had complimented him on the bicycle, had found grace in his eyes. Paradoxically, and despite his all-out offensive "to go native" in Creole company, it was all only appearance, as he explained to me. The disguise was meant to give him a temporary Creole essence for the duration of his contact with them. Literally, from his viewpoint, he was becoming a Creole when he had to cope with them. But the superficiality of his pretense was complete. In many respects, he was less on the path of acculturation than Domingo Barrios; Domingo Flores was merely overemphasizing the formality displayed in the contact situation. Marquito had summed up well the Creole expectations that had to be satisfied if the Panare were to cope properly with them. To be fed outside of the settlement, the Panare constantly had to appear and behave in a restrained and repressed way. Domingo Flores had gone one step further, but none of *tatto* culture had been internalized by him. The ridiculousness of his disguise was not the expression of an identity crisis, but only the misreading of *tatto*-ness. In this sense, it was—true to form—a pure, if poor, disguise behind which he had hoped in vain to escape the vaguely perceived aggression of the West.

I could multiply almost endlessly these examples of the range of variations of Panare reactions to the West. Instead, I shall point out two cases that I perceived as opposite extremes. Mirón, despite his youth, was undoubtedly the most conservative among the men of Turiba Viejo. His resistance to me might have another explanation, as indicated earlier, but it was also a reaction against the Western world which I represented. Many elements could be brought forth as proof, but a few will suffice. As I noticed on several occasions at Turiba Viejo, his command of trade-Spanish was minimal and at any rate inferior to that of any other Panare male adult. Whenever he had to deal with a Creole, he managed to do so through an intermediary, generally his brother Andrés. However, his competence was slightly greater than his performance had led me to believe, something I realized very late in my fieldwork, when I discovered that he intervened in a trade-Spanish conversation only when he was directly concerned by it. One day, at the Station, I witnessed the following. A Creole asked him,

"Where is Marquito?" He replied in trade-Spanish, "I do not understand," and then turned to Andrés and said to him in Panare, "The Creole asks where Marquito is. I do not want to talk with him."

But there were other indications of his fierce cultural resistance. He made fewer baskets than any other man in the settlement, which was a way of limiting his target marketing and his possibility of acquiring Western goods. Altogether, he was not eager to go to Caicara. On one trip that he had nevertheless undertaken with Marquito, he had preferred to walk all the way rather than get a lift in a truck. This was astonishing enough to me, but then he was also the only one to refuse to eat the beef I boiled once for the male common meal. In fact, every single outside good he could dispense with, he would. As far as Turiba Viejo is concerned, he was the only man I knew who had never tasted beer or Coca-Cola. As he put it, "It is good for the Creoles." With some sense, his attitude—which I had to respect—was that the least contact was the best, and contrary to most other Panare his curiosity about the outside world was minimal. It was clear that my "adoption" had displeased him deeply. For him, I was an invasion all by myself. And that is where communication between the two of us broke down.

In complete opposition to such a recalcitrant viewpoint, Felipe Casanova was one of my best informants, patient and cooperative. But he was also the man most tempted by culture change. Not unlike Domingo Flores, he too had his Creole disguise. But it was much more than that. It was not a mere appearance. Not unlike Domingo Barrios, he too could mock the Creoles. But again, it was different and certainly a much milder social criticism. He enjoyed the outside world, was curious about it, and saw advantages to it. Within the limits of the Panare cultural norms, he tended to be a more adventurous entrepreneur than anybody else. He was well aware that Pedro Castro's case represented an unacceptable position, in that he had gone too far. But Felipe Casanova had similar, yet contained tendencies, and thereby allowed himself to be vulnerable to the impact of the Western world. The missionaries, the civil servants, and I amused and intrigued him. He had no intention of "abandoning" his culture and was not even an incipient deviant. But anything new attracted him. With him, the profit-making principle of marketing had been perfectly internalized, although the Protestant ethic had not (yet) killed his *joie de vivre*. On the contrary, for him it was marvelous to bring back "gadgets" from the outside world. One day it had been *ñopo*, the Piaroa drug, that he inhaled as he had seen his southern neighbors do. Another day, he came back to the settlement with socks and shoes and asked me to

Pl. 19. *Felipe Casanova* (naxtö-*TV 17*) *and his immediate family, "dressed up" to visit a Creole* compadre

confirm that they looked really good on him. Another time, he had somewhere acquired a potato peeler, which was soon discarded, as one might expect. In addition, his target marketing was more active than that of the other men of the settlement.

So far, however, his peregrination on the path of acculturation was limited. It is not so much that he was changing, but that he was open-minded about culture change. His acquisitions in terms of outside goods were few and hardly distinguished him from Domingo Flores or Domingo Barrios. But his whole attitude was different. He wanted a medical doctor or at least a nurse at Turiba Nuevo so the sick could be cured by Western means. He did not discard shamanism, but he wanted both, tradition *and* Western medicine. He also wanted to learn how to read and write but did not have the patience to do so. Instead of learning from me, he would ask me for a notebook and "write" in it. He was also able to compare his life with that of the Creoles, who "eat plain rice, while we have plenty of meat and fish." At the same time, because his travel experience among the Creoles was extensive, he was in the best position to see a grim future for the Panare. He knew from the Creoles that the Venezuelan government had planned the construction of a road nearby, and he was apprehensive about it. He also knew that missionaries would arrive someday and settle in the vicinity, and of that too he was apprehensive. In general terms, he would have liked to go toward the Western world, rather than witness the latter's impingement upon his territory. He was prompt to point out that when all these *tatto* came, they would bring more cattle to which the Panare would have no access and kill game and fish, thus forcing the Panare out. Someday, he would drive a jeep, but he knew well that this was only mouth-talk. Meanwhile, he enjoyed riding the *kanowa*—any means of transportation—of the *tatto*.

The Panare future would pass to his children, and he had contradictory views about what they would be confronted with. At times, it was all rosy on the horizon—he foresaw an increased technological consumption but paid no attention to the production process that it required. At times, it was all grim, because it would no longer be the way it used to be. My own perception of the situation was closer to the latter viewpoint. So far, acculturation among the Panare had been minimal, and the Panare tradition had been maintained. But it was very obvious that the West was awaiting the occasion to absorb the Panare, that is, to destroy them as such. So far, the impact of the West, its effects and affects, had been slight, although noticeable. But the children were affected differently, as I could see in their play. Play, of course, reveals what children internalize as culture. As Erikson puts it, "creative make-believe creates belief just because of its consequence in dealing with the facts of geography and history, with ready social actualities, and with the inner lives of the people" (1977: 64).

Upon my arrival, boys who were weaned and not yet initiated played with toy blowguns, with which lizards were tortured. A cruel game indeed, but this was also the expression of their fantasy of the adult world. Such a ritualization was indeed "a major link between the ego's propensity for orientation in space and time and the world views dominating (or competing in) a society" (Erikson 1977: 83). It thus was extraordinarily striking when new toys were created by the children as my fieldwork was drawing to an end. I observed *ciköxpwö*-TV19 play with an airplane and *kanapwey*-TV39 with a truck. The toys had been made of leaves and bark; the wheels were segments of sugarcane, with broken darts for the axles which allowed the toys to roll on the ground. It was difficult not to notice the radical shift of orientation in these children, not to perceive that their enculturation would have a decidedly different coloration than that of their parents. Because they were in the process of internalizing values foreign to their culture of orientation and experiencing the Western world im-

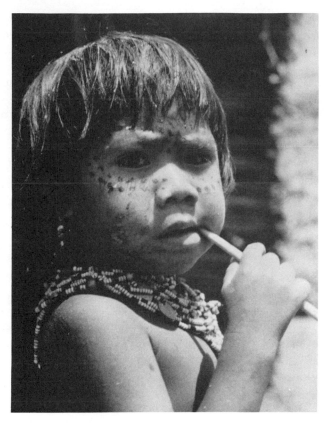

Pl. 20. *Felipe Casanova's daughter* nyamca-*TV*47

mediately, if only in fantasy, their vulnerability to it was becoming more obvious than ever. If the toys were the indicator that I believed they were, the future of the Panare was grim indeed.

It was mango time again—it must have been July 1969. I had spent the whole dry season of 1969 in and out of Turiba Viejo, visiting and taking censuses in other local groups. With the arrival of the rainy season, it had become more difficult to walk from settlement to settlement, but water transportation then became easier. So I decided to pay a visit to the Panare of the Candelaria area. It was my unfortunate experience to capsize with a good deal of irretrievable data (see Dumont 1976: 5). The experience was unforgettable. Suddenly everything was turning sour. I had not done much on this trip. The day before, in a Creole settlement, my whole supply of 5-Bolivar bills had been stolen. Now half my Panare culture had been engulfed by the waters of the Cuchivero. As my clothes were drying out, I cried, and felt relieved. I realized, too, that I was experiencing fieldwork fatigue.

The day before, I had felt overanxious to discover the who's who of the Panare settlement where I had stayed. I did not ask the right questions of Vicente, its headman, nor did I wander around as I usually did. I found the people there unpleasant and dirty. The boiled stingray they offered me had a muddy taste. The mosquitoes were biting too hard. It was too muggy. Most of this was a projection, and I came to realize it. I was longing for a fine Caracas restaurant, a bug-free environment, feminine perfumes, and metaphysical discussions. I just could not concentrate on anything at all and I could not wait to leave, which I did, an ill-fated trip indeed.

I returned once more to the people of Turiba Viejo. Now that I had decided it was time for me to leave, I found that it was not so easy. Mirón and Andrés were clearly relieved by my departure and, seeing me packing, they became more pleasant than they ever had been. With his usual poise, Marquito asked me if I was really leaving. Would I ever come back? I was not sure about that, but I replied that I would, two dry seasons from then. It was a plan, not a lie.

I had already been ferried across the Turiba River, and the whole group of men were on the other side with me. Guzmán commented, "You are leaving. Are your wives lonely at home? Are your children crying without their father? When you come back, bring them with you." Felipe Casanova enumerated the members of my French family that he knew of: a father, a mother, two brothers, two wives, and two children. Then he said, "Eight bearded people in your house." He raised another finger of his left hand: "With you, that makes nine." Domingo Barrios, who had remained squatting, spat between his legs. "That is a lot of people. Here we do not have much to eat. Make sure to bring rice and beef when you come back." I had distributed what was left of my bag of rice, kerosene, hooks, and fishing line. Domingo Barrios was to keep my table until my return. The son of Felipe Casanova, *tose*-TV18, stated, "*Panaxpon*, you are going to die if you leave us." To my "why?" he answered, "You will starve there; there is no tapir in your settlement." Andrés had a different opinion: "The *tatto* will eat you." Mirón added, "The jaguar, too." Domingo Flores saw a different fate altogether for me: "He is going to write about us, a lot of writing with all the pictures he took; bring it here, we want to see it." But Domingo Barrios fantasized differently: "My father is a big liar. He will screw a lot and make many little bearded babies." We all laughed together, and it was the memory I wanted to keep of my companions. I got up and said *utey*, "I am going." And I left and walked swiftly to the Creole settlement without turning around for the last look I preferred not to take.

I was not sure where to go. It made no great sense to go back to France before I had completed my Ph.D. dissertation. Since my English had deteriorated in two years of fieldwork, I decided to go back to the University of Pittsburgh to write up my material. But the department had moved, and the neighborhood had changed. There were new faculty and students, new books and new fads. The culture shock was so great that I found myself writing poetry, something I had taken up in the field to maintain my sense of identity, instead of writing my dissertation. Somehow, I could not "digest" Marquito and Domingo Barrios. I still had the taste of manioc beer on my lips and the sound of nose flutes in my ears when I was asked to act as a consultant for a British television film on the Panare. The escape was too tantalizing to be rejected, and I went back to Turiba Viejo for a last visit during January and February 1970. "You did not lie after all," was the first comment of Domingo Barrios. The son of Felipe Casanova, *ciköxpwö-*TV19, had died during the fall, in all probability of pneumonia. On February 12, Domingo Flores' wife, Soledad, gave birth to a son. Guzmán's wife was pregnant again. Marquito complained, "We see too many *tatto* now." In fact, there had been a diamond rush in Panare territory since the previous fall, and, with renewed vigor, Creole men had taken to the forest, hoping to make it big financially.

Revisiting the Panare under these conditions was more an escape than anything else. Chatting with my "brother" and the other people of the settlement was no longer fieldwork as I had undertaken it before. It was sheer involvement. I had the impression that I was visiting old friends, and the news and the gossip were only a pretext to maintain the flow of communication. Data collecting had now become epiphenomenal to the reality of my social experience. At the same time, revisiting Turiba Viejo as an old acquaintance rather than as an anthropologist was my way of demystifying my fieldwork. The revisiting soon came to an end. Then, and only then, could I begin to emerge from the opacity of the anthropological experience, upon which I could now begin to reflect with more serenity.

I have not returned to Turiba Viejo since, and in all probability I never will. The closing of this chapter is also the end of an anthropological experience. A chunk of my life is detached from me as I near the end in transforming anthropological praxis into anthropological logos. The existence of Marquito, Domingo Barrios, Felipe Casanova, Hortensia, Luisa, Elena, and the other Panare whose lives I have shared is suddenly rigidified in the essence of my writing. Familiar

faces have now turned into concepts whose concreteness remains un-
reachable forever. At the end of our physical and intellectual encounter, the Panare are left to grapple with their own cultural identity on
the fringes of the Guiano-Amazonian forest. I, enriched with their experience, have to rejoin the West and to question it as well, in search
of my own cultural identity. But to the reader is left the task of deciding for himself or herself whether I have answered the question from
which I started: "Who was I for them?" and whether I have done
justice to the thickness of the anthropologizing experience in these reflections on fieldwork.

Bibliography

Acosta-Saignes, M.
  1961 [1954] *Estudios de etnología antigua de Venezuela.* 2d ed. Caracas: Ediciones de la Biblioteca, Universidad Central de Venezuela.

Alvarado, L.
  1956 [1945] *Obras completas de Lisandro Alvarado. IV. Datos etnográficos de Venezuela.* Caracas: Ministerio de Educación, Dirección de Cultura y Bellas Artes.

Antolínez, G.
  1944 "Características típicas de la vivienda Panare." *America Indígena* 4: 201–210.

  1946a "El niño del llano frente al niño indígena." *Educación* 43: 54–61.

  1946b *Hacia el Indio y su mundo: Pensamientos vivos del hombre americano, etnología, mitología, folklore.* Caracas: Librería y Editorial del Maestro.

  1947a "Acuarelas Panare." *Revista Nacional de Cultura* 62: 80–83.

  1947b "Cuando fluye el barbasco." *Revista Nacional de Cultura* 62: 83–90.

  1952a "Interesantes aspectos de la cultura Panare." *Venezuela Misionera* 14: 279–282.

  1952b "Como viven los Indios 'Panares.'" *Venezuela Misionera* 14: 283–284.

Armellada, C. de
  1967 "La Primera Gran Feria del Orinoco." *Venezuela Misionera* 335: 92–95.

Arribas, J. M.
  1967 "Festival indígena en la Gran Feria del Orinoco." *Venezuela Misionera* 336: 100–103.

Arvelo-Jimenez, N.
  1974 *Relaciones políticas en una sociedad tribal: Estudio de los Ye'cuana, indígenas del Amazonas Venezolano.* Mexico City: Instituto Indigenista Interamericano, Ediciones especiales 68.

Basso, E. B. (ed.)
  1977 *Carib-speaking Indians: Culture, society and language.* Anthropological Papers of the University of Arizona #28. Tucson: The University of Arizona Press.

Bergson, H. L.
  1960 [1889] *Time and free will, an essay on the immediate data of consciousness.* (Transl. by F. L. Pogson). New York: Harper Torchbooks.
Berreman, G. D.
  1962 *Behind many masks: Ethnography and impression management in a Himalayan village.* Ithaca, N.Y.: Society for Applied Anthropology, Monograph #4.
Bohannan, P., and G. Dalton (eds.)
  1965 [1962] *Markets in Africa: Eight subsistence economies in transition.* Garden City, N.Y.: Doubleday Anchor Books.
Bowen, E. S. (pseudonym)
  1954 *Return to laughter.* New York: Harper and Bros.
Briggs, J. L.
  1970 *Never in anger: Portrait of an Eskimo family.* Cambridge: Harvard University Press.
Casagrande, J. B. (ed.)
  1960 *In the company of man: Twenty portraits by anthropologists.* New York: Harper and Bros.
Chagnon, N. A.
  1968 *Yanomamö: The fierce people.* New York: Holt, Rinehart and Winston.
  1974 *Studying the Yanomamö.* New York: Holt, Rinehart and Winston.
Chateaubriand, F. A. R., Vicomte de
  1964 [1827] *Voyage en Amérique.* Paris: Didier.
Deloria, V., Jr.
  1969 *Custer died for your sins: An Indian manifesto.* New York: Macmillan.
  1970 *We talk, you listen: New tribes, new turf.* New York: Macmillan.
Devereux, G.
  1967 *From anxiety to method in the behavioral sciences.* New York: Humanities Press.
Diamond, S.
  1969 "Anthropology in question." *In* Hymes 1974: 401–429.
Dumont, J.-P.
  1972 "Rapport pour la Commission Indigéniste Nationale du Vénézuéla sur la situation actuelle des Indiens Panare." *In* Renaud 1972: 79–98.
  1974a "L'alliance substituée." *L'Homme* 14: 43–56.
  1974b "Espacements et déplacements dans l'habitat Panare." *Journal de la Société des Américanistes* 61: 17–30.
  1976 *Under the rainbow: Nature and supernature among the Panare Indians.* Austin: University of Texas Press.
  1977 "From dogs to stars: the phatic function of naming among the Panare." *In* Basso 1977: 89–97.
Erikson, E. H.
  1977 *Toys and reasons: Stages in the ritualization of experience.* New York: W. W. Norton.

Evans-Pritchard, E. E.
1964   *Social anthropology and other essays.* New York: The
             Free Press.
Firth, R.
1975   "An appraisal of modern social anthropology." *Annual
             Review of Anthropology* 4: 1–25.
Freilich, M. (ed.)
1970   *Marginal natives: Anthropologists at work.* New York:
             Harper and Row.
Geertz, C.
1973   *The interpretation of cultures.* New York: Basic Books.
Godelier, M.
1973   *Horizon, trajets marxistes en anthropologie.* Paris: Fran-
             çois Maspéro.
Golde, P. (ed.)
1970   *Women in the field.* Chicago: Aldine.
Habermas, J.
1971 [1968]   *Knowledge and human interests.* (Transl. by J. J. Sha-
             piro). Boston: Beacon Press.
Hammel, E. A.
1976   "The matrilateral implications of structural cross-cousin
             marriage." *In* Zubrow 1976: 145–168.
Harris, M.
1968   *The rise of anthropological theory: A history of theories
             of culture.* New York: Thomas Y. Crowell.
Heisenberg, W.
1958   *Physics and philosophy: The revolution in modern science.*
             New York: Harper and Bros.
Hurtado Izquierdo, R.
1961   *Incorporación de los Indígenas de Guayana al progreso
             nacional.* Ciudad Bolivar: Instituto Agrario Nacional, Ad-
             ministración de la Sarrapia.
Hymes, D.
1974 [1969]   *Reinventing anthropology.* New York: Random House,
             Vintage Books.
Kaplan, J. O.
1975   *The Piaroa, a people of the Orinoco basin: A study in kin-
             ship and marriage.* Oxford: Clarendon Press.
Kimball, S. T., and J. B. Watson (eds.)
1972   *Crossing cultural boundaries: The anthropological experi-
             ence.* San Francisco: Chandler.
Koch-Gruenberg, T.
1922   "Die Völkergruppierung zwischen Rio Branco, Orinoco,
             Rio Negro und Yapura." *In* Lehmann 1922: 205–266.
Lehmann, W. (ed.)
1922   *Festschrift Eduard Seler.* Stuttgart: Strecker und Schröder.
Leiris, M.
1976   *La règle du jeu. IV. Frêle bruit.* Paris: Gallimard.
Lévi-Strauss, C.
1966 [1962]   *The savage mind.* (Transl. by anonym.). Chicago: The
             University of Chicago Press.

1967 [1958]   *Structural anthropology.* (Transl. by C. Jacobson and
               B. G. Schoepf). Garden City, N.Y.: Doubleday Anchor
               Books.
1969 [1949]   *The elementary structures of kinship.* (Transl. by J. H.
               Bell, J. R. von Sturmer, and R. Needham). Boston: Bea-
               con Press.
1974 [1955]   *Tristes tropiques.* (Transl. by J. and D. Weightman).
               New York: Atheneum.
1976 [1973]   *Structural anthropology. II.* (Transl. by M. Layton). New
               York: Basic Books.
Lizot, J.
1976   *Le cercle des feux: Faits et dits des Indiens Yanomami.*
               Paris: Seuil.
López Ramírez, T.
1944   "Visita a los Indios Panares en Venezuela." *Acta Amer-
               icana* 2: 254–255.
Lowie, R. H.
1937   *The history of ethnological theory.* New York: Holt, Rine-
               hart and Winston.
Malinowski, B.
1961 [1922]   *Argonauts of the western Pacific.* New York: E. P. Dut-
               ton.
1967   *A diary in the strict sense of the term.* New York: Har-
               court, Brace and World.
Mead, M.
1949   *The mountain Arapesh. V. The record of Unabelin with
               Rorschach analysis.* Anthropological Papers of the Amer-
               ican Museum of Natural History 41 (3).
1973   "The art and technology of fieldwork." *In* Naroll and
               Cohen 1973: 246–265.
Mintz, S. W., and E. R. Wolf
1950   "An analysis of ritual co-parenthood (compadrazgo)."
               Southwestern Journal of Anthropology 6: 341–368.
Monod, J.
1972   *Un riche cannibale.* Paris: Union Générale d'Editions,
               Collection 10/18.
Montaigne, M. E. de
1955 [1774]   *Journal de voyage en Italie par la Suisse et l'Allemagne
               en 1580 et 1581.* Paris: Garnier Frères.
Murdock, G. P.
1965 [1949]   *Social structure.* New York: The Free Press.
Naroll, R., and R. Cohen (eds.)
1973 [1970]   *A handbook of method in cultural anthropology.* 2d ed.
               New York: Columbia University Press.
Nash, D., and R. Wintrob
1972   "The emergence of self-consciousness in ethnography."
               [with *C.A.* comment]. *Current Anthropology* 13 (5):
               527–542.
Palmer, R. E.
1969   *Hermeneutics: Interpretation theory in Schleiermacher,*

Dilthey, Heidegger, and Gadamer. Evanston, Ill: North-western University Press.

Paul, R. A.
1976   "Did the primal crime take place?" *Ethos* 4 (3): 311–352.
Paul, R. A., and P. Rabinow
1976   "Bourgeois rationalism revisited." *Dialectical Anthropology* 1: 121–134.
Powdermaker, H.
1966   *Stranger and friend: The way of an anthropologist.* New York: W. W. Norton.
Rabinow, P.
1975   *Symbolic domination: Cultural form and historical change in Morocco.* Chicago: The University of Chicago Press.
1977   *Reflections on fieldwork in Morocco.* Berkeley and Los Angeles: University of California Press.
Read, K. E.
1965   *The high valley.* New York: Charles Scribner's Sons.
Redfield, R.
1953   *The primitive world and its transformations.* Chicago: The University of Chicago Press.
Renaud, R., P. Crime et al.
1972   *De l'ethnocide.* Paris: Union Générale d'Editions, Collections 10/18.
Riley, C. L.
1952   "Trade-Spanish of the Piñaguero Panare." *Studies in Linguistics* 10 (1): 6–11.
1959   "Some observations on the Panare language." *Boletín del Museo de Ciencias Naturales de Caracas* 4–5 (1–4): 87–96.
Roth, W. E.
1924   *An introductory study of the arts, crafts, and customs of the Guiana Indians.* U.S. Bureau of American Ethnology, 38th Annual Report: 23–745.
Ryle, G.
1949   *The concept of mind.* New York: Barnes and Noble.
Sahlins, M.
1968   *Tribesmen.* Englewood Cliffs: Prentice-Hall.
1972   *Stone age economics.* Chicago: Aldine-Atherton.
1976   *Culture and practical reason.* Chicago: The University of Chicago Press.
Salisbury, R. F.
1962   *From stone to steel: Economic consequences of a technological change in New Guinea.* London and New York: Cambridge University Press.
Scholte, B.
1969   "Toward a reflexive and critical anthropology." *In* Hymes 1974: 430–457.
Sterne, L.
1967 [1768]   *A sentimental journey through France and Italy. By Mr. Yorick.* Berkeley: University of California Press.

Wagner, R.
　1975　　　　*The invention of culture.* Englewood Cliffs: Prentice-Hall.
Watson, J. B.
　1972　　　　"Epilogue: In search of intimacy." *In* Kimball and Watson 1972: 299–302.
Wavrin, Marquis de
　1937　　　　*Moeurs et coutumes des Indiens sauvages de l'Amérique du Sud.* Paris: Payot.
Weinreich, U.
　1953　　　　*Languages in contact: Findings and problems.* New York: Linguistic Circle of New York.
Wolf, E. R.
　1964　　　　*Anthropology, humanistic scholarship in America.* Englewood Cliffs: Prentice-Hall.
Young, A.
　1969 [1792]　*Travels during the years 1787, 1788, and 1789. Undertaken more particularly with a view of ascertaining the cultivation, wealth, resources, and national prosperity, of the kingdom of France.* Garden City, N.Y.: Doubleday.
Zubrow, E. B. W. (ed.)
　1976　　　　*Demographic anthropology: Quantitative approaches.* Albuquerque: University of New Mexico Press.

Index